Thoughts Along The Way

Thoughts Along The Way

David Graham

Rutledge Books, Inc.  Bethel, CT

Copyright© 1996 by David Graham
ALL RIGHTS RESERVED
Rutledge Books, Inc.
8 F.J. Clarke Circle, Bethel, CT 06801

Manufactured in the United States of America

Cataloging in Publication Data
  Graham, David.
    Thoughts along the way/David Graham
    p. cm.
    ISBN 1-887750-15-0
    1. Conduct of life. 2. Christian life. I. Title.
248.4--dc20

Contents

Foreword xii

Introduction xv

I. A Global View

Africa: Cultural Lessons from a Trip Overseas. Travel and curiosity are good antidotes to narrow-mindedness, and a sojourn in Benin taught me a good bit about the impact that language and culture have on our way of life. 1

Encyclopedias are Dangerous. The diversity of the lives we lead and the very *way* we *think* never cease to astound me. What sorts of things do all humans share in common? Reading the encyclopedia entry on Kertanagara, King of Java, and comparing his life to mine had me wondering about two humans being so different—separated by such large barriers of time, space, climate, culture, religion and language. I am thankful that reading has at least made me aware of people whose lives are quite different from my own. Reading is an important means by which we enlarge our world view. Samuel Johnson was rather blunt on this matter: "You can never be wise unless you love reading."[1] 8

I Was Just Wondering: A few questions about humanity. The picture accompanying this essay was taken in the Canadian Rockies. It was beautiful there. And cold. I suppose the picture was chosen because it shows the openness and vastness of the region, and because people are supposed to ask all the "deep" questions of life when they are up on a mountaintop. 12

Footnotes. Explanations of why I was (and still am) wondering. 15

English Excursion. Thoughts from a trip to England. 20

Our Changed World. It daily amazes me. Technology has turned our planet into a global village, changing it in good and bad ways. But change it, it has. 25

II. Love

Wedding Tears. Why do people cry at weddings? The idea for writing my essays was conceived while I was in Washington state attending a wedding. This was to be the first of many questions that I would ask in my writings for which I felt there were no definitive answers. Imponderable questions, though, still beg responses, and musing about them seems to be the best thing to do for such elusive solutions. 29

Longfellow, Dumas, and Hatred. Frederick Buechner is right: Hatred is the ultimate consuming passion. "Evangeline" and *The Count of Monte Cristo* demonstrate, respectively, overcoming and being overcome by this passion. 31

The Shadowlands of C.S. Lewis. Little Tree's grandpa said that the only alternative to the grief of lost love was not to love anything, "which was worse because you would feel empty all the time." Lost love produces strong emotions, hopefully moving from initial grief to eventual gratefulness for the gift of experienced love. 34

Surprised by J: A few comments about marriage. The title comes as a bit of a parody of C.S. Lewis's spiritual autobiography *Surprised by Joy*. Indeed, I was surprised to find myself marrying at all. 38

III. Frailty

Frailty, Part I: The Conversation. Human frailty saddens me as much as anything. I never know what to say when someone like Dietrich opens up like that. As I've said before, sometimes there just aren't any answers. 42

Frailty, Part II: The Discussion. "Nothing softeneth the Arrogance of our Nature like a Mixture of some Frailties. It is by them that we are best told, that we must not strike too hard upon others because we ourselves do so often deserve blows. They pull our rage by the sleeve and whisper Gentleness to us in our censures." (Halifax [as quoted by Robertson Davies at the beginning of his novel *A Mixture* *of Frailties.*])[2] This essay was another musing to offer as a response to some vexing questions. ...46

What's Bred in the Bone. "What's bred in the bone will not out of the flesh,"[3] says the 13th century proverb. The prophet Jeremiah said as much when he claimed that it was as easy for an Ethiopian to change his skin color or a leopard his spots as it was for people accustomed to evil to change and do good. Ingrained habits do not change easily. Establishing good habits helps prevent bad actions. ...51

The Knowledge of Experience. After experiencing motion sickness myself, I could never again coldly dismiss someone as "only being nauseated." I know from experience just how miserable that feels. We can't learn everything vicariously. Some things have to be experienced; like empathy. ...53

Failure. Failure is something I don't like to experience. Profound failure seems to go all the way through the bones into the marrow. I am thankful that I can ask for understanding, forgiveness, and strength through prayer, and that there is a God who understands and hears me. Perhaps it is also good that failure is so humbling, lest pride make arrogant prigs of us all (especially me!!) ...56

Shame. It feels bad, but is healthy for us to have. It certainly points to a higher law, which, in turn, points to a higher being—God; (whom St. Anselm described as that "being than which nothing greater can be conceived.") [4] ...59

IV. The Dark Side of Life

This World Is Not a Friendly Place. . . Nature does not teach theology, but it certainly provides a lot to ponder when we puzzle over the character of God. My questions about scorpions, tarantula hawks, snakebites, crocodiles, parasites, floods, earthquakes, leukemia, kidney failure, and other assorted maladies are merely a few examples which invoke the age-old question: "If God is so good, why is there so much evil in the world?" On the other hand, much of what we view as "evil" may not really be bad. God's speech to Job and his friends suggests that God delights in the very wilderness of nature, much of which seems evil or cruel from the human viewpoint. For such an enigma, the best solution I can offer is this: in a harsh world, the offer of salvation to someone who must die (Job in particular, everyone in general) shows that even the harshness of God is kinder than the wildness of nature, and His compulsion is our liberation. (In his spiritual autobiography, *Surprised by Joy*, C.S. Lewis described God's relentless pursuit of himself to the point where Lewis finally, reluctantly, converted from atheism. He concluded, "The hardness of God is kinder than the softness of men, and His compulsion is our liberation.")[5] 62

The Optimist and Pessimist. An optimist and a pessimist visit Signal Point (overlooking Chattanooga and the Tennessee River) on the fourth of July. Each records what they "saw." Neither seemed to achieve the balance Philip Yancey wrote about in his book *Open Windows*, "Each spring when my wife and I open the windows of our Chicago apartment, fresh air rushes in. The streets outside are filled with happy sounds as people shed their coats and rediscover the outdoors. But open windows also let in city dust, the blaring horns of taxis, the throbbing music of a late-night bar. You'll find glimpses of both in this book: the lovely and the unlovely. I have tried to see both with a steady gaze."[6] 67

Morbid Fascination. Spider webs, disease, death, wars, and crime: why do humans love the morbid side of life? This fascination befuddles me. 71

The Human Sentence: Pain, Decay, and Death. The recurring question, "If God is good, why is there so much pain and suffering in the world?" takes on more significance when one sees suffering firsthand. My journal entry merely gave some specific examples of human pain that physicians come in contact with, only partially conveying how such disease can trouble the spirit. Sobering, isn't it, how thousands of years later, Job's questions still haven't been answered? 74

V. The Dark Side of Humanity

People Enjoy Complaining... We really do. We don't enjoy the things which cause us to complain, but there is pleasure in the griping and criticism that follow. The best antidotes for such morbidity seem to be forgiveness and self-appraisal of one's own shortcomings. Refusal to forgive is tantamount to spitting in the face of God's grace in forgiving ourselves. 78

Thoughts Along the Way

The Changing Autumn. Fall is my favorite season of the year. Mankind's population growth and propensity for destruction and noisemaking certainly threaten its charming existence. (Los Angeles, for example, has mushroomed in size over the last century, growing from only 11,000 inhabitants in 1880 to 3,485,398 by 1990.) Will we humans eventually outgrow ourselves—spiritually as well as physically? 80

Van Dieman's Land. History repeatedly records man's inhumanity to man. In 19th century Van Dieman's land, the cruelty was English extermination of Tasmanian aborigines. Such brutal acts either demonstrate that only the strong survive or that morally, mankind cannot save itself from destruction. (Perhaps both are true.) Studying history should make atheists or Christains of us all. 82

The Lessons of History: A Different View. "The first to plead his case seems just, until another comes and examines him" (Proverbs 18:17). As appalling as stories of injustice are, especially on the individual level, it is prudent to remember that "there is no one who does good, not even one."[7] G.K. Chesterton was right in maintaining that the idea of an innocent or sinless people is a fallacy. Australian aborigines, American Indians, Afro-Americans, Aztecs, Jews, and all other races that have been preyed upon are peoples who also demonstrated their *own* sinfulness repeatedly. 85

Reflections on the Tenth Commandment. Coveting does not receive much attention in the news media, but it lies at the heart of sexual lust, avarice (greed), jealousy, and many a war. 88

VI. Justice

Mudslinging and the Race for the Presidency. Character flaws do not automatically disqualify someone from performing a given job. As Lincoln once said, "A liar might be brave and have skill as an officer."[8] Along these lines, I have heard many quote Christ's statement, "do not judge lest you be judged," as a reason to refrain from passing judgment on others. Christ's own life refutes this notion, as He continuously passed judgment on people. He also encouraged His disciples to follow in His footsteps, and a good teacher teaches by example. Christ should be fully quoted. "For in the way you judge, you will be judged; and by your standard of measure, it will be measured to you."[9] This is the kind of judgment that encourages humility and caution, not arrogance and hatred, because we are to examine ourselves with the same scrutiny that we do others. 90

Righteous Indignation. Christians usually like to picture themselves as a peaceful lot, but they often aren't. Religious wars, whether it be killing physicians who perform abortions or fighting over a piece of land, are just as bloody as any human affair. Does God approve these zealous killings? The Old Testament records both religiously motivated slayings and divine lovingkindness, sometimes side by side. Indeed, the bottom line is that God often advocated the former while still proclaiming the truth of the latter. Justice and mercy are hard virtues to reconcile, and the God who practices both is ineffable. Not surprisingly, humans usually end up choosing one or the other. ...92

Firmness Without Malice, Justice Without Hatred. We humans do not mix such opposites easily. Abraham Lincoln was a rare exception of someone who did this well. 94

Lax Laws, Tardy Punishments, and Lawlessness. "Because the sentence against an evil deed is not executed quickly, therefore the hearts of the sons of men among them are given fully to do evil." (Ecclesiastes 8:11) 98

VII. Faith

An Amazing Moment. I surprised myself during a basketball game one night while I was in medical school. I somehow made a long, three-point basket that I thought I was going to miss. I made a split second adjustment during the act of shooting, and this changed the course of the basketball, which in turn produced the desired basket. I was awed and amazed at the human body's versatility and complexity. No wonder Sir Isaac Newton said that the thumb alone was enough to convince him of God's existence. 102

Cannibalism and the Gospel. This essay was my attempt to explain the basics of Christianity (spelled out in the long fourth paragraph) and to show that cannibalism and blood sacrifice are not as foreign to human decency as we often think they are. Hence my linking of Christ's quote (symbolic cannibalism) with the Namba, the Sawi, and the Kayagar tribal pratices (literal cannibalism). 104

Thoughts Along the Way

Revelation and Science Fiction. Sometimes it's hard to tell the difference between the two. The former is supposed to be an apocalyptic book of the Bible that was God-inspired when it was written. Its text, though, almost seems more like a script for a horror movie. One has to read it with symbolic (rather than literal) perspective to appreciate it. 107

Albert Schweitzer, Legend, and the Truth of the Gospel. People are fascinated by legends. (I know I sure am). They are sometimes more enjoyable to believe than the truth. The gospels, however, are historical accounts, not legends. 110

Family Trees and Pedigrees. They help generate interest for those parts of the Bible that are otherwise boring to read. They also help shape one's theology by demonstrating various subtleties such as intrafamilial marriages (among God's people, no less) and prophetic fulfillment (such as transferring a priesthood from one lineage to another). 115

Birthdays, Inheritance, and Booker T. Washington. What is it like to grow up without a past? Many slaves, like Washington, have done so. I found Washington's autobiography fascinating, being reminded again of how different our various lives are from each other. 121

The Missionary Spirit. It changes culture, but is this always better? "Success" is often not as profound as people would like to believe; but I support the missionary cause when it is appropriately enacted. 124

Holiness. I hear God's name treated casually so often that it makes atheism very unappealing and a desire for something holy quite strong. Holiness is very satisfying (even if unholiness is so often fun or exciting). Perhaps holiness is another example of humans wanting something that they can never have. Then again, it may just be the key to understanding reality. 130

Quoting. Quotation reflects our belief in authority. When a Christian debates a Mormon on a point of doctrine or a Jew confronts a Muslim on belief, what they basically differ about is which authority (the Bible, Koran, Book of Mormon, etc.) is "the truth." 132

The Unknowable Future. The future: how little we know about it. Steve Prefontaine and Michel de Montaigne were two men for whom the future turned out quite differently from what they were expecting. We, too, do not know what lies ahead of us, nor the moment our lives will end. It is best to trust the Being who knows these things. 134

Cultural Relevance and the Search for Absolute Truth. What we believe about life depends on the trust we place in our information sources (whether it be the Bible, the Koran or *The Wall Street Journal*) and how we interpret the data therein. Sometimes the line between what is permanently true and what is a temporary requirement is indistinct. 136

Motivation. Why write these musings? Why feed the poor, read a book, build a well, or translate a language? Why do anything? Because our actions matter—to God, to others in this life, and possibly to others in the generations to come. 141

VIII. The Printed Word

Samuel Johnson. Selections from James Boswell's *Life of Johnson*. (An attempt to recruit patrons for the book by sharing enthusiasm for the biography of a great man.) 143

A Book Sampler. Selections of some of my favorite and least favorite books. 145

A Heroic Bard. The unlikely hero: Henry Wadsworth Longfellow. 148

The Re-reading of Books. The re-reading of books marks the true lover of learning and entertainment. A book's qualities cannot be exhausted with a single reading. 152

Company Aytch—a rebel's report on the American Civil War. For we humans who seek comfort, who enjoy, as the prophet Amos put it, being "at ease in Zion," Sam Watkins' memoirs are a reminder that being cozy is not the chief purpose of living. 157

IX. Mystery

Crystallization. As in the laboratory, there are certain moments when a truth is suddenly realized. It is a quickening experience, fascinating and exciting all at once. 160

Thoughts Along the Way

The Puzzle of Sex. God is not embarrassed by human sexuality. We should not be either. It is puzzling enough and potent enough to merit open discussion and exhortation. 163

Hauntings. Most people have a dim view of being haunted by something. Indeed, nightmares and flashbacks to violent experiences can be dreadful. However, hauntings of another sort can be enchanting, mysterious, and wonderful. Indeed, a world without mystery is a world of boredom. 168

The Handicap of Divine Gnosis. Do idiot savants have the capacity to see a portion of the world as God sees it? They, too, seem to have an extraordinary sense of *feeling* knowledge (at least autistic twins John and Michael, as reported by Oliver Sacks in *The Man Who Mistook His Wife for a Hat*, seemed to.). In the gospels, Christ said, "even the very hairs of your head are all numbered,"[10] and one senses that a laborious counting process was not used to obtain that information. God simply "sees" and knows the number—just as John and Michael did with spilled matchsticks or prime numbers. The irony is that "normal" humans lack this gift of knowing (gnosis). We truly live in a mysterious world of wonder. 170

How We View the World. A seminal neurology lecture on vision was but one of many lessons on the human body that I heard in medical school, yet the intimate workings of vision seemed to have broader connotations, spilling over from anatomy and physiology to philosophy and religion. How *do* we see the world? Somehow, we see it through transformation: sensation—decomposition—recomposition—perception. This is as true in the "natural" world as it is in the "spiritual" world. The divine spark of reason, a gift from Providence, is what makes the transition from sensation to perception possible. As the psalmist said, "In Thy light, we see light."[11] 174

X. Observations

Requisite For A Surgeon 178

Work. Leonardo da Vinci created a study entitled "Allegory of Pleasure and Pain," in which he drew a picture of a male figure that split at the waist to make two torsos, two heads, and four arms, somewhat resembling Siamese twins joined at the waist. He wrote that

David Graham

"pleasure and pain are represented as twins, as though they were joined together, for there is never the one without the other...They are made with their backs turned to each other because they are contrary the one to the other. They are made growing out of the same trunk because they have one and the same foundation, for the foundation of pleasure is labor with pain, and the foundations of pain are vain and lascivious pleasures."[12] Work is like this in producing both satisfaction and fatigue. 180

The Unchanging Human Heart. R.K. Harrison's description of life during the reign of Jeroboam II in ancient Israel reveals that despite all of the technological advances mankind has made, the human spirit hasn't really changed at all. (For a different view on this, read chapter IX, "The Doctrine of the Unchanging Human Heart," in C.S. Lewis's *A Preface to Paradise Lost*.) 182

Studying the Little Things in Life. Samuel Johnson was right: "It is by studying little things that we attain the great art of having as little misery and as much happiness as possible."[13] 185

Sketch of a General Surgery Residency 187

Name-calling. Social titles are intriguing, and the ways we address one another are not governed by straightforward guidelines. One thing is certain, though: human pride loves entitlement, whether that title be 'Rabbi', 'Doctor', 'Professor', 'General', or 'Sir'. A healthy dose of humility—be it from Longfellow, Mathew's gospel, or anyone else—keeps things in proper perspective. 192

XI. Wisdom

Remember. Whether it be photographs, journals, or the Bible, it is wise to *remember* the past (without *pining* for it). C.S. Lewis wrote, "To study the past does indeed liberate us from the present, from the idols of our own market-place...I think no class of men are less enslaved to the past than historians."[14] The past is our teacher, even in lessons of severity. At the beginning of *The Rise and Fall of the Third Reich*, William Shirer quotes Santayana, giving an omen not to forget the atrocities of Nazi Germany: "Those who do not remember the past are condemned to relive it."[15] 195

Communication. This essay was sparked by a conversation with my older sister several years ago. She told me the story of the Barlig people in the Philippines, who had not traveled to see the ocean and therefore had trouble understanding certain aquatic terms (which made Bible translation a difficult task.) Communication must have meaning to be effective, and clarity aids the message (a lesson most doctors never learn). 197

Learning by Imitation. There aren't many sermons to be gleaned from a short book like III John, but this is a good one: "Do not imitate what is evil, but what is good." 200

Read Marcus Aurelius. An essay dedicated to the fleetingness of fame. 202

XII. Endings

A Panegyric for MJ and BB. (Michael Jordan and Bjorn Borg) This was written in November 1993, one month after Jordan's retirement and 16 months before his surprising return to basketball. 204

Endings. They are inevitable. 206

Footnotes 208

Foreword

by Philip Yancey

Names such as William Carlos Williams, Anton Chekhov, Richard Selzer, and Lewis Thomas demonstrate what fine literature can be wrought from the stuff of medicine. We should expect as much, after all, for doctors hold our hands—sometimes literally—at the most dramatic moments of life. Their own hands deliver us into the world, slap out our first breath, and tenderly release us into the next as we breathe our last.

Doctors break tragic news to families in the hallway, assist the disabled in adjusting to new boundaries, and listen like audiophiles to every twinge of pain. They live at those places most of us want to avoid, places where people are stretched, challenged, and defined.

Even so, the technical and reductionistic nature of modern medicine often squelches the sensitivity one might expect from those who spend their lives in the company of human suffering. Many doctors find time to read nothing besides medical journals and the daily paper. Many see so many patients each day that they function more as mechanics than as human healers. Some old-timers rue the loss of more reflective training in the philosophy of medicine, or on the subtleties of bedside manner. But who has time? A new version of MRI has just come out; ten new drugs were just released.

Somehow David Graham, both in his training and in his fledgling days of practice, has learned to restore a kind of balance to medicine, seeing it as an art as well as a science. He is an alert, literate human being, with receptors extending well beyond the range of medicine. He must not sleep more than an hour or two a night, for how else could he read so much of the likes of Tolstoy, Hugo, and Samuel Johnson? His insatiable curiosity carries him beyond the shores of the U.S., to places like Africa, Java, and Tasmania.

Moreover, Graham has not yet learned to hide experiences of failure and shame behind the physician's mask of hubris. He audibly wonders—about his patients, about the world around him, about himself—and out of his self-reflection come fine insights and a spirit that, astonishingly, seems almost like humility. His religious faith—how many doctors would dare acknowledge it?—enters in as well, sometimes like a flavoring spice and sometimes like a lens to enhance vision.

Graham has titled this collection *Thoughts Along the Way*, but that may give the wrong impression. Adventures, explorations, passions, maybe—but not mere thoughts. That distinction is what sets this collection apart from most writing by doctors and other scientists. By feeling as well as thinking, David Graham has brought medicine into the warm light of literature.

<small>Philip Yancey has authored such books as *Fearfully and Wonderfully Made*, *Where Is God When it Hurts*, *In His Image*, and *Pain: The Gift Nobody Wants*.</small>

Introduction

Being the reflective sort, I am thankful that I grew up in an age when reading and writing were widely taught. Writing is a tool that aids our thinking: it gathers scattered thoughts together, arranges and organizes them, then refines and edits them. In fact, it was during a writing course in college that I first began to regularly record my own musings about life. The professor, a former chemistry major named Paul Fromer, required his students to keep what he called an "intellectual journal" by making at least three entries a week in our notebooks about any subject that required some reflection. It is to him that I owe credit for the practice of keeping a journal and enjoying the therapy of recording my thoughts.

Within a year and a half after finishing that class, I moved a step further, from writing my thoughts in a journal to sharing them with friends (in the form of typewritten essays). This was really just an organized way of "talking" with them—somewhat like letter writing—and saying, "Hey, this is what I've been thinking about lately." And so it went until graduation dispersed us. I continued to write intermittently in my journal during the next four years in medical school, but it wasn't until I was preparing to start my residency that I began to send my musings out to others again.

This book is a collection of those writings, which discuss some of the things I was thinking about during that six-year general surgery residency. I believe that a writer is most likely to succeed if he or she writes the kinds of things that they themselves would enjoy reading, and since I like reading pensive essays, I have used this idiom to communicate my own thoughts. These musings reflect my fascination and satisfaction, as well as bewilderment and frustration, with life. There are many certainties and quite a few puzzles herein. Life has many mysteries, many enigmas, and many questions that do not have "solutions," so sometimes I write simply to make the reader aware of these problems. Socrates once defined "good" as "that which imparts truth to the known and the power of knowing to the knower." Thus "good," like sunlight, illumines things to give knowledge of their existence to us. I would like to think these essays "good" in that sense, in illuminating bits of our world, even if this sometimes means little more than questions or confessions of ignorance.

A Global View

Africa: Cultural Lessons from a Trip Overseas

What do Michael Jordan, microwave ovens, Ludwig van Beethoven, McDonald's restaurants, Richard Nixon, the stock market, William Shakespeare, Joe Montana, and compact discs have in common? The answer is that none of these mean anything to the average person in a Third World country. If you were to travel to a place where your particular interests in sports, music, food, politics, literature, or business were nonexistent, would your concept of culture change? Furthermore, if in this place, you could not speak the language(s) used for communication, would you feel isolated, frustrated, or stupid as well? How central is language to our life, our very being? Finally, if you knew nothing of the national geography or history, would that affect your opinion of the education you have acquired?

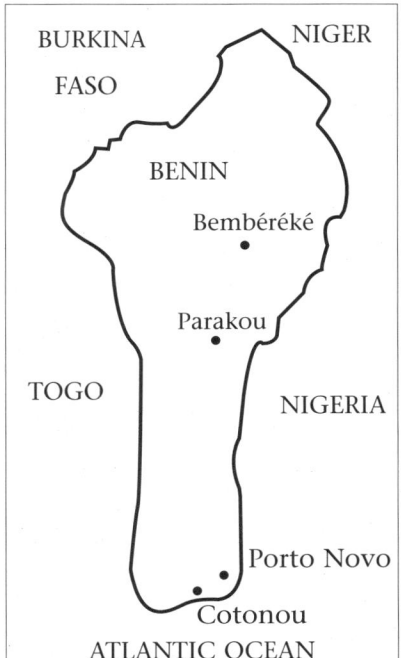

With these questions in mind, I would like to tell you a little bit about my life in Africa during January-February of 1990. As a medical student nearing the end of a four-year sojourn, my six weeks of international health studies at l'Hopital Evangelique in Bembéréké, Benin were profitable in several areas, the foremost of which were my increased knowledge of the local African culture, the French language, medicine in a Third World setting, and my world view (i.e., my Christian faith). These four factors—language, cul-

1

ture, job skills, and religion—strongly influence any work one might do as a Third World health care worker.

Many different parts are necessary for a body to work properly, and at Bembéréké I tagged along to observe the various bits of the mission work required to make the hospital run properly and provide good health care: the clinic (with its seemingly endless stream of patients), the operating room (with the seemingly endless stream of cases), the laboratory (for microscopic detection of disease), the pharmacy (for chemical treatment of disease), hospital wards (with 65 beds for patients), physical therapy (for rehabilitation), and village work by public health workers trying to educate people in the local towns about the importance of immunization, proper nutrition, good hygiene, and basic recognition and treatment of a few diseases. These departments also worked to meet the spiritual needs of the Beninoise by such means as praying with patients before operations, having a Beninoise pastor share the gospel message with locals following a public health lecture, or through conversations on the wards between the patients and fellow countrymen working as evangelists in the hospital. Luke 18:17 says, "Truly I say to you, whoever does not receive the kingdom of God like a child shall not enter it at all." Likewise, to enter into a world of knowledge in such areas as medicine or French or sociology, one must adopt a childlike attitude to learn, to put away pride and be willing to be instructed. I spent much time there observing, asking questions, and seeking to glean knowledge from all who would teach me.

Culturally, every society has its own advantages and disadvantages. Compared with Benin, Americans generally practice better hygiene, are taught to think rationally, and have open friendships between the sexes. On the other hand, Beninoise generally eat a healthier diet, don't get uptight or worry about time schedules, and don't wear neckties.

I found, as have others, that in many respects the African culture resembles the ancient near eastern Hebrew culture that we read about in the Old Testament: arranged marriages, life in a hot climate, importance of family bonds, respect for guests, desire for many children, and sometimes waiting to convey important news until the end of a conversation (*cf.* Genesis 18:16*ff*)[1] are just a few of the similarities. To read a book like the Bible, the western mind accepts on theory many things that Africans understand existentially with their hearts. For we who live with air conditioning, ice cubes, showers, Dr. Scholl's shoe inserts, leavened bread, trains, planes, and paved roads, what significance is there to phrases like, "the Lord was walking in the garden in the *cool* of the *day*,"[2] "As a deer *pants* for the *waterbrook*, so my soul pants for Thee O God,"[3] "Whoever drinks of the water that I shall give him shall never *thirst* again,"[4] "To what shall I compare the kingdom of God? It is like *leaven*, which a woman took and hid in three pecks of meal, until it was all leavened,"[5] "Then He poured water into the basin, and began to *wash* the disciples' *feet*, and to wipe them with the towel with which He was girded,"[6] "Now Ninevah was an exceedingly great city, a three

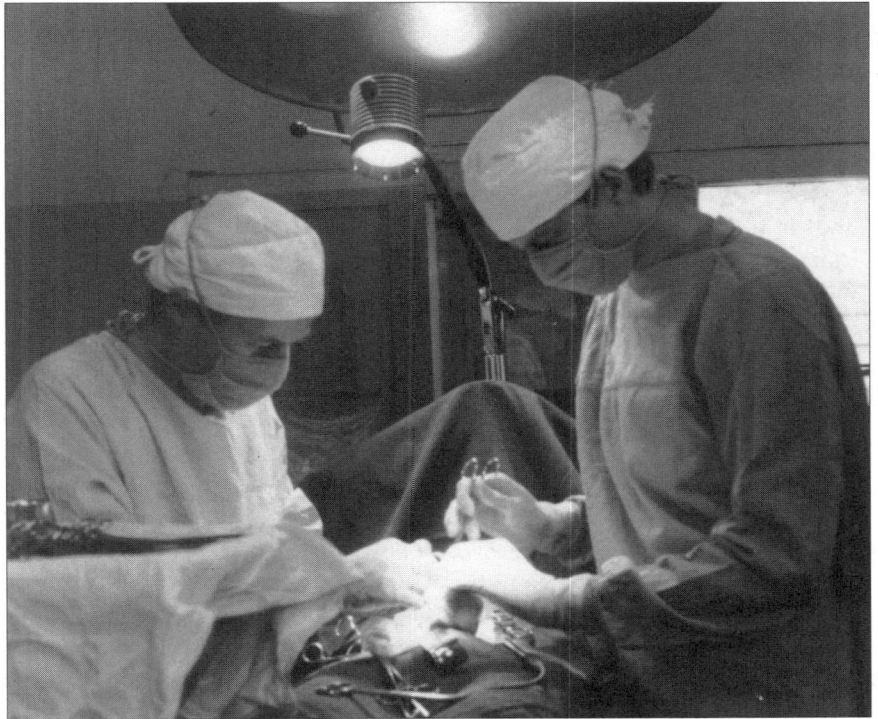

In the operating room at Hospital Evangelique near Bembéréké, Benin in West Africa. Dr. Andrew Potter (light gown) being assisted by the author (dark gown). February 1990.

days' *walk*,"[7] "So the king of Israel went with the king of Judah and the king of Edom; and they made a circuit of seven days journey, and there was no *water* for the army or for the *cattle* that *followed* them,"[8] "For the sons of Israel *walked forty years* in the wilderness"?[9]

David Graham

Today, many Third World countries are undergoing cultural changes because of the ever-expanding influence of twentieth century technology. Some of these, such as health education, are for better, while others, such as deforestation, are not. Just where these will lead and how they will affect the people they influence remains to be seen.

Missionaries face several challenges with these changes. At the same time, the Church has to tackle many of the problems that she also faces here in America, such as boredom with church services, lack of Christian growth in church members, ineffectiveness in sharing the gospel, or difficulties with church discipline. Additionally, there are cross-cultural decisions for the missionaries that are not easy to make. Too great of an involvement by the white western missionaries in terms of the number of members and money given in one particular community leads to an indigenous congregation unwilling to do things for themselves, since they know the missionaries can always do the jobs. Too little help and the church may struggle as well. The goal is to have nationals become self-governing, financially self-sustaining, self-taught, and spiritually self-serving in their churches; in a word: independent.

Like other countries, Benin also has language barriers to overcome. Though French is the official national language, there are about 50 different languages or dialects spoken throughout the country. Many people speak only their own language and do not know French. (It was not unusual to have 5-10 different languages spoken by hospitalized patients. All rounds and clinic work were done with the aid of translators.) Church services were always conducted in two or three languages at the place I usually attended. Time taken to translate a sermon disrupts the flow of a message, and language barriers make communication, and therefore fellowship, between the nationals and missionaries difficult. Bariba—the language most people around Bembéréké speak—is a highly nasal language and difficult to learn. It takes years of work to master it, and many missionaries were there for a short term, serving one or perhaps two years before returning home, thus not having time to thoroughly learn this language.

I cannot overstress the importance of language. At the beginning of this piece I submitted two questions about it to ponder. I felt the language barrier quite keenly, even among my fellow missionaries. Most of the missionaries at Bembéréké were Swiss, for whom English was

Thoughts Along the Way

their second or third language. Their English was better than my French, but French was the common language in which to communicate and I did my best to do so. However I may have communicated my various answers, questions, or ideas, with some people I could never have an in-depth discussion about anything—medicine, the market, the Bible, personal histories—because my lack of facility in that language prevented it. One cannot know another's personality well unless they speak the same language with ease. Perhaps I now know something of the *frustration* someone feels after becoming dysphasic after a stroke. Without language, I cannot communicate or acquire most of what makes me *Me*—my humor, my Christian beliefs, my meditations, my interests in medicine or literature or sports—all of that is stripped away. In fact, my deepest beliefs about the nature of reality—the natural world, the work of God in history, moral values, the supernatural—are all mediated through *language*. Language is the means for conveying images, feelings, knowledge, and ideas to my Self, my mind. This is why translating the Bible into someone's mother tongue is so important to do *well*. Thus, I came away from this trip very impressed by how much of our very *being* is tied to language. (For those of you who are skilled musicians, count your *international* 'language' abilities as a great blessing).

One difficult though valuable lesson that some of the missionaries shared with me was one that I had myself learned during the medical school years. It was a lesson about possession and permanence. Humans enjoy calling things their own and having some things that don't change. We enjoy the permanence of familiar surroundings, of familiar books, cars, landscapes, stereos, friends, musical instruments, spouses, family, and regular schedules. We like to have a house we can call our own. We do not enjoy having precious things—friends, homes, spouses, our autonomy—taken away from us. God often gives us much that we *can* keep for a long time—sometimes for a lifetime. All of us, however, must be *willing* to give up everything even if we are never asked to do so. We must learn to keep an open palm policy so that gifts God gives us are easily received and gifts God takes away easily removed without our clinging to them. "But Jesus said to him, 'No one after putting his hand to the plow and looking back, is fit for the kingdom of God,'" and "He said to them, 'Truly I say to you, there is no one who has left house or wife or brothers or parents or children for the sake of the kingdom of God, who shall not receive many times as much at this time and in the age to come, eternal life.'" (Luke 9:62;

18:29-30). A Third World missionary's life can be very unstable—moved around by the mission board from town to town because of job necessity, the ever-present possibility of being kicked out of the country at a moment's notice by the government, not being able to call any home one's own, sometimes not being one's own boss, constantly leaving friends and having friends leave them, and often lacking encouragement from anyone who can tell them that they are doing a good job and their work is appreciated. One physician I worked with had spent some time in Central Africa as a traveling eye surgeon, never staying in any one place longer than two weeks. Being single, it was evident that he had given up everything and everyone to serve Christ in that capacity. He only had himself (which, by the way, is more than many neurologically or psychologically impaired people have. *cf*. Oliver Sacks *The Man Who Mistook His Wife For A Hat* or *Awakenings*). A healthy attitude that sometimes must be adopted toward those we hold dear to us is that of Platon Karatayev, a character from Leo Tolstoy's *War and Peace* (which I re-read while over in Africa). Pierre Bezukhov thinks of him thus, "Karatayev had no attachments, friendships, loves, in the sense that Pierre understood them; but he loved and lived on affectionate terms with everything life brought him in contact with, and especially with man—not any particular man, but simply with those he happened to be with. He loved his dog, his comrades, the French, and Pierre, who was his neighbor; but Pierre felt that for all Karatayev's affectionate tenderness toward him (by which he instinctively gave Pierre's spiritual life its due) he would not have suffered a moment's grief at parting from him. And Pierre began to feel the same way toward Karatayev."[10]

Thoughts Along the Way

I have attempted to share a portion of my activities and reflections from my trip to Africa with the hope that this might stimulate you to remember the missionaries you know in your prayers and to encourage you to continue, or if needed, increase your involvement with your church. Language and culture are not preliminary barriers to overcome, and many needs are present if only we will inquire about them and fulfill what we can.

Shalom.

Encyclopedias are Dangerous...

They contain a wealth of information (most of which is true), capable of imparting knowledge to the reader. This in turn can lead to reflection, which jolts us out of complacency and causes us to ponder our ignorance.

I opened the encyclopedia to read one day and came across an article about Kertanagara, the king of Java from 1254 to 1292. Kertanagara was "the last king of Tumapel (or Singhasari) in Java and is still venerated by Indonesians as one of their greatest rulers. He was a zealous follower of Tantric Buddhism, which dealt with magic and demons and encouraged drinking and orgies of a ritual sort having nothing to do with pleasure-seeking. He believed that he was living in the Kali *yuga*, in Hindu cosmology the last of the four periods of world history, which was full of confusion, fear, and disaster, and that he, as a ruler, should save the world.[11]" His reign coincided with the expansion of Kublai Khan's realm in southeast Asia and he married a princess of Champa (southern Vietnam).

Kertanagara was a man who lived seven centuries before I was born. Kertanagara was a man who lived in a country on the opposite side of the world from the United States. Kertanagara lived in a culture that bears little resemblance to the modern, technology-dominated, fast-

Thoughts Along the Way

paced society where I dwell. Kertanagara was a man who spoke and thought in a language different from my own. Kertanagara and I are separated by huge barriers—time, space, culture, and language.

Kertanagara was a Buddhist and a king. I am a Christian and an ordinary citizen. Kertanagara wore kingly tribal garments. I wear a shirt, zippered trousers, and closed laced shoes. Kertanagara traveled on foot or an animal's back. I drive a car to work. Kertanagara lived in a hot climate his entire life. I have lived through many snowy winters near Chicago. Kertanagara lived in a world of tradition and manual labor. I inhabit a world of innovation, dominated by people whose hands are callus-less. Kertanagara sent messages through servants. I mail letters and talk into telephones. Kertanagara's culture was agrarian, mine urban. Kertanagara enjoyed music, but on a less spectacular level. The use of electricity had not yet been discovered so that microphones, amplifiers, stereos, electric guitars, or stage lights were not used to create "rock-n-roll" music and make people like Mick Jagger, Kiss, the Beatles, Elvis, U2 or Michael Jackson famous. (I doubt if any of the aforementioned people ever had an inkling of gratitude to people like Ben Franklin, Michael Faraday, Thomas Edison, or others whose discoveries of use for electricity made rock music, video and *international* recognition possible.) Kertanagara knew little of the world beyond Java, and probably did not even know of the *existence* of Europe, North America, Antarctica, South America, or Africa. Today, magazines, books, movies, television, and air travel have made the entire world knowable, something of a global village. Kertanagara had leisure activities, but sports, like music, were not addictive. The twentieth-century western world is addicted to sports and music, as evidenced by crowds at World Cup skiing races, the World Series, international soccer matches, or music concerts; by those who wake up, go to work, play, study, and go to bed listening to music; by the numerous compact disc and tape stores and ubiquitous use of athletes and musicians in the advertising industry; and by the media coverage of MTV, the NBA, NFL, Wimbledon, or the Olympics. If Kertanagara was typical of the people he governed, his thinking patterns worked more by association and superstition than by cold analytical reasoning. Kertanagara's historical studies centered around Java, whereas mine have focused on Europe and America.

Do you see why encyclopedias are so dangerous? A little article only one or two pages long can lead to a myriad of questions and a state of befuddlement. Encyclopedias remind us of our IGNORANCE. After this kind of encounter with the encyclopedia, I inevitably muse, "I know so *little* about the world."

Fortunately, there are some good lessons to be learned from this kind of encounter and they can be found in two books written by C.S. Lewis: *An Experiment in Criticism* and *The Abolition of Man*. The first lesson is that reading is a valuable gift and should be exercised accordingly in order to expand our world view and give us more insight into reality. At the end of *An Experiment in Criticism*, Lewis writes that the value of good literature is that

> "It admits us to experiences other than our own. Some, as we say, "interest" us more than others. It may be the typical (and we say "How true!") or the abnormal (and we say "How strange!"); it may be the beautiful, the terrible, the awe-inspiring, the exhilarating, the pathetic, the comic, or the merely piquant. Literature gives the *entree* to them all. Those of us who have been true readers all our life seldom fully realize the enormous extension of our being which we owe to authors. We realize it best when we talk with an unliterary friend. He may be full of goodness and good sense but he inhabits a tiny world. In it, we should be suffocated. The man who is contented to be only himself, and therefore less a self, is in prison. My own eyes are not enough for me, I will see through those of others..."[12]

The second lesson is that the differences of time, space, culture, language, and technology make people (and the lives they live) very different from each other. It should not be *assumed* that something is "normal" for everyone—it may just be a cultural peculiarity. We should not be *complacent* in our opinions about the nature of people or reasons for behavioral patterns. We should investigate before we formulate.

Finally, despite the differences, people do have things in common. Many women and men have never even heard of the Bible or the Christian faith to which I subscribe, yet all but the severely mentally impaired have a sense of right and wrong. In a letter to the church in Rome, the Apostle Paul wrote that one day, God will judge men's

Thoughts Along the Way

secrets and actions in accordance with the knowledge given each one. To those who know God's law, they will be judged by it, and to those who don't, they will be judged by their own obedience or disobedience to their own law; and people sense right from wrong.

In the appendix to *The Abolition of Man*, Lewis gives examples from all around the globe of people in different ages, cultures, geographical settings, and languages who have common laws (while living lives that often do not obey or acknowledge them). There are laws of general beneficence such as "do not murder" or "do not slander" or "show goodwill to others"; laws of special beneficence such as "love your wife and children" or "honor your father and mother." There are laws of justice: sexual justice (such as adultery), honesty (as in business practices or stealing property), or justice in court (not taking a bribe, for instance), laws of good faith and veracity (not lying, keeping promises), laws of mercy (feeding the hungry, taking care of the sick), and laws of magnanimity (sacrificing one's self on another's behalf). People sense right from wrong.

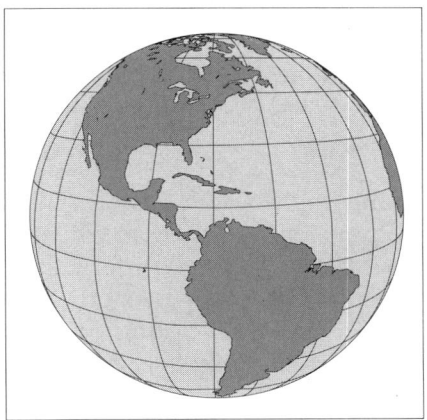

Near the end of his life, C.S. Lewis told his friend George Sayer that the best evidence for the existence of God seemed to be the moral sense, the desire for a way of life that is better and more just, for mercy and kindness, that so many people of different cultures share. If there was not something divine in us, we should be, as the animals seem to be, simply satisfied with what is.[13]

Amen.

Keep reading.

I Was Just Wondering...

Has it ever occurred to you that throughout history, including the present, individuals have spent their lives studying a subject about which you know nothing at all? That a man or a woman may spend their life interested in many things of whose very existence is unknown to you? That aside from consumption of food, bodily functions, and sleep, you may actually share NOTHING in common with a given individual?

How does the perception of the world differ for a blind, retarded child from the United States versus one from Ethiopia? How does perception of the world differ for a blind, retarded child versus a highly educated mathematician from Cambridge University, a hunter from the jungles of Brazil, or a veiled woman from a harem living in a male-dominated Arabian society? Can an enterprising single female on Wall Street carry on a meaningful conversation with an African mother from Liberia, whose sense of value as a human being is derived from bearing children?

How does the life and value system of a Christian theologian residing in a seminary community in America, who spends his life teaching and believing the same doctrines, differ from that of a Buddhist lama who spends his life studying Eastern philosophy in India? (Have you read any of Rudyard Kipling's novels, like *Kim*, which show some of the East-West differences?) Are people who pastor churches, write religious books, read only Christian magazines, or exclusively mingle in Christian circles ever guilty of not looking at all sides of an issue, or shrinking away from dispute in order to develop dogmatic ideas in an atmosphere of encouragement?

Would you admit that the vast majority of people who have lived on this planet have never heard of Beethoven, Michael Jordan, Nancy Reagan, or John Wayne? Is there any justification for a movie producer who has spent his life among Hollywood "stars" and whose keen interests lie in angles, lighting, scenery, plot, publicity, and the like, to feel more important than an elderly village grandmother from Thailand who has never seen a movie but who knows much about working in rice paddies, cooking over a wood fire, rearing a family, and speaking Thai fluently?

Is a mentally retarded child with cerebral palsy, who can neither talk nor feed himself, less human than a chimpanzee who can follow commands, climb, and eat with great dexterity? What is a human?

Is there any indication that a learned life in classical philosophy is in any way superior to that of a shaman, priestess, ship builder, or country farmer in gaining definitive answers to life's recurring questions, such as "Is there life after death?" "Does the supernatural exist?" or "What is right and what is wrong?" What do you think of C.S. Lewis's letter to his father, written after turning from a college teaching position in philosophy to one in English literature? "...I am rather glad of the change. I have come to think that if I had the mind, I have not the brain and nerves for a life of pure philosophy. A continued search among the abstract roots of things, a perpetual questioning of all that plain men take for granted, a chewing the cud for fifty years over inevitable ignorance and a constant frontier watch on the little tidy lighted conventional world of science and daily life—is this the best life for temperaments such as ours? Is it the way of health or even of sanity?... I am not condemning philosophy. Indeed in turning from it to literary history and criticism, I am conscious of a descent: and if the air on the heights did not suit me, still I have brought back something of value...At any rate I escape with joy from one definite drawback of philosophy—its solitude. I was beginning to feel that your first year carries you out of the reach of all save other professionals. No one sympathizes with your adventures in that subject because no one understands them: and if you struck treasure trove no one would be able to use it."[14]

Have you ever read something of which you understood very little and then pondered the fact that the person who wrote what you were trying to read was highly interested in it, had spent a great deal of time (*years*) studying it, and understood what was being said? Does it seem like the people who write about the Ancient Near East (such as Egyptian life around 2000 B.C. or Mesopotamian history before Hammurapi), sixteenth-century England, seventeenth-century Peru, or the nineteenth-century Soloman Islands somehow *inhabit* a world that you can only *see*? What other worlds have you seen that others inhabit? Mathematics? (Could you comprehend Pascal's *Traite du tri-*

angle arithmetique?) Physics? (Can you grasp the principles of Newton's *Principia?*) Cardiothoracic surgery? (Have you seen any television specials on medicine?) Music? (Are your skills of music appreciation matched by your skills of musical performance? Have you ever heard a musician perform and wished you could inhabit that world?) Art? (Have you ever glanced through a book of art history? Can you draw, paint, or sculpt the image in your mind's eye?) Are the innumerable subjects and complexity of our world overwhelming to ponder?

How does sexual attraction differ for someone with eyesight versus a blind man? How does sexual attraction differ for an Englishman versus an African who lives in a topless society? How does sexual interest differ for a playboy versus a quadriplegic? How would a playboy's world change if he became a quadriplegic?

Why are human beings inquisitive? What makes some people more inquisitive than others? How does a perpetual questioning of imponderables affect one's sanity? One's happiness?

Just thought I'd ask.

Footnotes

I often ask questions without explaining the reasons for my enquiries. Here are a few explanations to some questions posed in the previous chapter.

Paragraph 1—Have you ever spent a fair amount of time in bookstores or libraries just looking at all of the books and browsing through some of them? If so, you may understand how I feel rather overwhelmed by the sheer volume and extraordinary diversity of knowledge encountered there. I confront the same feelings when walking down a street in Chicago or in an airport in Miami or in a village in West Africa—so MANY people who are interested in so MANY things of which I know NOTHING. Conversely, some of the things that hold my attention and direct my studies are totally unknown to others. If I ponder the origins of romantic love, for example, the denizen of Chicago won't understand why I'm puzzled about something so "universal," whereas a woman from a West African village or city, whose marriage was *arranged* and who does all the domestic chores, bears children, and whose husband consorts with prostitutes, might hear of romance and not understand such a foreign idea.

Paragraph 2—A blind, retarded child in the U.S. may live in a climate comforted by air conditioning, eat a tasty diet and have regular meals, be kept free from the multitude of flies swarming around the face (a real *nuisance* and health hazard), learn to communicate via Braille (depending on degree of retardation), swim in a pool, or do many other things that a blind, retarded child in Ethiopia would not do. So how does this affect how they "view" the world?... I was actually thinking of a Cambridge physicist—Stephen Hawking—and not a mathematician when I posed the second question, asking how a scholar's world view differs from that of a nonliterate hunter from Brazil, whose hunting and survival skills far exceed a professor's, or a veiled Arabian woman who lives a life of obedient subordination as a "second-class" human, or a retarded child. One might also wonder how deafness affects someone's view of the world. Oliver Sacks explores this in his fascinating book *Seeing Voices*.

David Graham

Paragraph 3—It can be difficult to look at all sides of an issue and to consider each one fairly. It is often not easy to keep issues in their proper perspective, either. For example, denominational preference in the church is important and merits discussion, but to the legions of people in this world who do not subscribe to Christianity, this is a trivial affair. For myself, I find that for a person pondering whether or not God exists, the issues of denominational "allegiance," finding one's "gift," the "Lordship of Christ controversy," women's roles in the church, speaking in tongues, mode of baptism, "finding God's Will," predestination, eschatology (the end times), "holy living" (whatever that is), styles of worship, or modes of prayer are simply INSIGNIFICANT. Christian magazines, books, laymen, and pastors alike should discuss these things, but never to the point of disproportionate importance. *God in the Dock* contains C.S. Lewis's piece "On the Reading of Old Books," in which he writes, "Nothing strikes me more when I read the controversies of past ages than the fact that both sides were usually assuming without question a good deal which we should now absolutely deny. They thought that they were as completely opposed as two sides could be, but in fact they were all the time secretly united—united *with* each other and *against* earlier and later ages—by a great mass of common assumptions."[15] Surely one could take any two Christian groups who feel quite opposed to each other on one or many points and find that they both agree on several things. Would not any Christian (or Jew or Muslim) affirm a belief, for example, that the existence of God and His work in history is better than the absence of God in an atheistic universe built on chance or a Hindu universe smothered in Karma? When someone chooses to believe and enter the "narrow gate," the denominational clothes that she/he wears are not of import; the decision to enter is. "Mere Christianity" puts the controversies of the moment in their proper perspective, and humility blunts narrow-mindedness from preventing due consideration of other religious beliefs quite different from one's own.

Paragraph 4—While traveling through Benin in West Africa, I saw *thousands* of people in marketplaces, houses, along village streets, or under shade trees, and the thought kept going through my mind: "*None* of these people know who Michael Jordan is." Almost everyone in America knows who this sports mega-god is, yet if he wore plain clothes he could ride the train through Benin and no one would pay special attention to him. In this way, I would, comically,

Thoughts Along the Way

be more popular in Benin than Michael Jordan, Ella Fitzgerald, Mike Tyson, Whitney Houston, Michael Jackson, Carl Lewis, or Billy Dee Williams because my skin is white, and people would cater to me because they know that white people have money. Travel is good for gaining perspective. . . The second sentence in the paragraph was written with the show "Entertainment Tonight" in mind, though one could also watch the evening news, read grocery store magazines, attend movies, or view advertisements to see who garners the attention and glamour in our society.

Paragraph 5—I was thinking of a mentally retarded, cerebral palsy child I encountered during my pediatrics rotation in medical school.

Paragraph 6—One of the things that I particularly appreciate about C.S. Lewis was his ability to articulate things that I can only feel or poorly express. I laughed heartily when I read his letter to his father explaining the switch from tutoring in philosophy to English literature (which came about less by deliberate choice than by the need for a job, of which one in English was obtained.) I too feel that philosophy is important and do not condemn it. Indeed, most people need more philosophical training and exposure to the issues man has grappled with for ages. On the other hand, it does have its limitations in its usefulness to those who aren't "bookish" and in often ending in "inevitable ignorance." It is helpful in teaching one how to think and to some extent what to think, but it never taught anyone how to mend a boot, how to teach a child to read, how to sew an artery, how to build a wall, how to cook, how to balance to checkbook, how to ride a bike, how to shoot an arrow, how to be a friend, how to play an instrument of music, or how to navigate a boat.

Paragraph 7—This reiterates the humbling theme from the first paragraph of acknowledging human limitation in comprehending our complex world. One year, I found myself working through a few scholarly works whose erudition I certainly admired more than I understood. C.S. Lewis's brilliant *English Literature in the Sixteenth Century (Excluding Drama)* gave me glimpses of that unfamiliar world. G.T. Bettany's wonderful *Encyclopedia of World Religions*, compiled in 1892, gives a superb and fair-minded analysis of the hundreds of religions of various tribes and peoples before the influence of the white man came on the scene, in addition to discussing the more well-known religions such as Christianity, Hinduism, Buddhism, Islam, etc. It, too, was far more than I could digest. R.K. Harrison's extensive (1,325-page) *Introduction to the Old Testament* is a *thorough*, insightful, readable work that has substantially increased my confidence in the truth of Christianity. I recommend it unreservedly. Additionally, the encyclopedias and *National Geographics* that I peruse arouse my fascination yet heighten my sense of ignorance: the multiplicity of our existence is incomprehensible. Furthermore, I am not artistically gifted, and my skills of music appreciation exceed my skills of music performance so that I cannot, alas, *inhabit* those worlds. . . I'm only allowed occasional visits.

Paragraph 8—After I wrote this paragraph, I realized that Larry Flint would have been an excellent person to interview for this, as he was publishing the pornographic *Hustler* magazine when he was rendered paraplegic after a shooting. Sexual arousal seems to vary not just by bodily function but by cultural apprehension as well. In westernized countries, scanty clothing worn in a suggestive manner is a vehicle of stimulation. Compare this with the near naked Sawi of Irian Jaya who had heard that Caucasians "covered themselves with strange skins so completely that their actual persons were hardly visible! 'How difficult it must be to know them as they really are!'" they responded in Don Richardson's *Peace Child*.[16] Compare the imagery conveyed in Richardson's *Lords of the Earth* with the male image here in the West: "He [Selambo] stepped past Kugwarak, thigh muscles flowing, naked buttocks swollen yet hard. He turned to face the old man, barrel-chested torso arched vainly forward, achieving the swayback stance admired by Yalis. Like all mature Yali males, Selambo wore a penis sheath cut from a long, dried yellow gourd. Anchored to his waist by a length of string, the sheath craned at an upright angle, ostentatiously emphasizing his sexuality."[17] As for the female image, I recall viewing two movies on my return plane flights from Benin, Africa to the U.S. via Brussels, Belgium, which reflected the developed world's emphasis on sexual attraction and behaviour. Neither film was as explicit as some I've seen, but the talk, the innuendoes, and the connotations revolved around sexual intercourse quite a bit. It took being away from the American culture for less than two months to see just how inundated it is with visual and mental sexual imagery. In Benin, women casually bared their breasts to feed their children during the church services. In Brussels, they bared them for the pornographic magazines (of which many were on display at the newsstands). Such a contrast. . .

Thoughts Along the Way

Paragraph 9—Working in the emergency room of a very active trauma center and moving among a healthy cross section of society in the hospital has given me the opportunity to observe a broad range of humanity. I am thankful for this. Among the miscellaneous conclusions I have drawn are the following: some people are far more inquisitive than others; few people have a wide ranging curiosity; people enjoy talking about themselves and the things (such as their family life) that happen to them; much learning requires careful listening; prejudice, dogma, and assumptions are more easily and frequently practiced than inquiry, openness, honesty, and giving someone the benefit of the doubt; childish behaviour is not restricted to children; human frailty is universal; failure is difficult to accept; and an act of kindness is never a trivial affair.

Does a perpetual questioning of imponderables affect one's sanity? Or one's happiness? I certainly think it *can*. It doesn't have to, but it can. Discussing them with others is certainly a balm for those inclined to despondency over life's difficult problems. Near the end of his life, Sir Isaac Newton wrote his feelings about living in such a complex world. "I do not know what I may appear to the world; but to myself I seem to have been only like a boy playing on the seashore, and diverting myself in now and then finding a smoother pebble or prettier shell than ordinary, while the great ocean of truth lay all undiscovered before me."[18]

English Excursion

"In the summer of the Roman year 699, now described as the year 55 before the birth of Christ, the Proconsul of Gaul, Gaius Julius Caesar, turned his gaze upon Britain." Thus wrote Winston Churchill as he began *A History of the English Speaking Peoples*.[19] It's a splendid sentence, and when a friend extended the invitation for me to spend a holiday at his home on that island, I, too, began to turn my gaze upon Britain. One year after the offer, having "scouted" the island through consultation with previous inhabitants and several books, I arrived on the southern end of England, where I spent a week relaxing, observing, and visiting. This was my first journey to the "mother land" of America, and I came away determined that my next visit, whenever it would be, should be at least one month in length so as to better enjoy the treasures of exploration. I received several subjective, unscientific impressions on that trip, just the kind of things that are therefore fun to ponder and relate.

The first thing to make a striking impression upon the visitor can be seen when England first comes into view from an airplane or a boat. England is *green*. The grassy fields, the shrubs, the trees, and even the hedges are a stronger, more vivid green than anything seen anywhere in the United States during the late autumn months of November and December. The word "verdant" immediately sprang to mind upon beholding the land. Everywhere I traveled, this green intensity of life caught my eye and demanded consideration.

The English must love their flora, for everyone, it seems, has a garden. On the train rides from Hampton Court into London, I don't recall seeing a single house that was without a garden. Unlike the sporadically distributed gardens in the U.S., which are distinctly bordered, the ubiquitous gardens in England form what we would call a "backyard." Here in the U.S., the garden might be part of a yard. In England, the yard would be part of the garden.

England is crowded. The subways and trains in London were always closely packed, the streets of Oxford were filled with people elbow to elbow (or "cheek and jowl" as the English might say), and the shops in

Thoughts Along the Way

Windsor were lined with browsers and buyers—England struck me as a place with a high-density population. Statistics bear this out. The United Kingdom (England, Scotland, Wales, and Northern Ireland) has a population of 58 million people inhabiting 94,251 square miles of land, meaning that 612 people populate each square mile. By comparison, the U.S. is nearly nine times less dense, with 70 people per square mile. Unlike the rest of the world, though, the U.K.'s population has not mushroomed in the twentieth century. Growth has been steady but unspectacular: 40.8 million people present in 1911, 42.7 million in 1921, 44.8 million in 1931, then up to 50 million in 1951, and 56 million in 1981. Nevertheless, Great Britain (England, Scotland, Wales) squeezes its inhabitants on a crowded island. The population of London alone (exclusive of suburbs) is nearly 7 million. This leaves one wondering what it would have been like, for example, to walk the streets of Oxford with Samuel Johnson in the 1720s when only 5 million people inhabited all of Britain, and when horses and carriages roamed the streets rather than cars and buses. (Which is preferable, the smell of horse manure or exhaust fumes?) While at the Euston train station, I was accosted by a greybeard who spent the first 14 years of his life (1926-1940) in Oxford, while his father ran a photography business. He was returning from a visit to that city—only his third such since leaving a half century earlier—and remarked on the crowded condition of the Oxford streets. Far more people roamed them now than when he was a lad. Indeed the change was most remarkable.

The 1920s, as it turns out, were also C.S. Lewis's early years at Oxford. As an unknown University College scholar with ambitions of becoming a great poet, he was hardly less popular in England then than he is now. C.S. Lewis books abound in the U.S., with almost any bookstore in any city containing at least one or two of his books. Not so in England, where many a bookstore is devoid of his writing. Perhaps this is partly the result of "a prophet not being accepted in his own home town." Perhaps Brits aren't as interested in "religious matters." But mainly, I was struck by the fact that Britain is a kingdom of overachievers, and Lewis—while he does deserve some measure of attention—was but one among legions of "great" people who have come from its fold. He is but one star among a constellation, so is only the focus of relatively few people. Familiarity among a few book specialists, a sign and some pictures at his favorite Oxford pub, and a picture at the British National Portrait Gallery—these are the notices appropriated to him.

David Graham

A visit to the British National Portrait Gallery revealed something else besides Lewis's likeness. I was startled to find out that no one opened their mouth prior to the twentieth century!! Of the hundreds and hundreds of portraits I reviewed, I don't recall a single one done prior to this century that depicted any teeth. Talking, eating, all breathing (even when riding horses) seem to have been done with the mouth closed. Why do art critics not mention this astonishing fact more frequently?! Either something drastic happened in the evolution of human anatomy and physiology over the past century or illustrators and portrait painters finally learned to come to grips with reality. One painting, in particular, seemed especially absurd. It was done on a huge canvas that nearly covered the entire end-wall of one of the rooms in an upstairs gallery. Hundreds of men and women were seen crowded into a courtroom to witness the trial of Queen Caroline in 1820. Figures were seen leaning toward each other as if to whisper, gesticulating and pointing as if talking, and up walking around the room, yet they all had lips as closed as a Ziplock bag. Strangely, I don't recall my college art professor ever discussing this troubling matter. Perhaps an investigation should be launched. . .

England is rich in church buildings, but some of the larger ones are rather morbid. With an odd Anglican efficiency, the English have made some of their church buildings double as houses of worship and cemeteries (two for the price of one, so to speak.) During the candlelight Advent service in Westminster Abbey, despite being uplifted by its magnificent interior, the spirit of holiness and worship was somewhat dampened when I looked down to find my chair on top of the grave of a long deceased naval officer, interred in the abbey for admirable service to his country. Other cathedrals and chapels also combined sepulcher and altar—St. George's Chapel at Windsor Castle, the chapel at the Tower of London, and St. Paul's Cathedral, to name a few. External beauty and internal death. Christ's words to the Pharisees came back to me, "You are like whitewashed tombs which on the outside appear beautiful, but inside they are full of dead men's bones and all uncleanness." (Matthew 23:27) "For you are like concealed tombs, and the people who walk over them are unaware of it." (Luke 11:44). In a way, these churches were symbolic of the British people themselves—outwardly very polite and proper, but inwardly spiritually bereft. Yet these cathedrals, while simply part of tradition for many, are the center of worship for others, where the spirit of God moves in the hearts of the congregants. So too, the spirit of God is moving in the lives of many in a spiritually dormant country.

Sport has its heroes on both sides of the Atlantic, but the particular interests are different. When Michael Jordan retired from professional basketball, the announcement supposedly "rocked the sporting world." It would be more accurate to say "rocked the North American sporting world." Americans seem to have an overinflated view of their athletic achievements. NBA basketball, major league baseball, and NFL football teams that win league titles not uncommonly proclaim themselves to be the "world" champions. Yet these "world" champions have only beaten other teams from their own country. While basketball, baseball, and American-style football are gaining a wider following, the most popular sport in the world is *soccer* (also called "football."). On Sunday mornings in England, field after field after field is occupied by men and boys engaged in playing soccer. Cricket is another popular sport that makes news on television and in the papers there. Track and field events, while having limited popularity in the U.S., are followed on a more knowledgeable level in England (and all of Europe, for that matter). Seeing each country's sporting heroes and interests helps to temper the proclaimed self-importance of athletes and their fans. The claim, "We are the world champions!" may be properly countered with "That's an interesting claim, because most people across the ocean either don't know or don't care."

Obesity seemed less common in England than in America. While the people appeared well-fed, culinary indulgence didn't seem as obvious. This was not too surprising. The United States is a country of unrivaled opulence, and it is to be expected that the easy availability and excesses of food and luxury would create a population of overeaters. One remembers the message of Amos. "Woe to you who are complacent in Zion, and to you who feel secure on Mount Samaria. . . You lie on beds inlaid with ivory and lounge on your couches. You dine on choice lambs and fattened calves. You strum away on your harps like David and improvise on musical instruments. You drink wine by the bowlful and use the finest lotions, but you do not grieve over the ruin of Joseph. Therefore you will be among the first to go into exile; your feasting and lounging will end."[20]

Such are a few of the impressions from a brief interlude on the British isle. I look forward to the time when I can return to this kingdom and explore it more fully. The beauty of Wales, the lure of the Scottish highlands, the peacefulness of the English Lake District—these are but a few of the forces that will again cause me to turn my gaze upon Britain; and then, perhaps, another assault will be launched. . . I relish the thought.

Our Changed World

There is rarely a day that passes in which I am not cognizant of the changed world I inhabit. While the basic elements of my life are the same as those of my ancestors—I too eat food for bodily fuel, breathe air to live, clothe my body, and live in a shelter from the elements—my entire life is affected by technological advances that create a chasm between my existence and theirs. I tried to articulate some of these differences when I wrote about Kertanagara, a thirteenth-century king of Java. The way he dressed, traveled, thought, talked, worked, and lived then were so radically different from the lifestyles of today's western world. In reflecting on some of these specific differences, not merely with him but also with the rest of the world prior to the twentieth century, certain things seem to recur to the mind.

In considering the *millions* of airplane flights that presently occur on a *daily* basis, the great *size* of the large commercial planes, the *hundreds* of miles people travel in a few *hours*, the tremendous *speeds* and facile *maneuverability* of military jets, and the multitude of rocket flights and satellite launches that have sent mankind into space, it is truly amazing to think that at the beginning of this century—THIS century—no one had yet flown a mechanically powered aircraft! In less than 100 years, humanity has gone from earth-walking to walking on the moon; from earth-walking to flying several times the speed of sound; from earth-walking to crossing oceans and continents in a day. It is simply. . .astonishing.

The first successful human airlift actually occurred somewhat earlier than powered flight. On November 21, 1783, two Frenchmen named Jean-Francois Pilatre de Rozier and Francois Laurent, marquis d'Arlandes, took off in free flight for the first time, riding a hot air balloon for almost 10 miles. Over the course of the next century, others were also born aloft by this means. Even so, only a select few were able to do this. The vast populace did not become involved in generalized air travel for over a century and a half after that inaugural airlift; so that again, one is left with the astounding observation that every day, millions of people are now sent heavenward, traveling hundreds of miles from their homes in a matter of hours.

David Graham

The idea of never traveling more than 50 miles from one's front door during an entire lifetime was normal even through the end of the nineteenth century. In today's western world, this would be unusual.

The automobile has been no less of a life-changing experience. Again, successful efforts at self-propelled car engines predate the twentieth century, going back to the latter eighteenth century, but automobiles did not begin to be regularly manufactured until the 1880s, and widespread public use did not occur until *this* century. By the end of 1970, though, 243 million automobiles were in existence throughout the world. (In the United States, automotive emissions were producing 39% of the national tonnage of pollution.) The indelible changes that have come can hardly be described. There have been many more roads built and streets paved, and there is more of a "connectedness" today between the different towns and cities. From the developed world to the Third World capital cities, there is far more air pollution and city noise, as well as high-velocity crashes. Horse droppings have been replaced by tire tracks; and travel to work, worship, entertainment, and family has become much easier, with the distances traveled being much farther.

In the audiovisual sphere, the telegraph, then telephone were followed by moving pictures, radio, television, and more recently, computers, which have all "connected" people with each other. It is now possible to sit in one's own house, pick up a telephone, and speak to someone who is literally on another continent. It is now possible to drive a car across a city while listening to music composed, performed, and recorded thousands of miles away. It is now possible to fly hundreds of miles to visit a friend or discuss the same movie that was seen by both parties in separate cities. It is now possible to relax on a sofa, turn on a television, and in half an hour be informed, both visually and verbally, of current events across the nation and around the globe. In past centuries, knowledge of people in distant lands was scant, being infrequently transmitted by written or verbal description, with few visual illustrations available. Only the voyagers and travelers themselves had more than an imaginary—and often exaggerated or distorted—idea of the physical topography of a land, the smell of a distant country, the appearance of a strange people. Columbus, Pizzaro, Cortez, DeSoto, Madgellen, Cook, and Marco Polo knew these things firsthand. Those who heard their stories didn't: it was left to their imagination to paint the scenes, create the smells, and construct an

Thoughts Along the Way

idea of the faraway world. Today, there are photographs, radio broadcasts, television and computer images that daily—*DAILY*—depict the sights and sounds around the world. (Touch, taste, and smell are still not *immediately* communicated—only coming in delayed fashion through transported merchandise.) These pictures and broadcasts are not just available to privileged royalty or the literate few, either. They are now available to the far greater populace. When people speak about "our global village," they are referring to a twentieth-century phenomenon.

The effects of other revolutions still daily confront me. The role that antibiotics have played in our world is staggering. Antibiotics have had as great an impact on our life as anything in the world of medicine. Even though their use is commonplace, they still amaze me. Millions of people are still alive who grew up in the pre-antibiotic era and can appreciate their revolutionary impact. The first antibiotic, penicillin, was inaugurated during World War II, and soon came to be known as "the miracle drug." Reading the accounts of physicians working during that time reveals just how strongly the drug impacted patient survival. Infections such as cellulitis or pneumonia would have killed people 60 years ago, but today are routinely treated with antibiotics, often on an outpatient basis. Antibiotics, like immunizations, have strongly impacted the human lifespan (as well as the world's population.)

All of these changes—from airplanes to telephones to television—have increasingly led to a homogenization of society. Shelby Foote, a septuagenarian from Mississippi who is best known for his writings about America's Civil War, recently spoke of this during an interview aired on television. As a Mississippian who went to college at the University of North Carolina, he remembered breaking up his zoology class with laughter when he spoke about "oith-woims" (earthworms). The dialects of the various regions of the country were quite distinctive, and even though there is still a great variety in pronunciation of words today, Foote felt as though the differences had shrunk since the time of his boyhood in Mississippi. And perhaps they have. Even as the knowledge of and communication with the world has expanded, cultural distinctiveness is melting into the mainstream of humanity. This is not just true of language but of societal differences, too. For example, most African peoples have adopted a western style of dress, often even in areas of "bush country." Tribal garments are more for ceremonial show than daily living. School and schoolrooms, once nonexistent, are now ubiquitous. Common national languages are required learning. Food chains like McDonald's can now be found as far away as Asia and eastern Europe. On the gruesome side, head-hunting and cannibalism have all but disappeared from the planet, because even remote tribes are now under federal jurisdiction of their governments, which forbid such practices. After pausing to reflect on these widespread movements of conformity, the question inevitably arises: have we profited from all these advances, including this newer "connectedness?" Undoubtedly, yes. The benefits of exchanged knowledge are readily apparent. I think these technological advances have made our world even more interesting. (I'm *glad* I was born in the twentieth century.) I am aware, however, that technology has also served to impoverish the human spirit. Drug trafficking is more efficient and widespread with technological advancement. Pornography is much easier to distribute and access. Procrastination and distraction from work are more tempting to those with access to televisions and radios. Graphic violence, sexual promiscuity, open lying, and blasphemous language are broadly exposed to the numerous viewers of television and cinema. These all too often harden or "sear" the moral conscience. Many plant and animal species have been transported to new lands because of mankind's exploits, sometimes crowding out or destroying the indigenous flora and fauna through competition, predation, or disease. "Technology" is not a blanket blessing. Like wine or sex or language, it is a gift that may be used well or ill.

Be that as it may, our world is a vastly changed place because of it. Personally, I enjoy inhabiting such a world. I find it infinitely fascinating, amusing, and surprising. I also enjoy the benefits that come from living in the twentieth century, including the amenities of easy transportation, better health, and access to vast information. The only word I think of when pondering what it feels like to live here is

"Wow". . .

Love

Wedding Tears

Why do people cry at weddings? It's a time of joy, yet sometimes those with the greatest reason to rejoice are the ones most moved to tears. Why?

Three weeks before I began my residency, I attended a wedding out in Washington. A dear friend was marrying a man from the East Coast and people from all around the United States (and even one from Israel) flew in for the occasion. It was a time of exuberant celebration, for both the bride and groom were well loved by friends and family alike. After several days of festivities, the wedding crowned the time with a moving, beautiful ceremony. Two people exchanged solemn vows before God and a host of witnesses to remain faithful to each other always, even when they are not dressed up and standing in front of hundreds of people, are no longer newlyweds, or even young and healthy and full of erotic emotions. Their vows were so extravagant that they even pledged to be each other's spouse in sickness, in health, in good times and in bad till death did them part. No trivial promises, these two made. So the tears flowed, faces smiled, and the congregation reminded me of rain coming down from heaven while the sun shines.

Though I too had tears in my eyes and a lump in my throat, it was something that happened the night before the wedding that gave me the impetus to pen my thoughts. After finishing a picnic dinner in the park pavilion, friends and family gathered round to "roast" the bride and groom by telling humorous anecdotes about them. A friend of the bride—her roommate for three years in college—stood up and in her amusing fashion related some jocular things about the bride. It was funny though, said her friend, to see how close they had become as friends because their personalities were quite opposite in many respects. It was rather puzzling to see how their friendship had so bloomed. She did know, however, that the bride had been a very loyal friend, and it almost seemed as though the bride had *chosen* her to be her friend. She suddenly had to pause for a moment as her eyes welled up with tears. She was not the only one deeply moved.

"She chose her," I mused. It was a beautiful display of love. To be the recipient of such love evokes many emotions, not the least of which are gratitude and devotion: gratitude for the underserved gift, and devotion to the love giver. As I thought of this concept of choosing, I remembered the words of the Apostle John when he wrote, "We love because He first loved us."[1] We respond because He first touched. John also writes, "This is love: not that we loved God, but that He loved us and sent His Son as an atoning sacrifice for our sins,"[2] a thought that Paul echoed when he wrote to the Christians in Rome, "But God demonstrates His love towards us, in that while we were yet sinners, Christ died for us."[3] We love because He first loved, we speak because He first spoke, and we live because He gives us life. "In Him we live and move and have our being."[4]

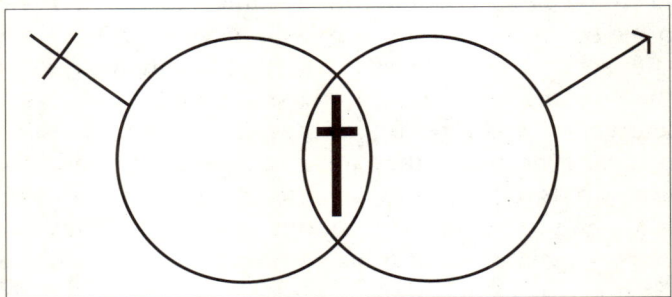

So why do people cry at weddings? I don't know; but perhaps it has something to do with the love we bear for the beloved and the joy we experience in seeing two people who have chosen each other and have pledged their faithfulness to that choice. It's not a bad reminder, really, of an earlier choice, when even before the earth was created, all of us were chosen to have life and the offer of salvation. Perhaps the best way to show gratitude and demonstrate our devotion is to share with others the love of one who loved us first.

Longfellow, Dumas, and Hatred

> This is the forest primeval. The murmuring
> pines and the hemlocks,
> Bearded with moss, and in garments green,
> indistinct in the twilight,
> Stand like Druids of eld, with voices sad
> and prophetic,
> Stand like harpers hoar, with beards that
> rest on their bosoms.
> Loud from its rocky caverns, the deep-voiced
> neighboring ocean
> Speaks, and in accents disconsolate answers
> the wail of the forest. [5]

Thus begins Henry Longfellow's "Evangeline," a tragic story of lost love that I first read disinterestedly in eighth grade. Partially based on a true story, it's the tale of an engaged couple from Acadie in French Canada. On what was to be the young nuptial's wedding day, all the men of the province were summoned by the authorities to assemble in the church to hear a proclamation. When assembled, they were all seized and shipped off to be distributed throughout New England—among them the bridegroom Gabriel. Afterward, his betrothed (Evangeline) set off in search of him—wandered a lifetime about New England then Louisiana and, at last, when she was old, found her bridegroom on his deathbed. He died in her arms, and she soon joined him in the grave. To a 14-year-old interested in sports, baseball cards, and having fun, it was just another reading assignment. The full impact of its appeal wouldn't hit me for another dozen years.

Shortly after my re-encounter with "Evangeline", I read Alexander Dumas's novel *The Count of Monte Cristo*. This tale also has its foundations in a true story and provides a thoughtful counterpoint to "Evangeline." In 1838, an archivist named Jacques Peuchet published six volumes of crime stories taken from the files of the Paris police. Contained therein was the story of a young shoemaker from Nimes who, in 1807, became engaged to marry a rich and beautiful orphan, but because of a despicable practical joke played by four jealous friends, was falsely arrested as a spy for the English against Napoleon and imprisoned until the empire fell in 1814. While still in prison, he met a dying Italian priest who told him where a great treasure was buried. Upon his release he found the treasure and, using various disguises, cold-bloodedly proceeded to wreak his vengeance on those responsible for his misfortune, one of whom had married his fiancee. The retelling of that real-life melodrama is, pretty nearly, *The Count of Monte Cristo* in outline.

Though dissimilar as stories, Longfellow's and Dumas's tales do share a common tragedy of a wedding-day separation, providing an interesting contrast in reactions to the tragedy. The Count of Monte Cristo, after finding his fortune, became a man of formidable learning, lavish wealth, and possessor of a cunning mind. He could be gracious, entertaining, likable, and even endearing, but his soul was motivated by one overwhelming desire: revenge. The goal of revenging his enemies and former fiancee never left his mind. Reading his slow, subtle, yet devastatingly thorough acts of vengeance produced mixed emotions in me. My sense of justice was vindicated, for here was a man greatly wronged, who turned the tables so that the evil of his enemies was returned back upon them. It gave me the same satisfaction as reading the biblical narrative of Daniel, whose malicious accusers were themselves thrown in the lion's den by order of King Darius. (The Count's actions wrecked not only his enemies' lives, but those of their families as well. Evil—even by association—has consequences. The families of Daniel's accusers were also, you will recall, cast into the lion's den.)

Yet it also saddened me to see a man so nearly consumed by hate that he could not forgive. His very character was transformed by his desire for revenge. Only after his vengeance bore fruit did the Count see the harm of his hatred to himself. By then, there was little left that reconciliation could mend.

Such deep-seated anger and hatred, the Count's driving passions, are well described by Frederic Buechner. Of "Anger," he writes,

> Of the Seven Deadly Sins, anger is possibly the most fun. To lick your wounds, to smack your lips over grievances long past, to roll over your tongue the prospect of bitter confrontations still to come, to savor to the last toothsome morsel both the pain you are given and the pain you are giving back—in many ways it is a feast fit for a king. The chief drawback is that what you are wolfing down is yourself. The skeleton at the feast is you.[6]

Of "Hate" he writes,

> Hate is as all-absorbing as love, as irrational, and in its own way as satisfying. As lovers thrive on the presence of the beloved, haters revel in encounters with the ones they hate. They confirm him in all his darkest suspicions. They add fuel to all his most burning animosities. The anticipation of them makes the hating heart pound. The memory of them can be as sweet as young love.
>
> The major difference between hating and loving is perhaps that whereas to love somebody is to be fulfilled and enriched by the experience, to hate somebody is to be diminished and drained by it. Lovers, by losing themselves in their loving, find themselves, become themselves. Haters simply lose themselves. Theirs is the ultimate *consuming* passion.[7]

Evangeline spent her life searching for her betrothed but, by contrast, the motive of her actions was love. Her love was of the highest order, so that even while she did not find her beloved Gabriel, she sought others to whom her love could be given. "Patience and abnegation of self, and devotion to others. This was the lesson a life of trial and sorrow had taught her."[5] At the very last, she did find her long lost Gabriel—on his deathbed. After spying him, she knelt and held his head to her bosom for one moment before he died, the hope of an agonizing lifetime's search realized and then quickly snuffed out. When this temporary bliss was swiftly snatched away, it did not produce what would seem to be inevitable bitterness. The response was a meekly bowed head and a soul that murmured, "Father, I thank thee!"

The Apostle Paul wrote to the Romans, "Do not be overcome by evil, but overcome evil with good."[8] Justice must be served, evil punished, and wrongs between friends righted. If in this process, however, the heart is enslaved by hate, then no justice can free that spirit from its prison. It's an incarceration of the soul.

God help us avoid it.

The Shadowlands of C.S. Lewis

I never lost as much but twice,
And that was in the sod;
Twice have I stood a beggar
Before the door of God!

Angels—twice descending,
Reimbursed my store—
Burglar! Banker—Father!
I am poor once more!

— Emily Dickinson[9]

It is not often that a man who spends his career as a scholar in the world of academia receives much attention from the public. Exceptions do occur from time to time, but by and large the arenas of politics, sports, and entertainment are the worlds that produce most widely recognized individuals. With the PBS (Public Broadcasting System) television release of the film *Shadowlands*, followed by a Broadway play and later a popular movie of the same name, the life of one such exception has gained more attention over the last few years. C.S. Lewis was the one featured in these *Shadowlands* productions, not so much for his writings or his well-attended lectures or his popular broadcast talks over the BBC (British Broadcasting Corporation) as for his marriage to Joy Davidman. The PBS film and the Hollywood movie show the agony and the ecstasy of Lewis's falling in love with a woman dying of cancer, her recovery, their joy together, then her relapse and death, followed by Lewis's sorrow. Throughout the dramas, Lewis's Christian faith is tested and matured as he faces the realities of pain and death of his beloved Joy.

While both films are very well done, they are nonetheless *dramas*—not biographies—and as such are often at variance with the factual reality of Lewis's life. Throughout both films (I haven't seen the play)

Thoughts Along the Way

Lewis is pictured as serious, somber, and later somewhat shaken in his Christian faith by Joy's illness and death. While Lewis was *sincere*, he was seldom solemn or morose, and although he did grieve over Joy and struggle with his concept of God, his faith remained intact. (His book *A Grief Observed*, written through the pain that followed Joy's death, was meant to be more than an anguished cry—it was something of an apologetic as well.) Those who knew Lewis (or "Jack" as he was known to his friends and family) on an intimate level spoke of him as a genial, even jolly person whose humor was often displayed even in his most serious discussions. Also contrary to the movie version, Lewis did not have a smug view of the theological problem of pain. The Hollywood film has Lewis lecturing to various audiences, giving moral platitudes to explain the problem of pain: "Pain is God's megaphone to rouse a deaf world." While Lewis did write this in his book *The Problem of Pain*, he also wrote, "For that very reason there is one criticism which cannot be brought against me. No one can say, 'He jests at scars who never felt a wound', for I have never for one moment been in a state of mind to which even the imagination of serious pain was less than intolerable. If any man is safe from the danger of underestimating this adversary, I am that man. I must add, too, that the only purpose of the book is to solve that intellectual problem raised by suffering; for the far higher task of teaching fortitude and patience I was never fool enough to suppose myself qualified, nor have I anything to offer my readers except my conviction that when pain is to be borne, a little courage helps more than much knowledge, a little human sympathy more than much courage, and the least tincture of the love of God more than all."[10] Indeed, Lewis himself knew what pain, suffering, and death brought to the human soul. He had lost friends and family members throughout the years, from childhood, when his mother died of cancer, to adult life, when he lost many friends (including his dear friend Charles Williams). Lewis's faith, however, was in the long run strengthened by these experiences, even the experience of losing his wife. They forced him to test the reality of his faith in God.

What Lewis did learn from his marriage was the personal meaning of erotic love and its loss. Having successfully and brilliantly written about courtly love in his thirties as a scholarly bachelor (*The Allegory of Love*), Lewis came to understand the matter with his heart as a happy newlywed in his fifties. "Years ago when I wrote about medieval love-poetry and described its strange, half make-believe, 'religion of love,' I was blind enough to treat this as an almost purely literary phenomenon. I know better now. Eros by his nature invites it. Of all loves he is, at his height, most god-like; therefore most prone to demand our worship. Of himself he always tends to turn 'being in love' into a sort of religion."[11]

"Tis better to have loved and lost than not to have loved at all," wrote Alfred Lord Tennyson.[12] Yes it is, but why? Forrest Carter probably gave the best answer to that question in his book *The Education of Little Tree*. Little Tree described what he felt like when one of his beloved dogs died in an accident. "I felt total bad about it, and empty. Granpa said he knew how I felt, for he was feeling the same way. But Granpa said everything you lost which you had loved give you that feeling. He said the only way round it was not to love anything, which was worse because you would feel empty all the time."[13] Indeed. Lewis, who chose to love, did grieve over Joy. Just how painful his mournings were can be seen in *A Grief Observed*. Yet he did not despair. He remained a genial man, still able to think and write and enjoy his friends, though with perhaps a deeper understanding of their own loves and bereavements. Although he might never have said so, his life after Joy certainly showed that he felt it truly was better to have loved and lost than not to have loved at all. Perhaps, with time, something of his love for Joy could be captured by a statement he once made about a friend that he lost to death years before—Captain W.O. Field ("Wof"), one of his companions on his annual walking tours. "Wof was the most completely lovable man, almost, I have known. I am so glad to have known him that it almost obliterates the loss."[14]

The *Shadowlands* productions are moving accounts of the love between a man and a woman who loved God. They show some of the anguish that Jack and Joy shared physically, emotionally, and spiritually. Death of the beloved is as sad as anything one can experience in life; yet *Shadowlands* can only tell a portion of one man's travail. It doesn't reveal the other gift of love, the one that is still left when the beloved dies. It is a gift that grows richer and deeper with time. For beyond the lingering sorrow is the blessing of a lingering love, of continued affection for the loved one and gratefulness for the love that was. For creatures who brought nothing into this world and who can carry nothing out of it, the *gratefulness* for having had such a love is a balm for the soul when the loved one is lost. Such gratitude is a healing salve. Especially for so deep a wound.

Thoughts Along the Way

To lose thee, sweeter than to gain
All other hearts I knew.
'Tis true the drought is destitute,
But then I had the dew!

— Emily Dickinson[15]

Surprised by J.

May marks the anniversary of the date when Joahnna Evans and I exchanged wedding vows. Anniversaries, birthdays, and holidays are meant to commemorate important events, to reflect on the past while celebrating the present; so for once I have decided to put my puzzlings, questionings, and diffident speculations aside and write instead about something reliable and meaningful, something about which I have no doubts: my marriage.

I spent my first 28 years on this planet being single, marrying Joahnna (or "J"as I sometimes call her) near the end of my second year of residency. Twenty-eight years constitutes a significant portion of my life span, contributing to the strong sense of individuality and independence I feel, a certain "I"-ness that pervades my view of the world. The "we"-ness of marriage is at times still more of an intellectual acknowledgment than a heartfelt reality. It takes time to adjust the mental stance from the "she and I" position to one of "us." Among other things, this position manifests itself in my writings, as, for example, when I wrote about my observations and reflections from a trip to England (cf. pp. 20-24). Because I was trying to maintain consistency in writing style, I wrote entirely in the first person singular ("I"), rather than combining a first person plural ("we") journey with first person singular ("my") observations. While this achieved stylistic unity, it unfortunately gave the impression that I went on the trip by myself, when, in fact, I was accompanied by my favorite traveling companion. Joahnna and I *both* had an enjoyable week "relaxing, observing, and visiting." The observations I shared were my own, but we talked and laughed about both mine and hers while we were there.

Among other reasons, Joahnna is a good traveling companion because she brings a complementary mode of thinking to our marriage. While I tend to view matters from a pronounced rationalistic, deductive point, she sees things from more of an intuitive, inductive angle. To illustrate, I am more apt to comment on the content of what a person says, whereas she is more likely to notice how that person is feeling when they talk or what sort of personality would say such things. I tend to focus on the results of a person's or society's work,

Thoughts Along the Way

while she finds herself pondering the motivation behind it. We have both admitted to each other that our different approaches have been mutually helpful. She has helped develop my intuition, while I have offered her rational stimulation.

Ideas and insights are, of course, only part of what we exchange. Part of the fun of a great marriage is sharing, be it histories, experiences, ideas, love, food, stories, beauty, books, or friends. For instance, we both enjoy walking outside and pointing out various things to each other. "Wow, look at that hawk!" "Isn't that tree beautiful?" "I believe that squirrel has been eating quite well here. He's huge." "Hey, what kind of bird is that?" We enjoy visiting cities together and trying out different restaurants—as well as regaling our friends and family about some of our adventures. (One of our favorite stories tells of a cultural faux pas while eating at an Indian restaurant in Hampton Court, England. Joahnna had asked—twice—for iced tea, a common drink in the southern United States, but a rarity in the northern U.S. and an absolute anomaly in England. After receiving a thorough explanation on how to prepare this novelty, our server turned and left. Much later, not one, but two waiters returned to the table, bearing with them their prize creation and beaming proudly at their success in preparing this oddity. They placed three small ice cubes in a generous tea cup, set it in front of J., and handed her a piping hot pot of tea, the contents of which promptly melted the miserable little cubes... We waited until they left the table before laughing.) A receptive audience, someone with similar interests and sense of humor, makes the good things in life even better. We both provide this for each other.

Similar interests should not be confused with identical ideology. We are both independent, strong-willed people, and when two such people marry, there are going to be disagreements. I enjoy being in a marriage where we can respectfully cross swords. (The key word is "respectfully." If there is not mutual respect, then disagreements become merely argumentative abuse.) Proverbs 27:17 states, "As iron sharpens iron, so one man sharpens another." The vast majority of the time, J. and I agree on things; when we do disagree, it almost always proves constructive for both of us, and I like that.

Joahnna is a vivacious, friendly, outgoing, extroverted person who, it may accurately be said, "never met a stranger." I am the opposite, a reserved and introverted person who clams up when in a crowd of strangers. Marriage to such an opposite has helped to prevent me from becoming a hermit. Surgery residency helps foster any underlying tendencies toward social isolation outside of the hospital because it places heavy demands on a physician's time and encourages a selfish attitude. I guard what little free time I have jealously and look detestably upon interruptions and social engagements as intrusions upon my life. For example, I might say, "This Saturday will be my last day away from the hospital for the next three months. I see people all day, every day at the hospital and I would like to be alone. I'm *not* going to have any visitors intruding on my free time." This, of course, is not like Jesus Christ who, even when tired, addressed the people who intruded on His free time. But it does reflect the reality of the attitude inculcated by residency. I realized even before I married that my hermit's attitude was too comfortable to change and might ultimately lead to a self-centered life of indulgence. (Charles Williams's novel *Descent into Hell* would sometimes come to mind.) Joahnna continues to help this poor, socially retarded soul in that respect, and I am grateful (sometimes grudgingly) for that.

Authors like C.S. Lewis and Philip Yancey have written of people and things that "fill words with meaning" for them. For me, Joahnna fills the words "love" and "loyalty" with meaning. In fact, the two go hand in hand. Her love and loyalty for me are constant: filling, surrounding and supporting me. I have said to some people that marriage is often either the best or worst thing that can happen to them. I am grateful that my own marriage has been the former. Some would say that for this gift, I should thank my lucky stars. But I don't. I thank God.

Frailty

Frailty Part 1: The Conversation

We were sitting in the park watching the sun set when a neighbor I'll call Dietrich changed the course of the conversation.

"You know, David, I just don't understand why our minds work like they do. It seems as though God could have given us brains that we could use to control what we think and how we feel. But things aren't like that. Yesterday I was readin' 'bout these people who have 'obsessive-compulsive disorders,' and how they can't make these recurring thoughts go away except by doing some action. This one lady was washing her hands 50-60 times a day 'cause she kept having these thoughts about dirt coming into her head. It took the psychiatrists two years to help her get over this problem. Two *years*!! She couldn't just command her brain to quit thinking these thoughts. Well, at least she got over it. Some people struggle a whole lifetime and never get control, even those who are smart and well educated. Weren't you the one telling me about C.S. Lewis's brother Warren?"

"Yes, I did," I replied. "He battled the bottle for his whole adult life. Sometimes he was successful—even for periods of over a year—and sometimes he failed and went on drinking binges. He never conquered it."

"He was a Christian even, and he never conquered it?!"

"That's right," I said. "Many others have been like him. Have you ever read Graham Greene's *The Power and The Glory*?"

"No," he replied, "never even heard of it...ya know, we can't control how we feel either. I had a friend of mine whose cousin had depression. She was a Christian and she used to pray and pray, asking God to lift this oppressive 'weight' off her chest, to give her motivation to work, to feel okay again, to have the Holy Spirit 'fill her' and overcome her depression. Think her prayers helped? They sure didn't help her overcome depression. She thought about suicide on a daily basis. She was rescued only because she finally quit her job and moved away to a new town and job. Seems like it was her circumstances that saved her, not her prayers."

Thoughts Along the Way

"Maybe God answered her prayers to overcome her emotions by having her move away," I offered.

"I suppose," he replied somewhat doubtfully, "though the way she talks about it, she wanted to succeed where she was (I think her phrase was "have victory over the situation").

"All of us struggle, Dietrich," I said, "though most people's problems don't vanish quickly. There do seem to be a lot of people, like Billy Sunday, who give testimonies to how their conversion to Christianity delivered them from struggles with alcoholism, greed, drug addiction, cruelty, sexual promiscuity, or other problems. Many times, though, it takes a while to overcome problems and some people have one or two big struggles that they never overcome. I don't have much sympathy for those who give up and give in to their struggles, and I hate to hear people trying to justify their caving in. On the other hand, my heart goes out to someone who keeps on trying and failing and trying and failing. As long as the effort is there to stand back up and start walking again, I can forgive a person who trips and falls."

"Like, for example, who?" he asked.

"Well, like Christians who struggle with their sexuality. If someone tells me they have difficulties because of homosexual attractions, I am understanding. But if someone tells me that they are homosexual and a Christian and that the bigoted church should accept this as a justified position, I tend to become angry since I disagree so vehemently with this. The Bible always rejects homosexuality as a justifiable lifestyle. You might say I have sympathies with them on personal, but not theological grounds."

Dietrich paused and sipped his lemonade. "You may be wondering why I'm tellin' ya these things." He paused again and then continued in his thick Southern drawl, which disguised the fact that he was a very intelligent, well-educated architect. "I have problems trying to control my own thoughts and feelings, which means I have problems controlling my actions. I have a recurring set of thoughts that I find repulsive and morally unacceptable. It's not like that lady whose obsessive thoughts happened all day long every day. Mine come back anywhere from two weeks to two months later, more or less I suppose, like an alcoholics' temptations. It is exacerbated if I read a certain sort of literature. You see, my problem of womanizing is founded upon a wild fantasy life that objectively I know to be quite fictitious. Imaginatively, this life is quite real. In fact, you would be shocked if I told you what my ultimate fantasy was."

He decided to go ahead and tell this to me, and when he finished, he looked at me to see any signs of surprise or disgust on my face. I simply nodded my head in understanding and when he received my reassurance, he continued.

"I do a good job most of the time evading overt pornography like *Penthouse* or *Hustler* magazines, and have even begun to skip a few movies I might normally see, just because they are sexually provocative. But I have problems when a friend loans me a modern novel or I browse through the bestseller or romance sections in a bookstore. You wouldn't believe how much trash gets printed. Hundreds or even thousands of books depicting some of the most unbelievable situations, conversations, human responses, and emotions. Somehow, though, it sells well, probably because people are attracted to fantasy worlds like those of James Bond or Star Wars. Well, a theme often found in modern fiction is that of a beautiful, voluptuous, innocent girl who loses her innocence and naiveté in several areas, one of which is always the sexual. Whether through seduction or rape or an affair, the initial sexual acts are spelled out in detail. . .*in detail*," he repeated. "Course, if the girl hated it initially (as in rape), she eventually comes to enjoy and desire it, and these subsequent intercourses are also spelled out quite graphically. Maybe a woman can read these books and not be permanently affected by them, but it doesn't surprise me that real-life rapists cannot identify with the feelings of the

victim, and why a lot of 'em think, 'Sooner or later a girl has to relax and just enjoy it.' Where do you think they get these ideas?!"

"Course, I know they are misleading. Even so, I know another man for whom I have a lot of respect, and though he is a Christian and a preacher with a devoted wife and Christian family and a good congregation to preach to—he's even written a few books that a lot of people have been helped by—his surroundings were somehow not enough to keep him from having an affair last year. I think it was some woman he had been counseling. How about that? Here's a woman he's supposed to be helping to control her own sin and he has adultery with her for six months. . .'Course, afterward he was pretty sorry and remorseful 'bout the whole thing. I really think he was sincerely sorry too, 'cause he didn't think what he did was right. But I wonder what was goin' through his mind when he started headin' down the lusty path to adultery? Whatever he was thinkin', he didn't seem to control it too well. I mean, here was a man who had everything to lose and only a few fleeting moments of pleasure to gain by this."

"Sort of like King David when he went after Bathsheba," I interjected.

"Yeah, sort of like that. Course I think that anyone who has been in Alcoholics Anonymous, or in therapy for depression, or even embarrassed by repeated public outbursts of anger probably feels a little sympathy for him. Which brings me back to the question of 'Why?!' Why do we think about and dwell on and do things we later regret? Why is it that the alcoholic, the obsessive-compulsive woman, the depressed girl, the angry man, the liar, the kleptomaniac, or the perpetually jealous or bitter person," he was talking faster and faster, "or even the everyday lustful like this preacher or King David or myself have the wish to stop but don't?! You know, even the Apostle Paul said that he did the very things he did not want to do. It is so frustrating, David! Why can't we always control our thoughts? Isn't the Holy Spirit," his voice was now rising, "supposed to help us when we ask? If it is demons that are tempting us, won't our prayers crying for help drive them away? I mean," he yelled, "WHY DOESN'T GOD GIVE US MORE *CONTROL* OVER OURSELVES???!!!"

I sat for a full minute in silence, and when I looked up at him, I gave him the only honest answer I could give. "I don't know, Dietrich. . . I don't know."

We drained our glasses, shook hands, and silently walked back to our homes.

Frailty Part 11: The Discussion

> "Nothing softeneth the Arrogance of our Nature like a Mixture of some Frailties. It is by them that we are best told, that we must not strike too hard upon others because we ourselves do so often deserve blows. They pull our rage by the sleeve and whisper Gentleness to us in our censures."
>
> —Halifax [1]

Life is queer. After my conversation with Dietrich about why God gave us brains that often produce thoughts we cannot control, I had yet another reminder that many things in life just can't be explained or discovered. We explain all that we can, we do research, and we make educated guesses, but in the end our ignorance gets the better of us and we shrug our shoulders and say, "*Je ne sais pas.*"

Why do humans dream? What makes a lemming join hundreds of other lemmings to jump off of a cliff into the sea during peak population spurts? Why do most women have reproductive systems that in theory work beautifully but in practice malfunction so often that ovarian cysts, ectopic pregnancies, menstrual cramps, urinary tract infections, or cervical cancer are common medical occurrences? How does language work? What makes laughter enjoyable? How does music evoke responses from its listeners? Why are there streaks of success or failure in sports (e.g., what makes a basketball player like Larry Bird have a game where he struggles, misses most of his shots for three quarters, then suddenly light up the scoreboard by making 9 of 10 shots in the final period?). Why are humans so conceited? If there is an omnipotent God out there, why did He create people with bodies that fart? Why don't we have digestive systems that internally combust our food, leaving no trace left over, instead of converting it to a product that causes us to build toilets? *Je ne sais pas.* I don't know.

Thoughts Along the Way

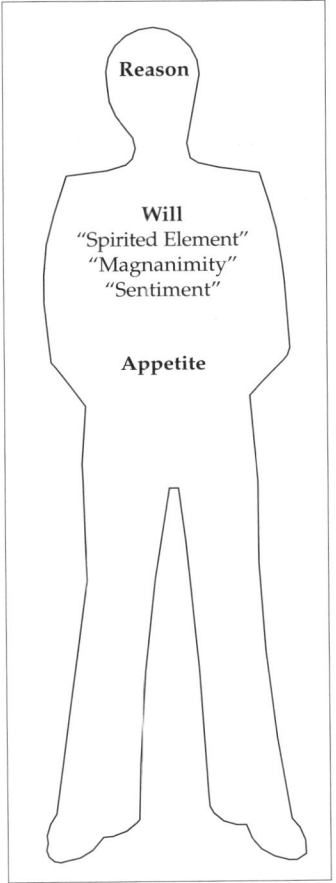

Life is queer. To many questions, the only answer is, "That's just the way things are."

As I continued to ponder my conversation with Dietrich, I thought about a trilogy of books I read back in March of 1990 near the end of medical school: C.S. Lewis's *Preface to Paradise Lost*, John Milton's *Paradise Lost*, and Lewis's *Perelandra*. *Paradise Lost* tells the story of Satan's and other angels' fall from glory, Satan's successful temptation of Eve and mankind's fall from sinlessness, and the loss of the garden of Eden ("Paradise Lost"). This book is an imaginative reconstruction of the past that is consistent with the scriptures, though not strictly history. It is a fictional treatment of a true story, somewhat like Irving Stone's biography of Michelangelo (*The Agony and the Ecstasy*) or William Shakespeare's *Julius Caesar* or perhaps the Old Testament book of Job. I gained much besides enjoyment from reading it, as it enabled me to feel the *appeal* of *holiness* (*Perelandra* did this as well) and to better understand the ideas of predestination, foreknowledge, freedom, and the presence of evil in the world. As C.S. Lewis said of George McDonald's *Phantastes*, *Paradise Lost* "baptized my imagination."

My conversation with Dietrich gave me the impetus to focus in on ideas that Milton wrote about and Lewis expanded upon. *Paradise Lost* painted an imaginative picture of the human psyche based on its description in Plato's *Republic*, where Reason, Will, and Appetite are likened to the head, chest, and belly. "As the king governs by his executive, so Reason in a man must rule the mere appetites by means of the 'spirited element,'" writes Lewis in *The Abolition of Man*. "The head rules the belly through the chest—the seat, as Alanus tells us, of Magnanimity, of emotions organized by trained

47

David Graham

habit into stable sentiments. The Chest—Magnanimity—Sentiment—these are the indispensable liaison officers between cerebral man and visceral man. It may even be said that it is by this middle element that man is man: for by his intellect he is mere spirit and by his appetite mere animal."[2] *Paradise Lost* depicted the Reason ruling the Appetites through Will *before* the Fall, but Appetite being the ruling faction *after* it. Milton gives an example of this by demonstrating the increased sexual drive of Adam and Eve immediately after eating the fruit.

> But that false fruit far other operation first displayed, carnal desire inflaming. He on Eve began to cast lascivious eyes; she him as wantonly repaid; in lust they burn.

Other passions also began to rule,

> They sat them down to weep. Nor only tears rained at their eyes, but high winds worse within began to rise, high passions—anger, hate, mistrust, suspicion, discord—and shook sore their inward state of mind, calm region once and full of peace, now tossed and turbulent: for Understanding ruled not, and the Will heard not her lore, both in subjection now to sensual Appetite, who, from beneath usurping over sovereign Reason, claimed superior sway. [3]

Perhaps the Apostle Paul explained this lack of control best when he wrote, "for the good that I wish, I do not do; but I practice the very evil I do not wish." [4]

> *For the good that I wish, I do not do; But I practice the very evil I do not wish.*

Fortunately, God is greater than everything and is able to use both good and evil actions to bring about a greater good in carrying out His will. In Books XI and XII of *Paradise Lost*, Adam is given a preview of the history of the world to come. Adam is astonished at the power "that all this good of evil shall produce, and evil turn to good." One can go directly from Milton to Romans 8:28. [5] Lewis's *A Preface to Paradise Lost* explains this well:

48

Though God has made all creatures good He foreknows that some will voluntarily make themselves bad and also foreknows the good use which He will then make of their badness. For as He shows His benevolence in *creating* good Natures, He shows His justice in *exploiting* evil wills...
As the angels point out, whoever tries to rebel against God produces the result opposite to his intention. At the end of the poem, Adam is astonished at the power "that all this good of evil shall produce." This is the exact reverse of the programme Satan had envisaged in Book I, when he hoped, if God attempted any good through him, to "pervert that end"; instead he is allowed to do all the evil he wants and finds that he has produced good. [And now Lewis delivers the coup de grace:] Those who will not be God's sons become his tools.[6]

Many of the biblical passages that had troubled me for so long became clear as I considered God exploiting evil wills for his purposes: Pharaoh hardening his heart, and God in turn hardening Pharaoh's heart for His glory, God using rebellious spirits for His purposes such as tormenting a disobedient King Saul, enticing King Ahab to fight and die to end a wicked reign, turning the evil of Joseph's brothers into good, using Satan's cruelty to Job as a means to reveal *Himself* to Job (Job responds, "I have heard of Thee by the hearing of the ear; But now my eye sees Thee"[7]) or even using the jealousy and hypocrisy of some Jewish countrymen to bring about His son's death, thereby bringing salvation to the world.

> *Those who will not be God's sons become His tools.*

It is sometimes hard to see why we continue to struggle with the same problems, especially when others seem to conquer theirs. Why does Dietrich, who loves God, continue to do battle with the lust within him? What good can come of it? Ultimately, I don't know. There are, however, two things he can learn from his problems: humility and empathy. Knowing his own inability to be master in all areas of his life (thus making him like me and everyone I've ever met) can help him to be more understanding of the struggles of others (something most people, including Christians, do not often do). The Apostle Paul writes, for this reason, to keep me from exalting myself, there was given me a thorn in the flesh, a messenger of Satan to buffet me—to keep me from exalting myself! Concerning this I entrusted the Lord three times that it might depart from me. And He said to me, "My grace is sufficient for you, for power is perfected in weakness." Most gladly, therefore, I will rather boast about my weaknesses, that the power of Christ may dwell in me. Therefore I am well content with weaknesses, with insults, with distresses, with persecutions, with difficulties, for Christ's sake; for when I am weak, then I am strong. [8]

Frustration and pain accompany us when we try and try again, only to keep failing, realizing that we are not rid of our struggles. Because of this, God can teach us humility and empathy. Moreover, God can and does use even our sins and errors to build His kingdom. It is indeed most comforting to realize that salvation is by faith in God's grace, not being in any way dependent on what we consider to be success or failure in adhering to an every-day-pretty-goodness. Thank God.

What's Bred in the Bone

Can the Ethiopian change his skin
Or the leopard his spots?
Then you also can do good
Who are accustomed to do evil.

Jeremiah 13:23

My mother has told me that I was spanked more than twice as many times as any of my other four siblings. I take a rather perverse pride in this fact. It gives me a place of distinction in my family, a sense that no matter how much the others did, they could not match my record. I required more disciplinary action than anyone else. I was the champion.

There does finally come a time, though, when the spankings cease. We gradually evolve our own standards, make our own decisions, and develop our own patterns of behavior, sometimes adhering to the canon we were reared by and sometimes not. Many things may influence our choices, including our conscience (usually conditioned by our upbringing), our friends, our family, social or political pressures as well as our ambitions. We certainly lead multifaceted lives.

It is peculiar how our minds can take an idea and continue to work on it "after closing time," for I had a dream in which I was discussing these things with a friend while taking a break from helping him build a new porch. As best as I can remember, I was telling him that one of my favorite novelists, Robertson Davies, once began one of his books with the quote, "What's bred in the bone will not out of the flesh."

"Well, that's a strange way of putting it," he said, "but there is a lot of truth in that. The values instilled into us—either by families, friends, or what we pick up ourselves—tend to stick with us, either outwardly or inwardly; I mean, we can change, but it ain't always easy." (chuckle) I guess that's what Davies' quote was saying—if somethin' is bred or buried deep in us, like bone, it won't leave just by wishing it would or by making superficial changes, like shedding skin off the flesh. Hard to get away from our breeding, isn't it?"

"Yeah," I replied, "especially on our own. If we have a bone tumor, it takes another person—a surgeon—to cut through the flesh and remove it."

"Like that Dravecky guy who use to pitch for the San Francisco Giants. He had a bone tumor in his pitching arm and the doctors finally ended up cutting his whole arm off. I bet *that* hurt."

"Physically and emotionally," I added.

"Yeah. . . Wow."

"Anyway, our habits are habitual...Uh, I guess that's redundant, isn't it? Well, I suppose it does underscore the truth of establishing—and keeping—*good* thinking and behavioral patterns. It's a lot easier to prevent illness than it is to cure it. That is a lesson I have learned from medicine and it applies to our moral choices, too."

"Yeah, yeah, 'An ounce of prevention is worth a pound of cure,' right? Well, the trouble is that human curiosity is pretty strong. Add peer pressure to that and prevention isn't as easy as you make it sound."

"You're right," I conceded, "but I still think it is better to establish habits that are *good*. Doing the right thing takes practice sometimes. That's why we are supposed to be accountable to others. Humans weren't meant to live in a vacuum. As a Christian I believe that we should tell others when we need help."

"Yeah. But that kind of thing hurts a fella's pride."

"Well, it sure beats getting spanked!" I replied.

I must have awoken shortly after that because I remember opening my eyes and thinking, "Spoken like a true champion. . . "

The Knowledge of Experience

We all subscribe thoughtlessly to many beliefs, the truth of which does not strike home to us until experience gives them reality. Wisdom may be rented, so to speak, on the experience of other people, but we buy it at an inordinate price before we make it our own forever.

Leaven of Malice by Robertson Davies [9]

As the plane continued to circle around the Pittsburg airport, waiting for the snowstorm to clear so it could land, I sat inside strapped to my seat, wondering when that time would come. The air turbulence and continuous circling were making me queasy. I had only experienced motion sickness once before—years ago on a sailboat in choppy waters off of Haiti's coast—and I wasn't tolerating it much better the second time around. I tried to distract myself by thinking of other things, but to little avail. Next to the nausea itself, the worst feeling was not knowing when the ride would end. The minutes ticked by like hours.

While I was trying to stoically endure the ordeal, a woman sitting next to me turned and asked, "You feelin' sick?" "Yeah," I nodded. "Me to," she replied. "Now you know what it's like being pregnant, only it's like this all the time." I could only reply by shaking my head in dismay. Then it was time to return to the business of trying to prevent my lunch from making a sudden bodily exit. After what seemed like days, the plane finally did land. Somehow, I managed to debark without ever using a "doggie bag."

The French essayist Michel de Montaigne once wrote, "There is no desire more natural than the desire for knowledge. We try all the ways that can lead us to it. When reason fails us, we use experience...Medicine professes always to have experience as the touchstone for its workings. So Plato was right in saying that to become a true doctor, the candidate must have passed through all the illnesses that he wants to cure and all the accidents and circumstances that he is to diagnose. It is reasonable that he should catch the pox if he wants to know how to treat it. Truly I should trust such a man. For the others guide us like the man who paints seas, reefs, and ports while sitting at his table, and sails the model of a ship there in complete safety. Throw him into the real thing, and he does not know how to go at it." [10]

No one can experience all maladies, but it is true that the things we experience, like motion sickness, give us a kind of knowledge that is unobtainable from any book, film, radio program, or TV show. Physicians are trained to look for signs and symptoms of illness. Most of what they diagnose and treat will be things that they have never experienced themselves, so they become detectives, drawing on the experiences of others and putting the signs and symptoms together to solve the puzzle of the illness's identity. Identifying the disease and its problems is important because this is often necessary for curing the patient. Because of the bulk of patients doctors see, common symptoms such as nausea, vomiting, or feelings of pain become unemotional points for discussion, pegs to hang one's hat on when attempting to make a diagnosis. These symptoms are spoken of glibly by the uninvolved parties—doctors, nurses, or others in good health. The sickness has no self-importance; until, that is, the doctor or nurse or friend becomes sick. Then the disease becomes personal.

Dr. Oliver Sacks, himself a neurologist, wrote about this when he sustained a leg injury which resulted in a significant neurological impairment. His tale about the experience of becoming a patient came out in *A Leg to Stand On*. Sacks stated that when he first became a doctor and decided to enter neurology, there was a part of him that wanted only the pure joy and challenge of concepts—abstractions divorced from any human reality. It was safer to keep a distance from patients, to keep from entering their strange and often terrifying world. In that way, the questions of existence, deep and terrible, were neatly excluded. That was safe, it was 'clean', it was 'pure' medicine—but it was also a sort of death because he was cutting himself off from the richness of experience. Only by entering into the experience of sickness himself could he begin to understand the phenomena of both sickness and health. Only when he became a patient himself did he know—existentially—what it was his patients were going through. It changed him, as nothing else had (or could). And in the end, it made him a better doctor.

Christians believe that their Creator also learned from experience, when He entered humanity in just such a manner through His son. "Christ Jesus...although He existed in the form of God, did not regard equality with God a thing to be grasped, but emptied Himself, taking the form of a bond-servant, and being made in the likeness of men."[11] It is an astonishingly paradoxical concept to ponder: an *omniscient* Being capable of *learning* (??!!!). Yet experience does indeed bring a reality, a knowledge, and an empathy all its own. This is a truth repeatedly born out by our life's events, such as my own experience over Pittsburg or Sacks's experience as a patient. Experience gives us empathy, "the capacity for experiencing as one's own the feelings of another."[12] We may ignore this. We may forget this. Or we may use this. For if empathy produces sympathy and compassion, then the experience is not tossed aside uselessly. It is converted to profit. In this way, we do not just address the pain—physical, emotional, spiritual—but understand it as well when we find it in our fellow humans. And this is how we enrich both ourselves and the souls we encounter.

Failure

Failure produces feelings that defy description. Individual reaction to failure varies, but as for me, I don't take it very well. In its mildest form it disappoints, and when severe it cuts all the way to the marrow. When profound, it seems to surround and overwhelm me. I feel engulfed by disappointment and frustration, as though this were some sort of gas that could envelope and penetrate me. It surrounds and devours, just as a macrophage phagocytizes bacteria. Of all the disappointments in life, personal failure hurts the most. I usually refrain from discussing it because failure hits too hard—athletes who have "the wind knocked out of them" seldom talk. Failure is not easily shaken, and a steady diet of it weighs with increasing heaviness until some success can break through the storm clouds, disband the darkness, and unload the disheartening burden.

Failure does bring disappointment, but the two are not synonymous. If a patronized sports team loses, or a movie doesn't live up to its expectations, or I don't make all the trips I wanted to take while on vacation, I feel disappointed. But failure—personal failure—goes beyond this: it hurts. In that setting, there are rarely any words of encouragement that can make things better. Words may sometimes be palliative, but they cannot cure. Only time and success can really help.

Professionally, failure is something that every physician encounters periodically, and dealing with it is part of the job. Internship—a doctor's first year out of medical school—is usually the period of greatest tribulation. In the ensuing years, experience breeds success, though it does not guarantee it. Failure will still come, and each time it does, it brings disappointment. It often brings discouragement, too. No one should ever like it.

If I think back to my own past failures, I can, thankfully, look on them without remorse (though I do not forget the pain that they caused.) My failures have not been few: my academic letdowns, from my struggles in high school calculus to the miserable trials of organic chemistry in college to the frustration of mediocrity in microbiology in medical school, were all sources of despondency because of the immense amount of work and study I put into them. So much effort for such low results. No one enjoys a low yield in their endeavors. Athletically, I wonder if anything is worse than a strikeout in baseball? I have missed lots of shots in basketball games, missed blocks or tackles in football, hit poor shots in racquetball and tennis, and run poor races in cross country and track, but striking out somehow seemed the worst. It always made me feel bad. Moral failures bring more shame than anything else and are often the hardest thing to face or confess, let alone live with. I can only remember my own with embarrassment. Musically, my performance skills always fell short of my aspirations. Many times I found myself puzzled in trying to understand why I could not translate the notes on the page into the music they encoded. My skills of musical performance were inadequate to match my skills of musical appreciation. Professionally, my failures and shortcomings have been, as I stated, disappointing and disheartening. They have been humbling, too (especially since I enjoy success so much).

Of the many things that help to cope with failure—subsequent success, a "strong constitution", the support of friends or family members, etc.—the one that has proven to be the greatest help to me, and my strongest consolation, has been my belief in God. It may sound trite to say so, but it is true nonetheless. The same things the psalmists were saying nearly 3,000 years ago are the things I seem to latch on to now when I fail. "Blessed be the Lord, who *daily bears* our *burden,* the God who is our *salvation.*" "Behold, God is my *helper;* the Lord is the *sustainer* of my soul." "*Be gracious* to me O God, according to Thy lovingkindness; According to the greatness of Thy *compassion* blot out *my transgressions.*"[13] God is the source of consolation because I want someone to *understand*: myself, my failure, my situation in life. I also want to feel worth, even in failure. Knowing that it is God's Being—not my actions—that bestows worth is comforting. This explains part of the efficacy of prayer. It is comforting to believe in and pray to a Being who understands our nature, our efforts, and our failings. It is comforting to know that trying my best counts for something with someone, even when I fail. It is comforting to feel forgiven for my shortcomings, knowing that this Being gives me my worth as a human. And so I pray. Prayer for help and forgiveness assuages some of the pain of our humanity. And what prayer cannot assuage, humility can redeem.

As Halifax said, "Nothing softeneth the Arrogance of our Nature like a Mixture of some Frailties. It is by them that we are best told, that we must not strike too hard upon others because we ourselves do so often deserve blows. They pull our rage by the sleeve and whisper Gentleness to us in our censures."[1]

Shame

Shame is a powerful emotion. The dictionary states that shame, like humiliation, implies "painful feelings caused by lowering of one's pride or self-respect. Shame is a painful feeling caused by the consciousness or exposure of unworthy or indecent conduct or circumstances."[14] This "painful feeling" of unworthiness comes over me whenever I am confronted by stories of those in countries who suffer because of their commitment to their Christian beliefs. Their sacrifice, especially if it involves prison or physical torment, stands in stark contrast to the ease and complacency of my own life. It is only too easy to take for granted the thing that is denied to so many—the chance to believe in the religion of one's choosing without losing friends, jobs, family, self-esteem, or physical well-being. Real-life encounters with those who have sacrificed these things do indeed lower "one's pride."

The feelings of shame are not unlike those of embarrassment, but how does one put them into words? A warm feeling in the face? A sense of bodily restlessness? A tightening in the throat? (These could just as easily describe the act of putting on a necktie.) However one phrases it, it is easier to describe what causes it than to describe the feeling itself. Philip Yancey, for example, described his reaction in *Praying with the KGB* after hearing the testimony of a former Soviet gulag prisoner named Basil. Basil had ended his revelation by encouraging Yancey and his group of fellow Christians (who had been invited to Russia by the ruling elite to help build moral character after the Soviet downfall) to be strong in their witness to the Russian government. "Suddenly, I burned with shame. Here we were: nineteen evangelical professionals who made a comfortable living from our faith sitting in one of the most luxurious hotels in Moscow. What did we know about the kind of bedrock faith needed in this nation of people who had endured such suffering? What gave us the right to represent the Basils of the land before Mikhail Gorbachev and the Supreme Soviet, let alone the KGB?" [15]

Seeing the pious sincerity and steadfast commitment of those in thankless positions, also engenders feelings of shame. While in college, I traveled each Sunday with a group of fellow students to the south side of Chicago to teach Sunday school in one of the first-floor meeting rooms in the Dearborn Housing Projects. This ministry had been founded and presided over by a widow from Mississippi, and although she had ample funding in her bank account to leave the projects for a better life, she chose to stay and work with the community. Rather than changing her environment by moving out, she chose to change it by staying in and transforming it. By the time I happened to come on the scene, Mrs. Harris was in her seventies, with several teeth missing, a bent and twisted spine, and rather severe emphysema. Her difficulties were brought home to me one day when I walked back to her apartment with her to exchange some supplies. As we stopped outside of her door, she fumbled with her keys, taking some time to find the right one. Her breathing was so heavy that I was amazed at her ability to get out and about at all. As I contemplated her faithfulness, in the mist of all her hardships, I felt that burning sense of shame for the ease of my own participation in a "ministry." It was a convenient commitment for me, one that only involved participation for a *few* hours on *one* day a week for nine months of the year. For her, it was a full-time commitment. Her faith was manifested in her actions and prayers—I don't believe I have ever heard a more sincere soul petition the Almighty for His help in our world. Waves of shame would hit me as I listened to her pour her heart out, knowing how tepid my own prayers were by comparison. In some ways she was, with all of her imperfections, as close to a saint as anyone I've ever met.

Shame in itself accomplishes very little if not accompanied by a desire to improve. "Faith without works is dead," wrote James.[16] So is shame without resolution. Yet even if shame bears no fruit, it does at least point to a moral law. A sense of shame implies that there is something better, a higher standard, than what we have attained. A moral law, in turn, points to a lawmaker. It is with the ability to feel shame that we understand Paul's letter to the church at Galatia, especially when he writes, "Wherefore the law was our schoolmaster to bring us unto Christ, that we might be justified by faith."[17] The Old Testament law brought shame by revealing humanity's shortcomings. In that sense, it prepared us as a schoolmaster would for the justification from sin by faith in Christ. This gift is given by grace alone, something I appreciated more fully after befriending a devout Muslim physician.

Thoughts Along the Way

In Islam, a sense of shame helps to guide the follower of Mohammed back to the righteous path that pleases Allah, but since salvation is ultimately based on weighing a person's good works against the bad at the end of life, shame may bring as much despair and uncertainty as it does hope. For the follower of Christ, shame should bring hope, since salvation is based on grace, not works. It should also bring the desire to improve. This, as much as anything, makes me thankful for shame, a feeling I never enjoy.

The Dark Side of Life

This World Is Not a Friendly Place...

According to my encyclopedia, if you are an animal small enough to be caught by a scorpion, this is your fate: Most scorpions are sit-and-wait predators who remain motionless until a suitable prey moves into an ambush zone. Once you, the prey, are detected, the scorpion orients, runs to you, and seizes you in its pincerlike claws. While you struggle, the scorpion lifts its lethal tail and plunges its dagger-like stinger into your body to inject a potent neurotoxin. After raping you of your health, the scorpion begins its unusual feeding. A pair of toothed, pincerlike appendages and sharp edges of adjacent jaw-like structures macerate you, as quantities of digestive fluids secreted from its small intestine pour over you. Your soft parts are broken down, liquefied, and slowly sucked into the scorpion's stomach over a few hours. You are gradually reduced to a ball of indigestible material and cast aside.

Lest you think yourself above this horror, you should note that about 25 species of scorpions possess venom potent enough to kill humans. With the exception of snakes and bees, scorpions cause more deaths than any other nonparasitic group of animals. More than 5,000 people are thought to die each year from scorpion stings. The process of dying is quite painful as the neurotoxin injected typically produces severe convulsions, paralysis, and cardiac arrhythmias before death. Even the majority that produce lesser effects similar to a bee sting can instill caution: I always used a flash light to illumine my path at night when I was in West Africa.

Be thankful that you will not suffer the fate of some spiders. Many species of spider wasps exist, the most notorious of which is the Tarantula Hawk. These little wasps often attack spiders many times their own size. If successful in battle, the wasp's sting will completely immobilize the spider. While still alive, the paralyzed spider is dragged to the nest, where the wasp lays eggs on it. When the larvae emerge, they feed on the flesh of the still living but paralyzed spider. I am amazed how each year, thousands of larvae grow to be wasps who—without any instruction or continuing education courses—know who their prey is (tarantulas, not flower nectar or crickets), how to kill it (with the stinger, not the mouth), and what to do after the kill (drag it home and lay eggs on it rather than feasting on the spot). Of course, the tarantula does not share my awe, nor I its agony.

There are plenty of dangers for humans, though. In the United States, fewer than 20 people die each year from snakebites. The world Health Organization, on the other hand, estimates that as many as 300,000 snakebites occur throughout the world each year, causing perhaps 30,000 to 40,000 deaths. About 25,000 of these occur in Southeast Asia (India, Burma, Thailand, etc.), with Burma and Brazil being the hardest hit countries (having about 2,000 fatalities apiece.) Snake venoms, which vary from species to species, are complex mixtures of polypeptides, which contain a number of enzymes and toxins that are quite specific for destroying tissue and causing toxic effects on the cardiovascular, nervous, and respiratory systems. These venoms slay effectively and make the snake—along with striking speed, fang structure, and limber body movements—an efficiently designed *killer*.

Venom is but one means of producing death. Imagine swimming in a lake among the reeds when suddenly your arm is savagely ripped off in the jaws of a 10-foot crocodile. If you don't escape so that you can bleed to death, the leviathan may grab another limb and pull you under until, after vainly gasping for air, you finally drown. The croc will drag you off to its lair and stow you away to be eaten at a later date. A swifter fate may occur in the jaws of a shark, one species of which has been known to tear a human *in half*. Just as painful are the maulings of a bear or death in the jaws of a lion. Even a pit bulldog is capable of taking the life of a screaming child...These are not fairy tales. These things really do happen.

Less dramatically, but with more prolonged agony, it has been noted that the average individual in the western, developed world suffers an infection of the gastrointestinal tract from one to six times a year, depending on location, living conditions, and age. In the world as a whole, the problem is enormous. Apart from a bacterial or viral GI tract infection, A.C. Cuckler calculated that in 1975 alone, there were more cases of *parasitic* infections in the world than there were people (!!). Even if it does not kill from dehydration, malnutrition, or sepsis (as cholera often does), diarrhea is difficult to live with. For many in this large world, it is more a way of life than an occasional, short-lived discomfort.

A round of applause would be appropriate for public health organizations that have eradicated mosquito-born malaria from their countries. Malaria still infects between 250 million and 300 million inhabitants of 104 countries throughout Africa, South America, Latin America, Asia, and the ocean islands. Approximately 1 million people die each year from this disease. As with so many other protozoal or parasitic organisms, the malarial organisms are fit to thrive inside the human (the liver and red blood cells, in this case) and to destroy. The design for destruction is, once again, quite effective.

Mother Nature is often neither a beautiful nor benevolent mother. On August 21, 1986, a lethal cloud of carbon dioxide gas issued forth unexpectedly from Lake Nyos in Cameroon, Africa, killing more than 1,700 people. Heavy rains in September and October of 1887 caused China's Hwang Ho River to inundate 50,000 square miles, destroy 300 villages, and kill up to 2.5 million people. A 75-foot tidal wave (tsunami) scoured 170 miles of Japan's coastline on June 15, 1896, killing more than 28,000 people—drowned, crushed by falling buildings, or impaled on debris driven by the relentless wall of water. On May 8, 1902, 30,000 people perished when the volcano Pelée erupted. A superheated cloud of gas—more than $1,000°$ F—covered the city and many objects were instantly carbonized. For humans, a single breath meant death. A howling hurricane made September 8, 1900, a day to remember as 12,000 people were killed in Galveston, Texas. Messina,

Thoughts Along the Way

Italy was rocked by an earthquake that claimed more than 85,000 people during the Christmas holiday of 1908..."*MOTHER*" Nature???

Of course, the internal environment is just as threatening as the external. For millennia, malformed and retarded babies have been born. For millennia, little children have suffered and died from cystic fibrosis, leukemia, lymphoma, and deficiencies in the immune system, among other things. Adults too have succumbed to brain tumors, Hodgkin's Disease, mental derangement such as Alzheimer's Disease or schizophrenia, kidney failure, or pancreatic cancer. "Homeostasis" is the word taught to physiology students to describe the "integrative action of the systems of an organism that result in the maintenance of the optimal internal environment."[1] In plainer words, our insides are working right to keep us healthy. The problem with homeostasis is that no one has it: we are all programmed to age and die. Some have died at 100 days of life and others at 100 years, but homeostasis never lasts.

A man named Paul once wrote a letter to a group of people living it Italy. This letter was later collected with other writings in a book known as the Bible and given the title of "Romans." Paul wrote that the sin of Adam brought death into the world. He also wrote that the whole of creation was subjected to change because of this sin and became enslaved to corruption. Paul stated that God himself subjected it and that someday it will be set free from its problems of imperfection. Other apostles, such as Peter and John, wrote about a new Jerusalem or new earth and a new heaven that will one day come about. Christ himself maintained that our present world will not last forever. It seems, then, that throughout the ages, whether we realized it or not, mankind has been waiting for deliverance; all that stuff I wrote about scorpions, snakes, parasites, the food chain, crocodiles and the forces of nature are examples of how bad our world is, how much evil has influenced it. While it may be amazing to see the ability of a bird to dive from 50 feet above the water to catch a fish, it should be remembered that this is because we live in a fallen world where animals eat each other and hopefully this practice will one day cease.

Except. . . except. . . except I'm not sure that this is how God views things. Rather than despair at the harshness and brutality of nature, God seems to delight in it. In the last few chapters of the book of Job,

God speaks almost boastfully about the stupidity and cruelty of the ostrich, the stubbornness of the wild donkey, the ability of hail and snow to destroy, the untamable behemoth, or the lethal terror of the leviathan. The very *wildness* of creation gives a sense of pride to its Creator and a sense of awe and astonishment to many of its inhabitants (like Job). It is a universe of one master and no rivals.

"The fear of the Lord is the beginning of wisdom," states Proverbs.[2] Perhaps the only thing more fearful than the harshness of creation is the Creator who made it. It is no wonder, then, that Job cowered before God when He answered Job out of the whirlwind. And yet, upon encountering the Omnipotent, the offer of salvation to a man who must die shows that even the harshness of God is kinder than the wildness of nature, and His compulsion is our liberation.

An Optimist Visits Signal Point

Signal Mountain, TN
July 4, 1994

After intermittent showers and overcast skies, it has finally turned out to be a glorious day. The clouds have lifted and are moving off to the west, where the late afternoon sun shines through in brilliant white. Gone with the clouds is the haze that had settled throughout the region over the last week, and I can now see clearly all the way over to Chattanooga and the green-covered hills beyond. It's a beautiful city, cozily nestled among the hills and semicircled by three mountains—Lookout, Racoon (or "Elder"), and Walden's Ridge, where I am standing. One can't help but reflect on the rich history here—the founding of a trading settlement by Cherokee chief John Ross in 1815, still commemorated by Ross's Landing on the Tennessee River, the Civil War battles fought on Lookout Mountain and Missionary Ridge to my left, the old tracks of the Chattanooga Choo-Choo and the Signal Mountain trolley service established by Charles James—this heritage is still visible in the fertile river valley before me.

Down below on the left, a great cloud of steam is rising from the Prentice Cooper State Forest, no doubt issuing from the rainwater on the trees and bushes that the sun is quickly heating. It floats phantasmally through the valley, driven westward by the wind softly blowing between the ridges. Around the bend of the river to my right, I can see where one such mist has gathered to form a cloud that is peeping out from around the corner of Raccoon Mountain, as if trying to spy on the valley.

The wind between the mountains and the thermals from heat rising off the rocks make this a good day for a hawk flight. There aren't any out here today—it's not quite the right time of year. I wish they would come anyway, riding the currents and soaring majestically—as I have so often seen them do—through the valley and over the river, dipping and rising, their wings spread far apart as they make lazy circles over the river. Some of the smaller creatures, though, have managed to make an outing today. Just in front of me, a butterfly unfolds itself and

David Graham

flaps its beautifully patterned wings, perhaps trying to dry them out. The familiar buzz of a wasp or a fly can often be heard as the cicadas make their familiar summer songs. An occasional swallow even skips across my view, winging its way across the treetops.

Down below, the Tennessee River just keeps lazily rolling along, twisting and turning as it moves on down to Bridgeport and Guntersville, Alabama, before turning north, heading back up into Tennessee and then Kentucky, where it joins with the Ohio River at Paducah before emptying into the mother of American rivers, the mighty Mississippi. Several people are out in boats, enjoying the sunshine and the warm weather. Down on the riverbanks at the foot of Racoon Mountain, a spattering of firecrackers igniting shows how several people are celebrating the fourth.

Until now, I have taken all of this scenery in solitude, surveying the views before me and reminiscing on its history. A couple finally joins me at the Point, looking out across the stone retaining wall at the sea of green trees before us. They too watch in silence, reverently preserving the peacefulness of the moment. They too must know that the soul relaxes at such times, not by talking but rather by listening, seeing, breathing, hearing, feeling.

It's good to be alive.

A Pessimist Visits Signal Point

Signal Mountain, TN
July 4, 1994

It rained practically all day today, and now that the sun is out, the heat and humidity are oppressive. After being cooped up in that wretched house all day, I just had to get out. Yet here I am, sweating already after only a few minutes of running to get to this tourist spot.

I can see most of Chattanooga from here. It's a growing city—more trees cut down each year, more fields plowed up, more people crowding the roads with more cars to create more exhaust (which is probably why it's been so hazy around here)—this place sure has changed a lot since the Civil War. Not that anyone could recognize the battlefields—they're covered with houses, streets, and the marks of suburbia. Part of the view of Chattanooga is being obscured by this billowing steam cloud, rising up like some sort of sulfurous miasma from Hades itself. I'm glad the wind is blowing it away, otherwise I couldn't see the dirty, traffic-laden river road and those noisy speedboats incessantly cruising up and down the Tennessee River. Nothing like having another bunch of party seekers out for a good time on another fourth of July. I wonder who puts more trash in the river—them or the sewage-dumping industries. Those boats are almost as annoying as the riff-raff across the way setting off firecrackers—probably had to go to Alabama to buy them, since they are illegal in Georgia.

Gosh, can it get any more humid out here? No wonder there aren't any hawks flying today—their wings would probably melt. On the other hand, it shouldn't be too long before the flies, gnats, and mosquitoes start stopping by to bug me. What good are mosquitoes anyway? What do they contribute to our world besides disease and itching? They are good for nothing but spider food. Bunch of blood sucking pests. . .

Oh great, here comes a couple to spoil the solitude. Looks from their dress like they're Georgia Bulldog fans. This means they must have double-digit IQs. They are probably the same ones who came by earlier and threw that plastic bag and macaroni over the edge of the lookout here. Littering is so selfish. But then again, to say that is to say that littering is human, because humans are selfish. They are so disgusting. Speaking of which, I suppose I better go on back and entertain the cretins waiting in my yard for a barbecue. Sheesh. What a rotten, boring world this is. Makes me wonder why I even bother with anything sometimes. I guess that's why we all like to stay busy until we die: so we don't have to stop and ponder our miserable existence.

I hate this place.

Two men looked out from behind prison bars;
One saw mud, the other saw stars.

I doubt either of them saw the whole scene.

Morbid Fascination

Not long ago, while out walking around Signal Mountain one day, I came upon a spider, busily engaged in building a web of commodious proportions. The orb's dimensions themselves were impressive enough—perhaps six or seven feet in height and three or four feet in width—but it was the precision and speed of creation that were amazing to behold. That one-inch arachnid was creating a masterpiece of design at breakneck speed, pulling out all the stops as it climbed around its scaffolding, "spot-welding" anchoring points, throwing out drag lines and safety lines with some legs, while molding the silk with others. (Silk is produced as a liquid when emitted from a spider's spinnerets. The liquid silk is believed to be set by the spider pulling on it; the harder the pull, the stronger the silk.) The web was yet another masterpiece, done with a swiftness and accuracy that any engineer should envy. The affect on this viewer was one of paralyzing intensity: I stood frozen in my tracks, watching it work. It was the single most convincing performance I had ever witnessed for demonstrating that "instinct" in animal behavior could not possibly be the product of chance. An intelligent being programmed that spider's ancestors to make webs, designing the genes for webmaking that would be passed down from generation to generation. The result was impressive to behold.

The web, though, was built to serve as something more than a living quarters or impressive architectural display. It was built to catch food. In other words, it was a trap. A *death* trap. This lair is something that many people find fascinating. I know I certainly do. The previous autumn I had read a colorful introductory book about arachnids entitled *The Book of Spiders and Scorpions* by Rod Preston-Matham. It was entertaining and informative, discussing everything from defensive adaptations and the lifecycle to courtship and mating, with the text being richly supplemented by photographs and illustrations. (As a physician, I found the sections on anatomy and physiology particularly interesting.) Yet a spider's world involves more than mating, egg laying, and web building. Spiders inhabit a harsh world of killing and dying, eating and being eaten. Whether in courtship or capturing prey, the presence of death is always close; and this has provided the substance for countless journal articles, magazine pieces, research projects, scientific publications, and illustrated books. For many, the life and hard times of spiders are intriguing, a subject too morbidly interesting to ignore.

In the zoological realm, the spider is but one example of the food chain's "eat or be eaten" dictum, which rules the natural world. In the human sphere, the spider is but one example of our interest in the morbid side of life. The zoological and botanical worlds reveal that life lives on life, which means that the death of one party brings life to another. So botanists and zoologists make it their business to study death (whether they realize this or not). But biologists are not the only ones with interest in the morbid side of life. To live well, everyone must be knowledgeable of the results of sin and be aware of—if not downright interested in—mistakes, errors, and death. From the villager in New Guinea who knows which foods are poisonous to the physician in New York who spends his life studying disease to the detective in New Delhi who spends his time tracking crimes, the study of sin and wrong is important. More than being important, it is universally appealing.

Near the end of my first year of medical school, one of my classmates told me that he was looking forward to the next year in school, when the focus of our studies would shift from normal physiology to pathophysiology, from health to disease. "I'm tired of all this normal stuff," he remarked. His statements probably reflect the sentiment of nearly all those who venture into the world of medicine. I, too, have found that the focus of my professional time has been spent studying the things that go wrong with the body. Quite frankly, I find this pathophysiology fascinating and even fun to deal with. (It is fun to fix a hernia, remove a diseased gallbladder, bypass a closed-off blood vessel.) At times, I find this interest disturbing. Why should I, and others in the medical profession, thrive on the diseases of others? (Comments on a patient with unusual symptoms or disease are usually congratulatory—"Good case.") Are we aware that in a utopian, disease-free world, no job market for us would exist? Would we be bored in a world where doctors weren't needed?

It is said that everyone loves a good mystery; and most mysteries involve death or robbery. The best-selling mystery writers, from Arthur Conan Doyle to Dorothy Sayers to Agatha Christie, have used people's fascination with these matters to sell their books. The most frequently discussed mysteries from the "real" world also involve death—the assassinations of John F. Kennedy and Martin Luther King, Jr. being but two examples. Death and disease also make up part of various religious rites around the globe—usually in the form of sacrifice for curing physical illness or atoning for spiritual wickedness. War, too, shows our fascination with killing and maiming. Legions of books are written about the multitudinous factions among humans. Wars occupy the prominent places in history books (including biblical history). Once a month, a pamphlet arrives in my mailbox that is entitled, "Military History." The most recent issue advertised over 1,200 books, including 400 first-time "offerings," ranging from the American Civil War (always popular) to British military history to historical fiction, strategy/weaponry, and military videos. The titles reflect our fascination with the subject. *Celtic Warriors 400 B.C. to 1600 A.D.; Alexander the Great and the Logistics of the Macedonian Army; How to Build Your Own Flintlock-Rifle or Pistol; Gunshot Injuries* ("a seminal work on wound ballistics"); *On the Origins of War*. And then there is the Osprey *Men-at-Arms* series, over 100 volumes produced as "an unrivaled series of volumes which make an excellent source for authentic, detailed, and attractively presented information on the history of the fighting man."[3] Why are humans so enamored with this?

I find people's fascination with morbid or repulsive subjects to be in itself intriguing. Why are humans so enchanted by disease? Why are we so enchanted with war? Why are people so enchanted by sexual excess or aberration? Why are we lured toward mysteries of robbery or death? Why does a spider eating a fly in its web prove so attractive to many people (children and adults alike)? Why does the study of sin and error prove so intriguing? If I knew the answers to these questions, this article would not have been written.

The Human Sentence: Pain, Decay, and Death

Over the years, I have often been bothered by the same issues that mankind has been wrestling with for ages innumerable, the same enigmas discussed in college religion courses and philosophy textbooks alike. The questions are both fascinating and troublesome: "Does God exist?" "Which world view is the most accurate? Judaism? Islam? Atheism? Christianity?" "What is beauty? Is it real or is it a mirage, the subjective creation of an individual's imagination? Is it merely a judgment made 'in the eyes of the beholder'?" "Is there life after death?" "What is 'normal' in human sexuality? Is there a 'normal'?" "Are there absolute moral values of right and wrong? Can some things *always* be right and others *always* wrong?" I vacillate in my feelings of confidence or doubt about these issues. I can, for example, read a book of comparative religions and come away befuddled, feeling the force of atheism's tenets, only to make a ramble around the mountain on a beautiful autumn day and come upon a spider building an orderly web with a speed and precision that an engineer would envy, clearly demonstrating that "instinct" in such organized animal behavior cannot possibly be the product of mere atheistic chance. The world does indeed give mixed signals about the divine.

Of course, the issue of pain comes up when considering many of these questions. As a physician, I see the good side of pain when it alerts someone to seek medical help for something threatening, like appendicitis. From that viewpoint, one can say, as missionary surgeon Paul Brand has said, "Thank God for pain." But I also see the questions raised by pain, such as "Why do we live in a world where we are afflicted by appendicitis?" We may rejoice and "thank God for pain", but how do we thank God for the appendicitis that caused it? What about this bad side of pain, the pain that results in suffering? How does one think theistically about disease? Although I believe in God and the truth of the biblical story—with its explanations about suffering and death[4]—this faith can, ironically, make the darker side of life less palatable and more difficult to swallow. It helps in trying to provide answers to life's existential puzzles, but it raises others questions that a godless world needn't ask. "Why is there so much disease and suffering in the world?" The atheist does not need to ask that question, and if he does, the answer is easy. ("That's how we evolved.") The theist, by contrast, *must* ask that question, and the answer is elusive.

I spent the last half of 1994 studying the literature on melanoma in preparation for speaking at a conference about this particular form of skin cancer. The incidence of melanoma is continuing to rise throughout the world, having already tripled in the last four decades, and continues to kill thousands of people each year. After studying—in detail—all of the lethal effects of melanoma, I sat down one night and recorded my thoughts about disease and dying, with the memory of recently diagnosing and treating two people having advanced, metastatic cancer to the liver also weighing heavily upon me. (Both patients were jaundiced, weak, emaciated, nauseated, and in pain.) Without attempting any answers, here were my questions.

September 15, 1994

It all continues to bother me. The world I live in discourages and saddens me, leaving me pensive and forlorn. The whole medical profession centers around and indulges in the study of disease. Like parasites, we feed and prey upon those who come to us for help. We criticize certain lifestyles and practices: "He's a smoker, so he's having a hard time coming off of the ventilator." "We have much more colon cancer in developed countries because we eat so much red meat and have *low*-fiber diets." "We see volvulus [twisting of the intestines] more commonly in undeveloped African countries because of their *high*-fiber diets." "You have already had one heart attack. You need to change your eating habits and eat a low-fat diet. You also need to start exercising." "If you don't stop drinking, you'll get pancreatitis again or cirrhosis of the liver, and it might kill you." "These people get guinea worm infections because they don't filter the water they drink." "He contracted schistosomiasis from swimming at that water hole." "You need to brush your teeth more and start flossing or you'll get more cavities." "The parasite you have is called *diphyllobothrium latum*. It's your reward for eating sushi." "You haven't taken your insulin regularly, so now you are losing your sight." "You don't inspect your hands every day, and since you have leprosy, your negligence has cost you your fingers." "Your child died from diphtheria, something that would not have happened if he had been immunized," "She's only 35 years old and she is dying from metastatic cervical cancer. A simple yearly Pap smear could have easily prevented this."

Why should we have to inhabit a world like this? Why can't we eat whatever we please, swim wherever we want, drink whatever we desire, walk however and whenever we wish, smoke what seems good, and live without needing injections from painful needles? In other words, why can't we live *freely* in the world? In an atheistic world formed by chance, we expect such "imperfections." In a world created by an all-powerful God, I don't. If all of the cancer (a *miserable* way to die) and other diseases are "the result of sin entering into the world," then why would an all-knowing God create a world where sin *could* cause this? Why create a world where sin *would* cause this?

In thinking of the lifespans recorded in the book of Genesis, I am saddened even more if I compare them with ours today. There is a tenfold difference in length. I can't help but wonder if there were other quantitative differences that would draw parallels as well. What about the length of their youth and good health, for example? In keeping with the tenfold discrepancy, are we to assume that one of these ancient forefathers was in their athletic prime between 150 and 300 years of age?!! It is amusing to think so. Yet it is disheartening, too. By comparison, our lifespans are so *short* now. Has "sin" really changed the world so much? Are we such victims of sin's effects that we are now slaves to the natural world—carefully watching what we eat, what we drink, what we wear, and what we do? If the biblical account is true, then we have degenerated immensely in a few thousand years. It is depressing to ponder. Even one small area like melanoma highlights the differences. Melanoma is a widespread, menacing problem for our world today—did it even *exist* in Noah's or Methuselah's age? I doubt the ancients had to act like us—monitoring how intensely the sun's rays hit the skin over the years. Who needed sunscreen in such a world? Today, I see daily examples of our pathetic frailty, be it an 80-year-old, weak, toothless grandmother on a ventilator who is struggling just to breathe, or a bloated, jaundiced soul with pain, itching, nausea, and vomiting from metastatic cancer to the liver. The hospital reminds me of just what a PITIFUL condition humanity is in. I can't help but ask, "Were we created for <u>this</u>???"

Thoughts Along the Way

In the biblical book of Job, where pain and suffering are so extensively discussed, we are told that after a stern rebuke from the Almighty, Job spoke what was right of God; and in the end, God honored Job's belief. Job's belief and repentance can be viewed in two ways. Either God's presence satisfied Job, or Job was cowered into submission. Whichever it was, Job still never had his questions answered. Instead, they were left to be passed down to his descendants, inherited anew by each generation. Millennia later, we are still struggling with these ancestral enigmas.

The Dark Side of Humanity

People Enjoy Complaining...

They do not enjoy the thing that causes them to complain, but they do enjoy complaining. There is something of a perverse pleasure involved in hating someone, holding a grudge, remaining bitter, returning to self-pity, or complaining. These practices do not appear attractive to the person doing them because the light of attention shines on the person or people being hated, complained about, or despised, while the person's self-reflection lurks in the shadows. It is a subtle truth to acknowledge, but hate has its own loves.

During my sojourn in medical school, I was able to learn a bit about medicine. What I also learned was that the world I was stepping into was one in which most of its inhabitants were very adept at complaining. It was only too easy to do the same, and unless a conscious effort was made not to, one joined in the criticism. Working conditions, no matter how good or how poor, always provided stimulation and ammunition for verbal abuse, and this usually led to derogatory remarks about the source of work production: people. People are easier targets for criticism than environmental working conditions, probably because it is more gratifying to step on others in order to build one's self up. It takes little effort to criticize others' mistakes, shortcomings in character, body habitus (usually obesity), or personality.

> By this all men will know that you are my disciples, if you have love for one another.
>
> John 13:35

I was fortunate enough to spend six weeks at a mission hospital during the winter of my fourth year of medical school. It was there in West Africa that I saw people who loved each other, who loved the patients, and who did not complain and criticize just to satisfy an old habit. When problems arose, they were dealt with in a sincere yet understanding manner—no sarcasm, no flippancy, no superiority, no malice. They did indeed have love one for another, and for their patients. People knew these missionaries were Christ's disciples.

In his essay "Miserable Offenders," from *God in the Dock*, C.S. Lewis speaks of the Christian's honest appraisal of his own sinfulness. He then writes, "Does that sound very gloomy? Does Christianity encourage morbid introspection? The alternative is much more morbid. Those who do not think about their own sins make up for it by thinking incessantly about the sins of others."[1] Have you known the love of hating, holding a grudge, remaining bitter, returning to self-pity, or complaining? I have. I have been guilty of all these, and for this reason can say that it *is* a subtle truth: hate has its own loves. It is difficult to realize that one area of an otherwise placid life may be bitter, or that one may feel hatred towards those who criticize or treat us poorly; harder still to forgive others and correct ourselves once we realize these symptoms. Yet refusal to do so is to spit in the face of God's grace. For this reason, Christ not only said to love one another, He also said, "For if you forgive men for their transgressions, your heavenly Father will also forgive you. But if you do not forgive men, then your Father will not forgive your transgressions."[2] It's that simple.

The Changing Autumn

From my journal...   November 4, 1990

The colors were brilliant and the weather magnificent this weekend. It is no wonder that autumn is my favorite season of the year. Autumn stands for cross country season. It means Friday night high school football games and exciting college football rivalries on Saturdays. It is the season when school resumes, friends are reunited, and previous test records are wiped clean—a chance to start anew. The Fall issues in more agreeable weather and bids good-bye to mosquitoes and snakes. It's a time for couples to snuggle warmly and share the comforts of companionship. Autumn means color—especially the color of leaves: fiery red, brilliant yellow, sumptuous orange, vivid green, and mellow brown set against the background of a sea blue sky with the sun's golden rays bringing light and warmth to the crisp, cool, invigorating climate. *J'aime l'automne.*[3]

Among the inhabitants of twentieth-century urban America, the beauty of the season is often sacrificed to noises that destroy tranquility: automobiles incessantly driving by, airplanes droning overhead, stereos blaring out rock tunes in a neighbor's yard, or lawnmowers, chainsaws, and leaf-blowers with their loud roar destroying the songs of a bird, the crunching of squirrels, or the sound of leaves scraping the ground when blown along by the wind. Signal Mountain is a beautiful place to live, but even on Sabbath, people had lawnmowers and leaf-blowers and hedgetrimmers screaming aloud—whatever happened to a day of rest, peace, and relaxation?

Sometimes, often after reading Longfellow, I feel a nostalgic tug to visit the world that he knew in the nineteenth century. Geographically, the world was similar, though demographically it was quite different. The world's population was about one fifth of today's with far fewer cities on the planet. (Los Angeles, for example, still only held 11,000 inhabitants by 1880.) It was a harsher place—a world with more untamed beasts, no antibiotics, less indoor plumbing, and poor hygiene—but it was also a world without atomic bombs, radio waves, booming stereos, or high-speed car wrecks. It was a world with less pollution from exhaust pipes and smokestacks, where fewer cities had so many irritating noises, one in which an escape to the "silence" of Nature (really, the *sounds* of Nature) was not that difficult. I would rather hear horses' hoofs and smiths' hammers that could be left behind by a trip to the farm than the steady stream of traffic noise and machinery that are almost inescapable now.

Perhaps I am too influenced by a cultural desire for quiet and solitude. Many from other lands enjoy the constant stir and bustle of the manswarm of humanity with no inner urgings to ever "get away from it all." Even so, I can't help thinking that it is in some of the quiet moments that people can relax. In them, people can stop to think or daydream or become, as Lewis put it, "a mere sponge to sense impressions."[4] Solitude provides the environment to reflect on life or to stimulate creativity. It is difficult to imagine some of the Psalms being written in a room full of people. The imagery is replete with sights, sounds, and observations from the natural world.

The solitude of Nature cannot turn a churl into a poet nor make a sadist forget his cruelty. Its splendors will not pierce every heart. Yet a walk in the autumn woods freshens my spirit while the sights, sounds, and smells of the season bring happiness to my heart. I can only hope that man's population growth and inventions will not destroy it.

Van Diemen's Land

Historical interest can come from unusual sources. In 1988, *Rattle and Hum*, a documentary film about the Irish rock band U2, was released. As the opening credits rolled on the screen, guitarist Dave Evans—known as "The Edge"—sang a solo entitled "Van Diemen's Land." The lyrics and Edge's voice left something of a haunting impression on me. This, combined with a desire to discover where on earth Van Diemen's Land was located, led me to read about some of the history there.

Van Diemen's Land, or Tasmania as it is now called, is an island state of Australia lying about 150 miles off the southeastern corner of the continent. A Dutch navigator named Abel Tasman first sighted the island in 1642 and named it after his commander Anthony van

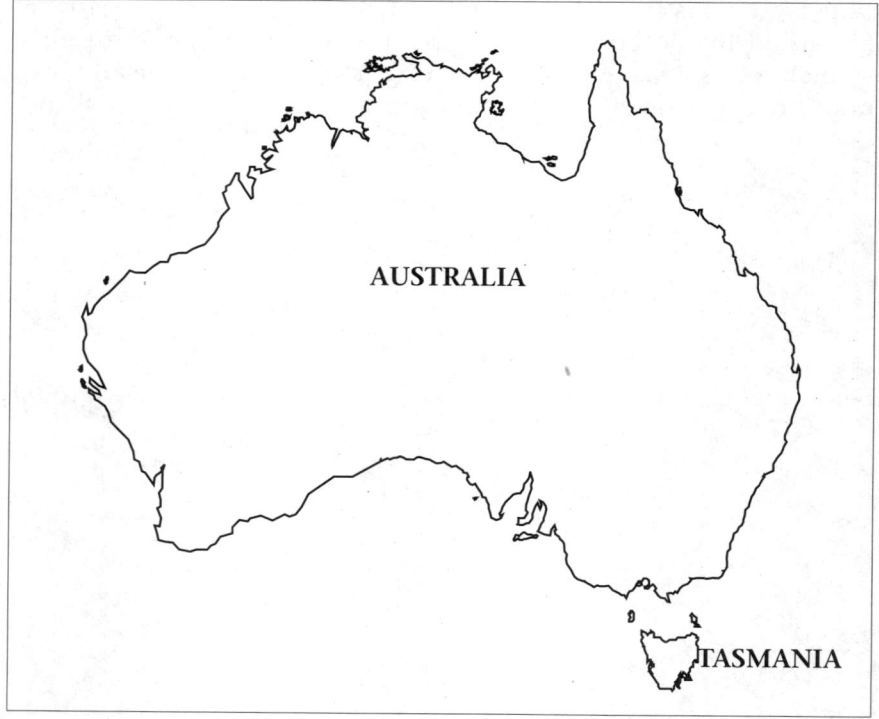

Thoughts Along the Way

Diemen, the governor general of the Dutch East Indies. The original inhabitants of the island were aboriginal Australians, a negritoid race (negroids of small stature) having the widest nasal span ever recorded and short, broad heads. Radiocarbon dating from two sites in northwest Tasmania has shown that aboriginal people occupied that region about 8,000 years ago. Their numbers were estimated to be between 1,200 and 5,000 prior to the establishment of the first Caucasian settlement in 1803. This settlement was a British group, numbering only 49, and from this European colony came the source for what would be known as the Black War (1804-1830) resulting in the virtual extermination of the Aboriginal population of the island. The whites treated the Aborigines as subhumans, seizing their hunting grounds, depleting their food supply, kidnapping many, raping the women, and murdering the men. Attempts to resist were met with superior weaponry and force from the Europeans. By 1830, only 200 aborigines remained. The next five years were spent resettling these few to Flinders Island. With their social organization and traditional way of life destroyed, subjected to alien disease and attempts to "civilize" them, they soon perished. The last known full-blooded aboriginal survivor died in 1876, leaving only a few colonies of mixed descendants behind. Having survived the elements of nature and the "thousand natural shocks that flesh is heir to"[5] for 8,000 years, they were destroyed in less than four score by the Europeans.

The story of Van Diemen's Land is a familiar one. Books such as John Ehle's *Trail of Tears: The Rise and Fall of the Cherokee Nation* or Dee Brown's *Bury My Heart at Wounded Knee: An Indian History of the American West* chronicle the rape and destruction of indigenous peoples by those of superior might. Voyages of "discovery" led the way for Spaniards like Pizarro to conquer the Incas of Peru and Cortez the Aztecs of Mexico, while the Portuguese invasion of Brazil led to enslavement of the populous and the Negroes shipped there from Africa. The tone of the Mongol conquest of Asia in the thirteenth century was tersely expressed by the statement accorded to Genghis Khan, "The greatest joy a man can have is victory: to conquer one's enemies armies, to pursue them, to deprive them of their possessions, to reduce their families to tears, to ride on their horses, and to make love to their wives and daughters."[6]

Nature itself is not spared from mankind's exploitation. Hunting, poaching, cutting, slashing, burning, burrowing, and killing have brought extinction to legions of animals, plants, forests, and ranges while polluting rivers, lakes, oceans, mountains, valleys, woods, and parks. Animal species are disappearing from the face of the planet by the hundreds every month, and while one only has to read the news to find out how swiftly mankind is destroying the natural resources most valuable to him, a walk along a garbage-strewn river is evidence enough of how little man cares for his world.

C.S. Lewis astutely noted, "We know what our race does to strangers. Man destroys or enslaves every species he can. Civilized man murders, enslaves, cheats, and corrupts savage man. Even inanimate nature he turns into dust bowls and slag-heaps. There are individuals who don't. But they are not the sort who are likely to be our pioneers in space. Our ambassador to new worlds will be the needy and greedy adventurer or the ruthless technical expert. They will do as their kind has always done. What that will be if they meet things weaker than themselves, the black man and the red man can tell. If they meet things stronger, they will be, very properly, destroyed."[7]

One may view the world, ponder its history, then conclude that God does not truly exist. Atheism is not built on a weak foundation. Human behavior repeatedly demonstrates that "only the strong survive." The wise are those who do not rely on some unseen power to care for them but who learn to live shrewdly, fend for themselves, "go for the gusto," and grab what they can while they can. Self-centeredness and exploitation of others for one's own personal gain is not immoral in an amoral world. It's smart. To be weak is to be eliminated.

Conversely, one may view our world and conclude that God does exist, for the very reason that our world needs saving from destruction, and if anything is evident, it is that mankind cannot save himself. Those who know this realize that in being weak, salvation and the strength to be good must come from a source outside of man.

Whichever view one takes, it is still evident that man has been as effective in spreading disease and destruction as he has knowledge and help. Unfortunately for the inhabitants of Van Diemen's Land, the former engulfed the latter.

The Lessons of History: A Different View

In history, as in the natural world, the strong prey upon the weak. The greedy adventurer or ambitious soldier will enslave or rape or destroy whoever or whatever he desires. The victims occasionally have their stories told, but most remain anonymous. When the truth of the matter does make that rare entrance into the public eye, it tends to evoke strong emotions such as anger, sadness, or shame. Sad are the tales of the millions of Russians slaughtered under Stalin's regime or Jews under Hitler's, the decimation of the Aztecs and the Incas by the Spaniards or the Australian aborigines by the English, the betrayal of the North American Indians by the conquering Caucasians, or the Slave Coast trade in West Africa. The injustice is appalling.

One of the basic truths of the universe, however, is that all humans are flawed. No one lives forever and no one is morally perfect. Everyone does wrong.

Historical scholar Kay Brigham has said, "If you look at the history of the world, you see the expression of man's desire to dominate and control his world as each rising culture displaces the one that preceded it. This was true of the American continent before Columbus came. The Indians that he found had displaced cultures that existed before them, sometimes in a violent manner." To the belief about the New World (the Americas) being a paradise before the coming of Columbus, she replied, "There was the same greed and violence over here as there was in all the rest of the world. In fact, on Guadeloupe, on the second voyage, Columbus discovered widespread cannibalism. The Carib people would raid the gentler Taino groups on the island, enslave them, and eat them. And later on in Mexico, Cortes, for all his cruelty, was horrified by the human sacrifice that was practiced on a grand scale in the Aztec culture."[8]

In *The Everlasting Man*, G.K. Chesterton notes:

Those who criticize that central civilization (which is

always their own civilization) have a curious habit of not merely doing their legitimate duty in condemning its crimes, but of going out of their way to idealize its victims. They always assume that before the advent of Europe there was nothing anywhere but Eden. And Swinburne, in that spirited chorus of the nations in "Songs Before Sunrise," used an expression about Spain in her South American conquests which always struck me as very strange. He said something about "her sins and sons through sinless lands dispersed," and how they "made accursed the name of man and thrice accursed the name of God." It may be reasonable enough that he should say the Spaniards were sinful, but why in the world should he say that the South Americans were sinless? Why should he have supposed that continent to be exclusively populated by archangels or saints perfect in heaven? It would be a strong thing to say to the most respectable neighborhood; but when we come to think of what we really do know of that society the remark is rather funny. We know that the sinless priests of this sinless people worshipped sinless gods, who accepted as the nectar and ambrosia of their sunny paradise nothing but incessant human sacrifice accompanied by horrible torments...

It is very right to rebuke our own race or religion for falling short of our own standards and ideals. But it is absurd to pretend that they fell lower than the other races and religions that professed the very opposite standards and ideals. There is a very real sense in which the Christian is worse than the heathen, the Spaniard worse than the Red Indian, or even the Roman potentially worse than the Carthaginian. But there is only one sense in which he is worse; and that is not in being positively worse. The Christian is only worse because it is his business to be better.[9]

There is not one race of people of whom it can be said that they were free from injustice or immorality. Slavery, for example, is bondage and the subservience of an individual's rights and self-control to a domi-

Thoughts Along the Way

nating power; something usually viewed (except by slave owners) as unjust dominion over a human being. Yet slavery has been present on six continents throughout the ages. It has, at various times, been practiced in China, Korea, India, Thailand, Burma, Philippines, Nepal, Malaya, Indonesia, Japan, England (about 10% of the population entered in the Domesday Book in 1086 *A.D.* were slaves), France, Germany, Poland, Lithuania, Russia, Babylon, Egypt, and the United States. Slaves have been owned in black Africa throughout recorded history. (Approximately 18 million Africans were delivered into the Islamic trans-Saharan and Indian Ocean slave trades between 650 and 1905). Many Amerindians owned slaves, such as the Creek of Georgia, the Comanche of Texas, the Callinago of Dominica, the Tupinamba of Brazil, the Inca of the Andes, and the Tehuelche of Patagonia (modern day Chile/Argentina.) Murder and thieving were not absent from these societies/peoples either. The dominion of rape has always been a part of history. Unjust power plays and bribes, of course, have always been ubiquitous.

While movies such as *The Killing Fields* or *The Mission* and books such as *Bury My Heart at Wounded Knee* chronicle man's inhumanity to man, the Bible reminds its readers that no one is completely innocent. Even in an overthrown society, the victims were not without faults. The Cherokee Indians, for example, were subject to the conquering injustice of the Caucasian government of the United States, and forced by the army of that nation to march the "Trail of Tears" in the late 1830's; yet only one century earlier, history reveals the Cherokees themselves to be waging war with many people—the Creeks, the Catawbas, the Tuscarorans, the Yuchi, the Choctaws, the Shawnees, and the Iroquois. As the Psalmist once wrote, "There is no one who does good, not even one."[10] A candid look at one's own life will reveal the number of times when the veracity of this statement is affirmed.

Books commonly have quotes either on the title page or isolated on a separate page in order to set the tone for the text. It would not be inappropriate to begin a history book, which must often tell the story of man's inhumanity to man, with this quote, "For all have sinned and fall short of the glory of God."[11]

Reflections on the Tenth Commandment

Until recently, I had not given much thought to the sin of coveting. The newspaper editorials, public health warnings, sermons, and journal articles that I encounter rarely even use the word "covet" when delivering moral statements. (This word seems to turn up more often in the world of sports, where it is a term of approbation—"the coveted Olympic gold medal," for example.) The misuse of alcohol, drugs, cigarettes, sex, natural resources, finances, political power, and improper familial or vocational conduct reap the lion's share of ethics discussions. But what of coveting?

Liberty allows the opportunity for choice. With the downfall of communism in many countries in the late 1980's and early 1990's, coupled with the increasing influence of capitalism abroad, many people began to experience what those of us in profit-conscious countries grew up with: desire. There has been an increased exposure to the buyer's market—and the temptations that accompany it—in my own life since graduating from medical school. Since then, the volume of mail placed in my mailbox has greatly escalated, entirely due to business offers. Being a M.D. makes me a prime target for almost anything—dozens of magazine subscription offers, thousands (literally) of book deals, scores of music, electronic, and clothing magazine advertisements, numerous bank, loan agency, and insurance appeals, and multiple sweepstakes entries. Many of these are attractive, inciting the wish to obtain what they offer. This is what the seller seeks, for like many television food advertisements, the offer must plant a desire, a want in the breast of the potential buyer. The temptation for the buyer is to do what the seller wants him to do: covet.

Buddhist belief in the cause of all unhappiness—desire—is based on the result of The Buddha's observations in India 2,500 years ago. He saw that the ills of life flowed from the lust for power, success, sex, and material pleasures. He concluded that the only way to attain truth was to give up desire. Suffering can be overcome by eliminating the cravings for pleasure, existence, and prosperity. This is done by following an Eightfold Path. Buddha did not take the issue of coveting lightly. Neither, for that matter, did Christ. "Take heed, and beware of covetousness: for a man's life consisteth not in the abundance of the things which he possesseth."[12] When covetousness comes to fruition, it leads to obtaining a nonessential, a luxury. We don't covet general necessities like clothing, but we might covet *particular* clothes such as a designer suit or high-profile tennis shoes. Purchasing luxury items is not wrong in itself, but poor use of financial resources is foolish. Habits of coveting lead to patterns of spending.

> You shall not covet your neighbor's house. You shall not covet your neighbor's wife, or his manservant or maid-servant, his ox or donkey, or anything that belongs to your neighbor.
>
> Exodus 20:17

It was with wisdom that God's command in Exodus was directed toward one's neighbor. Many moral downfalls occur because one's neighbor, like one's mail, offers something to be viewed again and again. "We begin by coveting what we see everyday," states Hannibal Lecter.[13] This may range from the lust at home for a friend's car to a lust at work for a secretary's body. Coveting, indeed, does not always lead to a cash transaction. In addition to prodigality, it can result in thievery, fornication, envy, or ulcers. It is not a sin of desire, but of inordinate desire. That is important to remember, whether looking at the mail, the neighbor, or the neighbor's possessions.

Justice

Mudslinging and the Race for the Presidency

It was late June in 1862 when Abraham Lincoln decided to unite all of the troops that were to comprise the Army of Virginia under one commander. The man chosen for this post was John Pope, someone Lincoln had known since his days as a prairie lawyer in Illinois, when he pled cases in the district court judged by Pope's father. As usual, there were objections to Lincoln's choice of commander. Pope's character was called into question, one man going so far as to state that Pope's father, old Judge Pope, "was a flatterer, a deceiver, a liar, and a trickster." "All the Popes are so," he added. Lincoln conceded that perhaps this was true. However, he did not see any reason why this should prevent Pope from being a good general. "A liar might be brave and have skill as an officer," he laconically noted.[1]

During the 1992 Presidential elections here in America, I thought of this anecdote from the Civil War era rather often, since so much of the "discussion" (i.e., mudslinging) by the warring parties centered around "family values," "integrity," and "character." After the election was over, for example, *Penthouse* magazine published nude photographs of one woman along with the graphic account of her former affair with the newly elected President. Republican opponents were quick to capitalize on this by commenting how low America had stooped by voting for a man with such a well-known record of womanizing (forgetting that many popular presidents, from Jefferson to Roosevelt to Kennedy, had fornicated without repercussion). "How can such a man ever make a decent president?!" they opined.

Politics is a dirty business, and continually reminds us that everyone is flawed. While not excusing the wrong, I believe that our own mixture of frailties should cause us to be honest and look for, then consider, the better qualities in others, especially those we despise. We might still think them evil or lazy or despicable, but we should also be reminded again that no one is wholly good nor entirely bad. Even tyrants are capable of acts of kindness, just as saints are able to commit atrocities. Henry Adams, grandson of America's sixth president, alluded to this when, after America's Civil War, he ruefully wrote of the South's most famous hero, "I think that Lee should have been hanged. It was all the worse that he was a good man and a fine character and acted conscientiously...It's always the good men who do the most harm in the world."[2]

Kings and presidents are just as flawed as generals and commanders, musicians and carpenters, pilots and athletes, housewives and gardeners, college professors and cooks. A perfect record of demonstrating "family values" or "leadership" or "boldness" is never going to be found in any candidate. The question, as Lincoln realized, is whether or not a person is qualified to perform the job. Is it necessary to be a teetotaler to compose great music? If not, you may hire Mozart. Is humility necessary to win wars? If not, you may hire Genghis Khan or Julius Caesar or Alexander the Great. Is honesty, though a good quality, necessary to be a good naval war captain? If not, you may hire a pirate like Jean Lafitte (who, along with his crew, preformed quite well for Andrew Jackson in the war of 1812.) May a poor disciplinarian be a good king? If you think not, read the Old Testament to see how successful King David was in building a kingdom, yet how poorly he performed in rearing Absolom, Amnon, and Adonijah, or how lax he was with his murderous army commander Joab. Is social grace needed to write great poetry? If so, then why is a recluse such as Emily Dickinson so widely read? Is it possible for a good nurse to be mean or socially withdrawn? The life of Florence Nightengale may cause you to say yes.

On the contrary, could not drunkenness, egotism, infidelity, cruelty, introvertedness, disorderliness, or clumsiness disqualify one from a post? Are not some qualities detrimental to a job? The answer, of course, is yes, and therein lies the rub. A discriminating mind detects truth from error and is able to place faults in perspective, but this practice may not—and many times does not—result in the best choice. (Pope, for example, turned out to be the wrong man for the job.) This is so because people are not mechanical, rigid, and emotionless, but changing, flexible, multifaceted, and impossible to know entirely.

Christ said, "Do not judge lest you be judged. For in the way yo judge, you will be judged; and by your standard of measure, it wi measured to you."[3] Christ meant for us to judge and to do i with discernment, fairness, tenacity for truth, and, mindfu own frailties, to keep all the facts in their proper perspe keeps us honest. It should also keep us humble. I ho merciful, too, especially when other elections roll aro

Righteous Indignation

Ehud. Both his name and his handedness were unusual, since most warriors were right-handed swordsmen. As a southpaw, however, his delivery was lethal. His actions as a God-given deliverer of the Israelites earned him a perpetual position in the book of Judges. Perennial readings tell of him being the man who craftily maneuvered himself into a private audience with King Eglon, killed him with a sword thrust, then led the Israelites in the battle to overthrow their Moabite suppressers. His actions, recorded in graphically gruesome detail, are seen as a means of providential favor.

One chapter later, Jael, a Kenite woman, plied the trust of a tired Canaanite general into her hands by luring Sisera to her tent. There, she gave him some milk (a somnolent drink, cleverly substituted for the water for which he had asked), covered him up, and promised to stand guard at the doorway for him. As he finally dozed off, she decided to to give him a splitting headache—literally. When the warring Israelite leader Barak eventually wandered in and saw the general nailed to the floor, even he must have been impressed with the sight of a human head spiked by a tent peg. The prophetess Deborah was too. Having told Barak before the war what an honor Sisera's death would be, she then spent the day singing (crowing?) with him about how great a feat this was that Jael had performed and what a blessed woman she was for doing this. Judges 5 records their "duet."

These stories came to mind while watching the television news report the shootings of physicians at two different abortion clinics. As a Christian, I found both the shootings and the bombing repulsive. However much one disagreed not the right way to stop it. That these so self-evident that I questioned the balance Christians. How could they do that? I

any Muslims who wage "jihad" or "holy people acting violently because they are convinced right but *holy* behavior. Being an instrument of God sometimes means being a sword, a hammer, a gun, or a torch, just as much as being a Sunday school teacher, a voter, or a counselor. Doing God's will in all things requires forceful measures in some—even if it means killing. The Old Testament abounds with examples of this; not just in the deceitful Ehud or the cunning Jael, but in leaders like Gideon, Joshua, Othniel, Shamgar, David, or Jephthah. They were all men of bloodshed. Of Phineas, who speared an Israelite and his Midianite lover after barging into their tent, God said to Moses, "Phineas...has turned My anger away from the Israelites; for he was as zealous as I am for my honor among them, so that in My zeal I did not put an end to them...He and his descendants will have a covenant of a lasting priesthood, because he was zealous for the honor of his God and made atonement for the Israelites." (Numbers 25:11-14) Millennia later, devout Christians such as "Stonewall" Jackson, Robert E. Lee, and Joshua Lawrence Chamberlain were seen as heroes for directing this kind of enthusiastic slaying while fighting in the American Civil War. So why should I feel disgust when a Christian kills a man who kills unborn babies for a living? What's the difference?

Perhaps there isn't any; but I believe my discomfort lies in the fact that we today are not ancient Israel, a nation that had a special covenantal relation with God. Physician-killing is also not part of a national war—a circumstance of special exceptions in human affairs—unlike the killing done by David, Jephthah, and their men. We are living in peacetime, when it is better to oppose someone without maiming them or destroying their property. In former times, God did indeed use the Israelites' wars to accomplish His punishment on those who forsook Him. At other times, He also allowed people, and their very human cruelty, to use their own wicked means for Israel's deliverance. But God's family now extends to all nations and His lovingkindness, as always, to all peoples. The Incarnation ushered in a new covenant (also established by bloodshed—Christ's blood). Christ, who instituted the new covenant, did not tell His followers to kill the enemy. He said to pray for them. When He declared the means by which the world would recognize His disciples (Christians), it was not by deeds of righteousness, nor righteous indignation, nor justice, nor charity—as necessary as these things are—but by love. Love even in, especially in, the face of hatred. Followers of Christ, as such, are told that "the wrath of man worketh not the righteousness of God."[4] If I ever become the target of an attack on my life, I hope my assailant will think of that. . . but I doubt he will.

Firmness Without Malice, Justice Without Hatred

> Grant us so to put away the
> leaven of malice and wickedness,
> that we may always serve Thee
> in pureness of living and truth
>
> The Prayer Book[5]

While sitting in the doctor's lounge one day, a fellow surgery resident began complaining about the amount of trash in the room. Doctors in our hospital commonly eat a meal or snack in the lounge, and rather than throwing away the waste products such as cups, ice cream wrappers, wadded up napkins, yogurt containers, sandwich wraps, aluminum cans, and whatnot, they leave them lying around. This creates a daily pigsty with trash on the couches, lampstands, tables, and floors. The hospital custodial service daily cleans up the mess only to have the process repeated. It is shameful to see adults display this type of immature behavior. The surgery resident expressed his disapproval of this kind of carelessness, yet even as he spoke, he tore two strips of paper off of a computer printout in his hand and absentmindedly tossed them onto a table. Surprised that he could be so boldly hypocritical, I pointed out his littering to him and then asserted that he was part of the problem. No one, especially in a moment of self-righteousness, enjoys being told that they are two-faced, and this fellow quickly rounded on me, claiming that what *he* had done was "not the same thing." ("Our *own* case is always different, isn't it?" I rejoined.) Still annoyed, he then tried to shift the blame, blurting out, "Well, *you're* one of the worst ones!" This angered me because it was not true, and I let him know what I thought of his judgment before I turned to other affairs. It was neither the first nor the last time that I had felt misunderstood, a hazard not restricted to my vocation in particular but present throughout life in general.

No one wants to be misjudged. We all want to be understood.

Thoughts Along the Way

When we feel that someone has misjudged us, we may be angry, sad, worried, depressed, annoyed, or anything but pleased. Our feelings are intensified if the assertion against us was made with malice, as it often is. Thoughts of popular church songs—"you can talk about me just as much as you please, I'll talk about you down on my knees, all my sins are washed away, I've been redeemed"—don't seem to pop up at such times; nor do Christ's admonitions to "love your enemies, and pray for those who persecute you." Peter's statement that "if when you do what is right and suffer for it you patiently endure it, this finds favor with God," seems outrageous when all one wants to do is fight back. Our sense of justice, and often our pride, is offended. Having had a series of confrontations earlier that summer, I felt anger and the desire to "battle" far more appealing than prayer. The statutes of scripture don't seem nearly as pertinent as something like "Don't get mad. Get even."

In the cooler, less emotionally charged moments, one can more rationally reflect on these matters. Christ, of course, is the model for Christian love and long-suffering. His motives were questioned and His actions repeatedly misinterpreted. He endured much: misunderstanding, loneliness, betrayal, desertion, and ultimately death, all because He loved us and was obedient to His Father in heaven. His name was degraded ("A good name is to be more desired than great riches, favor is better than silver and gold." Proverbs 22:1) and His character was mocked ("and they kneeled down before Him and mocked Him, saying, "Hail, King of the Jews!"[6]), by soldiers who baited and buffeted Him. As C.S. Lewis once said, he endured many such calumnies and indignities that soldiers, in all their cruelty, could give. "That's him!" "Hypocrite!" "Serves him right!" "That's what he deserves!" "Dirty traitor!"[7] He was long-suffering, indeed. But though He remains a perfect model of Christian charity, His life is not the example for all Christians to follow when seeking justice. He did not defend Himself against injustice; He submitted to it. He did so because his calling, his purpose in life, was to die. For most of us, that will not be the case. Christ was the supreme example of a martyr, but for examples of *combating* personal injustice, we had better look elsewhere.

As the Bible shows, God desires justice just as He desires long-suffering and kindness. As the catch phrase has it, Christians are to be "speaking the truth in love." One of the best examples of someone exercising this principle was Abraham Lincoln. Lincoln was by no means universally popular during his presidency. Many, including members of his own cabinet, criticized him, calling him everything from a clod to a tyrant, a clown, or a monster. One critic wrote, "His soul seems made of leather, and incapable of any grand or noble emotion. Compared with the mass of men, he is a line of flat prose in a beautiful and spirited lyric. He lowers, he never elevates you...You ask not, can this man carry the nation through its terrible struggles? but can the nation carry this man through them, and not perish in the attempt?" Another added, "He is thickheaded; he is ignorant; he is tricky, somewhat astute, in a small way, and obstinate as a mule...He is wrong-headed, the attorney not the lawyer, the petty politician not the statesman, and, in my belief, ill-deserving of the soubriquet of Honest. I am out of all patience with him. Is there no way of inducing him to resign, and allow Mr. Hamlin to take his place?"[8] Lincoln was well aware of these criticisms, yet he did not allow them to impede his sense of justice or rouse in him the leaven of malice. One cabinet member named Salmon P. Chase, for example, had practiced backhanded political tactics and was seeking a spot as a justice in the Supreme Court. Several White House visitors voiced their objections about him to the President. Lincoln simply commented, "I know meaner things about Mr. Chase than any of these men can tell me," and then went on to nominate him for Chief Justice of the Supreme Court. In response to one of the worst of his own name-callers, Lincoln privately remarked, "What's the harm in letting him have his fling? If he did not pitch into me, he would into some poor fellow he might hurt."[9] Conversely, Lincoln was not deterred from any reprimand that he thought necessary, which included relieving six ranking generals from duty, signing death warrants for several criminals, and removing one of his dishonest cabinet members by effectively banishing him to Russia. In performing his duties in a just fashion, yet without malice, he demonstrated Micah's dictum, "He has told you, O man, what is good; And what does the Lord require of you but to do justice, to love kindness, and to walk humbly with your God?" [10] Lincoln ended his second inaugural address by saying, "With malice toward none; with charity for all; with firmness in the right, as God gives us to see the right, let us strive on to finish the work we are in. . ."[11]

Firmness without malice, justice without hatred. These are the requirements regardless of the circumstances, be it in doctor's lounges or presidential cabinets, marketplace booths or hairdressing shops, family kitchens or community schoolrooms. The difficulty in doing right, hating wrong, but not hating those who do wrong is that humans are not made to blend opposites easily. It tends to give us moral indigestion. Yet that is the divine command. Just try to do it, and in the end, you will either be a saint or a schizophrenic. The fact that none of us is either shows just how often we succeed.

Lax Laws, Tardy Punishments, and Lawlessness

> Because the sentence against an evil deed is not executed quickly, therefore the hearts of the sons of men among them are given fully to do evil.
>
> Ecclesiastes 8:11

Over 20,000 people in the United States alone die each year because of accidents involving intoxicated drivers. This rather unsettling statistic is impressed upon the families of those killed, the law enforcement agencies, and health care workers who try to save many of the victims. Because surgeons are involved in the care of trauma patients, they are afforded a close and very personal view of the effects alcohol abuse has on society; and it is not a pretty sight. Anger, disgust, and frustration are probably the most frequently experienced emotions. The anger and disgust are directed against the intoxicated individual. The frustration is that of not seeing justice done. The drunken individual—if a patient himself—will often escape prosecution or incur only light punishment. A disturbing article that appeared in *The American Surgeon* journal one year reported the results of an 18-month period of study on drunk driving and criminal prosecution in the state of Michigan. The authors found that 100% of *un*injured intoxicated drivers involved in car wrecks were convicted of drunk driving during this time span. By contrast, only 59% of injured drunk drivers were successfully prosecuted. The article concluded that injury and hospitalization for drunk drivers after motor vehicle crashes afforded protection from prosecution, and may be enabling ongoing risk-taking behavior by the drunk driver. Before its publication, this paper was presented in a conference at the Midwest Surgical Association to other surgeons involved in trauma care. Discussion afterward was sympathetic and heartfelt. One surgeon said, "I recently cared for two patients admitted to our regional trauma center. One was a 26-year-old man with a ruptured aorta and a ruptured spleen. His 24-year-old fiancee had died at the scene with a high cervical spine injury. The other patient in the accident was a 32-year-old intoxicated driver with seven previous DUI

(Driving Under Influence of alcohol) convictions who had run a stop sign and struck the couple's car broadside into a telephone pole. His driver's license had been revoked. His only injury was a fractured ankle and a fractured sternum." Another added, "When I was in Australia, I was told that Queensland had a big problem with deaths from drunk driving until they passed a law that imposed a fine of $1,000 with a first conviction of driving under the influence, and the next year the number of fatalities from drunk driving dropped by one-half."[12]

"Because the sentence against an evil deed is not executed quickly, therefore the hearts of the sons of men...are given fully to do evil..."

When Dr. A. first came to the United States from Iran several years ago, he was shocked to see the number of people murdered each day. Nearly every night, the news carried a new homicide story. Dr. A. finally picked up the telephone and called his brother, who had arrived in the United States several years earlier, and asked him if there was a war going on. His brother laughed and said no, that this kind of thing happened all the time. Dr. A. was surprised. His previous experience in Iran had not prepared him for such widespread murder. Persians have strict laws concerning homicide. The penalty for someone convicted of murder is death, sometimes by public execution. Dr. A. was 21 before he ever heard of one taking place: a hanging of one man who had stabbed another to death in a fight. People flocked from miles around to witness it. (Public executions are held before sunrise so that no children can attend.) Dr. A's surprise at the high homicide rate in the United States, though, is somewhat deceiving. True, the reported assault rate in America is nearly 10 times that in Iran, and the murder rate nearly 20 times higher (424 assaults and 9.4 murders per 100,000 in the U.S. versus 48 assaults and 0.5 murders per 100,000 in Iran).[13] However, the unreported slaying, raping, and terrorizing of thousands by the Iranian government—often for trivial offenses or trumped up charges—has greatly skewed their figures. On the one hand, the laxity of punishment in the United States against most felons—drawn out court hearings, red tape filibuster delaying execution, modest sentences for heinous crimes—is disheartening. On the other hand, the swiftness to punish in Iran shows the limitations often present in such a strict system, where power is so easily abused. If the warning for the western world is "because the sentence against an evil deed is not executed quickly..." then the one for the East is "a ruler who oppresses the poor is like a driving rain that leaves no crops." (Proverbs 28:3)

Lex talionis or "law of the talon" (talon meaning a claw or hand) was the law of retribution and retaliation found in the ancient Near East among the Jews and the Babylonians, with examples given in the Torah and the Akkadian Code of Hammurabi. This "law" held to the principle of an eye for an eye and a tooth for a tooth, meaning that there should be appropriate punishment of a criminal so as not to be too lenient nor too strict. It could serve to restrain the punisher from being excessive or to uphold justice by preventing an inadequate penalty. The punishment was to fit the crime. "But if there is any further injury, then you shall appoint as a penalty life for life, eye for eye, tooth for tooth, hand for hand, foot for foot, burn for burn, wound for wound, bruise for bruise." (Exodus 21) "And if a man takes the life of any human being, he shall surely be put to death...And if a man injures his neighbor, just as he has done, so it shall be done to him: fracture for fracture, eye for eye, tooth for tooth; just as he has injured a man, so it shall be inflicted on him." (Leviticus 24) "And the judges shall investigate thoroughly; and if the witness is a false witness and he has accused his brother falsely, then you shall do to him just as he intended to do to his brother. Thus you shall purge the evil from among you. And the rest will hear and be afraid, and will never again do such an evil thing among you. Thus you shall not show pity: life for life, eye for eye, tooth for tooth, hand for hand, foot for foot." (Deuteronomy 19) Because human nature seeks revenge when wronged, these laws came to represent a basis for retaliation, a means for continuing never-ending feuds and acts of violence. What was originally provided as a means to exact public justice eventually became an excuse for private vengeance. Christ refuted the idea of a private vendetta when He spoke of turning the other cheek and praying for one's enemy. The corporate judicial principle of making the punishment fit the crime was still as valid as ever. (Be assured, any principle or precept that can potentially be abused will always be so. This is one of the inglorious truths about humanity. Societies like those of Iran or the former Soviet Union or communist China, for example, show that the kind of society with strict laws and low tolerance for crime tend to be oppressive. Loss of freedom and injustice are often the prices paid for living in such conditions, where the ruling few profit from their abuse of the many.)

Lex talionis isn't practiced to any great degree here in America for violent crimes. It is discouraging to see the extent of recidivism that comes from lenient punishment and from sentences that are not executed quickly or decisively. Sadly, a sense of justice being done is more often experienced in a movie theatre than it is in the real world. Drunken homicide, robbery, rape, kidnapping, murder, pedophilial sexual abuse—these criminal problems will always plague humanity, but instead of appropriately punishing them under a system of *lex talionis*, they are too often underpunished or not punished at all. This contributes to propagating lawlessness and hardening of the criminal conscience. It is unfair to the victims. And it is unwise for society.

Thankfully, change can come through persistent efforts of reformers. Mothers Against Drunk Driving (MADD) and Justice Fellowship (a branch of Prison Fellowship involved in legal reform) are two such examples here in America. Sometimes the changes may only come when a coup overthrows a government or persistence changes the legislature (such as the termination of the slave trade in the British West Indies in the nineteenth century or the abolition of racial apartheid in modern South Africa). But they do come—eventually. In the meantime, the widow whose husband was gunned down by two thieves, the young woman who contracted AIDS and hepatitis from a stranger who raped her, the child who was sexually molested by his teacher, the man whose wife was killed by a drunk driver, the pharmacist who was bound and gagged at gunpoint before his store was robbed—they must all try to pick up the pieces and move on in life. They are the ones who need the aid of others, to love them, support them, and to help lobby for judicial change. In so doing, restoration from the lack of punishment against an evil deed can begin. It is worth the effort.

Faith

An Amazing Moment

From my journal...　　　　　　　　　　　　February 10, 1989

B asketball is an amazing game. I wonder if anyone has ever proposed the "basketball argument" for the existence of God? Would this take its place alongside St. Anselm's ontological argument or Thomas Aquinas's cosmological or William Paley's teleological argument as a classical apology for a reality that transcends time and space, is the ground of all being and value, and is worthy of worship?

...So there I was with both feet off of the ground, my right hand cocked backward with the basketball resting gently yet firmly against my fingers, my left hand steadying the ball, and my eyes fixed on the goal 20 feet away. Something in my visual field and sense of position in space (the vestibular apparatus in my inner ear) relayed a lightning-fast message to my brain that a slight adjustment in launching trajectory was needed. Memory from similar adjustments made through years of playing the game was recalled, the information fed into the computer located somewhere in the frontal or parietal regions of the brain, results quickly tabulated, and a decision for the degree of change based upon these calculations was swiftly relayed through the cerebellum and pyramidal cell neuron cable system out to my arm via the radial, median, and ulnar nerves, where the elaborate flexor and extensor muscle and tendon systems responded by changing the timing of the release and force of acceleration that would change the flight of the basketball so as to slightly decrease the arc on the ball in order to provide the necessary power for the sphere to reach the middle of the hoop 20 feet away. . .

SWISH!!

"Amazing!" I mused with a sense of awe and wonder as I turned to run to the other end of the court with the emotional afterglow that always comes after making a basket. "It all took place in a fraction of a second."

The three-point shot I just described took place in last night's game. It was but one sliced moment from a game that *fascinates* me. Even apart from the competitive aspect, the kinesiology and physiology are marvelous. My last paragraph was a SIMPLIFIED description of what happened. I did not describe *in detail* how many more muscle units of the triceps I recruited for making that extra arm extension. I talked nothing of the microphysiology of the actin-myosin cross bridge filaments or the biochemistry of calcium or ATP involved in this. I did not mention all of the muscles involved in this adjustment such as the flexor carpi ulnaris, flexor digitorum superficialis, flexor digitorum profundus, the lumbricals, flexor digiti minimi brevis, or the flexor carpi radialis. I left out the detailed saltatory conduction of myelinated nerve sheaths, the membrane potentials and electrolyte gradients, and the many complex neural pathways in the brain that allow a person to learn and perform movements in a generically similar or varied way; and still, it was mind-bogglingly complex. The glory lies in the adjustments that allow the player to put the ball closer to the hoop—even if it doesn't go in—than if no adjustments were made at all. This phenomenon may be found in other sports such as tennis, baseball, soccer, or rugby.

The question, then, is, "Could such complex beings have evolved by chance, the governing force of such a process being *randomness*?" Would not a creator, a prime mover, seem to be the more logical force behind our existence? I think Isaac Newton was on the right track when he said that in the absence of any other proof, the thumb alone would convince him of God's existence. So, too, an adjustment in mid-air on a basketball court.

Cannibalism and the Gospel

Jesus therefore said to them, 'Truly, truly, I say to you, unless you eat the flesh of the Son of Man and drink His blood, you have no life in yourselves.'

John 6:53

While browsing in the hospital library one summer, I came across the January 1972 issue of *National Geographic*, which featured a story about the Namba people on the island of Malakula, east of Australia.

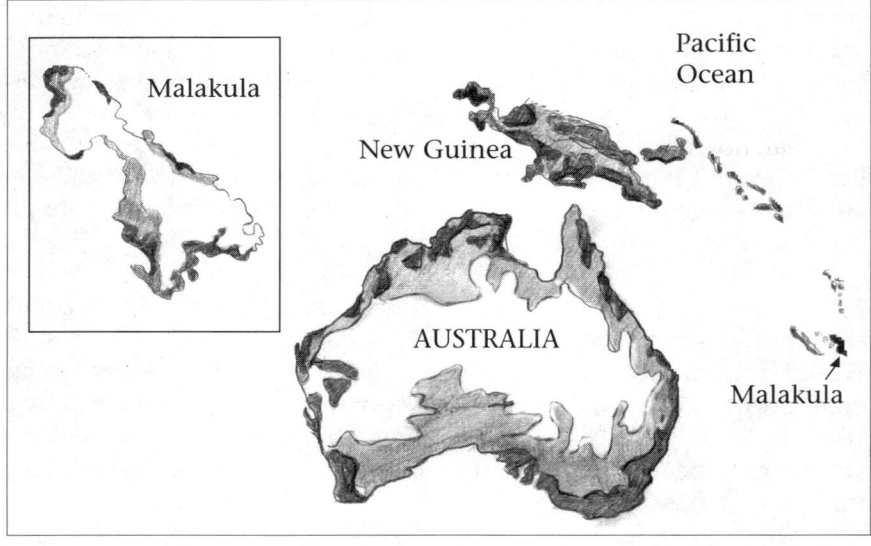

The author of the article was the first white man ever to visit the Namba, and he reported some portions of the tribal life, including a rarely discussed subject: cannibalism. The governments of France and Great Britain, which jointly ruled the island, had outlawed it years earlier, and it was no longer an active practice but a nostalgic memory. In speaking of it, the Nambas stressed to their visitor that it was never done for hunger but always for ritualistic purposes such as settling a quarrel or revenging an enemy. It was never a casual means of feasting.

Thoughts Along the Way

By comparison, Don Richardson reports that the Sawi of New Guinea enacted their cannibalism through treachery. The great game was to fatten the enemy with friendship before the slaughter. In his book *Peace Child*, Richardson tells the story of Yae, a man from an enemy tribe whom the Sawi had befriended for seven months. Then came the great day, when Yae made his last visit to the village for a feast with all of the Sawi tribal leaders—men who had befriended him for over half of a year. In the middle of conversation, the moment of truth came. At a hidden signal, the men stood, weapons in hand, gloated victoriously in beholding the terror on their victim's face, speared him as he screamed and tried vainly to escape, then feasted on his cooked flesh that evening.

Richardson found that there was only one means of making peace between two such warring tribes—a peace child. The exchange of a child from one tribe to the other provided peace, as long as that adopted child lived. Unfortunately, this custom did not always work. One such failed case particularly piqued my interest. Apparently, the Kayagar people had once accepted a peace child from the Sawi. The Kayagar, however, killed the peace child, cooked him, and cut him up into sections for all the tribesman to partake. In this way, they said, the peace child was living inside of everyone. . ."Truly, truly, I say to you, unless you eat the flesh of the Son of Man and drink His blood, you have no life in yourselves."

Over 3,000 years earlier, and nearly 7,000 miles away in the land of Canaan, Leviticus records God's command to the Israelites, "and any man from the house of Israel, or from the aliens who sojourn among them, who eats any blood, I will set my face against that person who eats blood, and will cut him off from among his people. For the life of the flesh is in the blood, and I have given it to you on the altar to make atonement for your souls; for it is the blood by reason of the life that makes atonement."[1] Because life was in the blood, and because justice requires a penalty for sin, the shedding of blood was the means of payment for doing wrong. An Israelite could only be pardoned to maintain fellowship with God by offering, in faith, a blood sacrifice to pay for his or her sin. The blood of a slain animal thus became a substitution for one's own. These sacrifices, however, were continually needed because of ongoing sin. They pointed to the need for a permanent sacrifice for

> *For the life of the flesh is in the blood.*

forgiveness; and this, Christians say, was accomplished by Christ's death as the martyrred, perfect son of God. While the Christian's faith looks back to the cross, the Israelite's faith looked forward. The standard for all is the same—without the shedding of blood there is no forgiveness, and by grace we are saved through *faith*.

When Christ said, "unless you eat the flesh of the son of Man and drink His blood, you have no life in yourselves," he spoke figuratively, using symbolic cannibalism to describe the *total* commitment involved in following him, the *only* commitment that will give *life*. A tribesman from Malakula or a Sawi warrior would understand this concept well, without any grimacing that a typical American might demonstrate at the thought of eating flesh or drinking blood. They could understand this truth: Christ was the perfect, permanent Peace Child, the one whose flesh we "eat" and whose blood we "drink" when we pledge our allegiance to Him, a choice we are reminded of whenever we have communion. For those who have practiced literal cannibalism, symbolic cannibalism poses no stumbling block to accepting the tenets of Christianity.

Richardson was correct in noting that as God has prepared the gospel for all peoples, so He has prepared all peoples for the gospel.

Even Americans.

Revelation and Science Fiction

You are stationary, watching the succession of images in front of you. A woman, pregnant with child, cries out as the labor pains foretell the birth of the baby. She looks uncomfortable. As always, the agony comes before the ecstasy. Horrifyingly, you realize a hideous monster—it looks like a dragon—has crept to the foot of the bed and is waiting with expectant jaws to devour the newborn. Terrified, you want to warn the woman of the harm awaiting her child, but as a spectator, you are helpless to intervene.

A few scenes later, another beast—this one unlike any you have ever encountered—arises out of the sea, similar to Godzilla's emergence from the deeps to face King Kong in battle. This ghastly creature has seven heads and long horns with a formidable countenance. While still gaping at this monstrosity, a second beast makes its appearance by breaking through the earth's surface. Though this one has only one head, it has a startling ability to use the forces of nature as fire bolts from the sky at its bidding. As the scenes continue to roll, you see blood, fire, smoke, lightning, earthquakes, hailstones, fighting, and people dying everywhere. All hell seems to have broken loose. What is going on? This is the most devastating movie you have ever seen, right? Right???!!

Au contraire.

Your name is John and you are watching a heavenly vision, the record of which people are still reading nearly 2,000 years later as the book of Revelation in the Bible.[2] It is the most bizarre thing you have ever seen, yet its validity as a vision of truth is unquestioned. "*C'est formidable!*" you gasp.

I must admit to a relative disinterest in eschatology. Eschatology is the study of the future or "end times", and I have had friends (not many) and heard pastors who relish studying eschatology, especially as found in the book of Revelation. To me, however, the Bible's depictions of it have seemed vague, mysterious, occasionally contradictory, and often unintelligible. If there is one word that describes the overwhelming quality that apocalyptic passages in Daniel, Ezekiel, Joel, Zechariah or Revelation all share in common, it would be "unreal." If Revelation were separated from the Bible and read as a pamphlet, or made into a movie, it would seem more like a Stephen King novel or a horror flick: *Nightmare on Armageddon Street*. It just doesn't have the feeling of historicity to it that other biblical books like I Kings or Matthew have.

However.

Intellectual honesty demands that evaluation of a book, person, idea, or finding be based upon fair-minded judgment. Revelation does not sound historical because it *isn't*. It was not written as a document recording the events of history. It was a vision, and one in which imagery, symbolism, and metaphor permeate the scenes. Like poetry, metaphor is its forte.

In *Fifth Business*, Robertson Davies tells of an atheist named Sam who, steeped in Biblical studies, would ridicule the teachings of the churches in a small Canadian town. Davies' protagonist, Dunstable Ramsay, reports, "His imitations of the parsons were finely observed, and he was very good as the Reverend Andrew Bowyer: 'O Lord, take Thou a live coal from off thine altar and touch our lips,' he would shout, in a caricature of our minister's fine Edinburgh accent; then, with a howl of laughter, 'Wouldn't he be surprised if his prayer was answered!'"

"If he hoped to make an atheist of me, this was where he went wrong; I knew a metaphor when I heard one, and I liked metaphor better than reason. I have known many atheists since Sam, and they all fall down on metaphor."[3]

Metaphor and figurative language, then, provide the keys for understanding a book like Zechariah or Revelation. This is important to bear in mind, for it gives reason to show more than just recreational interest in these books for their ability to entertain. The "take-home message" they impart is that God will come to the earth some day, wipe the slate clean, judge all men, and begin life forever with His people in a new world. That is Revelation in a nutshell. Knowing this engenders hope: hope that the "day of the Lord" will be one in which good permanently triumphs over evil and our bonds of mortality and slavery to sin cut free. Hope for the future gives encouragement for today, that despite all that goes wrong in the world, God is the one in control, not Fate or Satan. These books also give admonishment, a word of caution. As God is just, Christians await His return with the motivation to do God's Will, lest they be found wanting in their efforts to "work out their salvation with fear and trembling."

Though I'm not a big fan of either science fiction reading or horror movies, maybe you are. If you like either, perhaps you'll unwind from the next experience by reading a book like Revelation before you go to bed. It may be helpful in showing that this medium can be used for more than entertainment; it can be used to convey truth and instill hope. Reading eschatology instead of watching a horror movie may even help you sleep better—no one likes to retire after a film thinking about a guy named Jason hiding in the closet with an ax in his hand.[4]

Albert Schweitzer, Legend, and the Truth of the Gospel

After returning from Gabon in French equatorial Africa, photographer W. Eugene Smith wrote this about the man he had gone to observe:

> Albert Schweitzer. The man and his place are difficult to confine or define within the fabrics of their legend—for actuality is conceived in paradox, while legend is an exaggerated simplification as conceived by the imagination. Remoteness is important to legend (although closeness can distort with excessive detail) and, at both extremes, the narrow mind is susceptible to blindness.[5]

When I first read this, I immediately acknowledged its truthfulness even as I admired its penetrating insight. Actuality is indeed conceived in paradox. Humans can be innocent in some things and crooks in others, wonderful lovers or terrible haters, steadfastly committed or wavering and unfaithful, reasonable at times and irrational at others. I don't consider it odd, for example, to enjoy being in a big crowd, shoulder to shoulder, at a popular sporting event while valuing isolation, even when conditions are harsh, while hiking in the mountains. Throughout history, the

wisest minds have understood this and freely admitted it. Plato, through the mouth of Socrates, wrote that "the most extreme opposites have some qualities in common," and "on the one hand a man cannot be continuously good, but he may become good and may also become bad."[6] The Apostle Paul commented on paradox likewise, "For the good that I wish, I do not do; but I practice the very evil that I do not wish."[7]

What made an even deeper impression on me were Smith's comments about legend. Remoteness is important to legend, and allows the imagination freedom to make an exaggerated simplification of a person or events. Remoteness may come in the form of distant time or distant space, so that Britains can be enchanted by the old tales of King Arthur as Americans can be enraptured by the distant work of adventurers to the jungles of Brazil or physicians in the "wild" reaches of Africa. Such is the means by which active lives can be transformed into extraordinary legends, to be studied and analyzed and written about by succeeding generations of pupils and admirers. Abraham Lincoln, of whom more books have been written about than any other historical figure except for Jesus of Nazareth and William Shakespeare, is one such example. He ate, slept, wrote, walked, urinated, and groomed himself just like others. He made not a few mistakes in his political career. He was considered by many of his day—including some of his own cabinet members—to be inept and ungainly. Yet for most Americans who know of him, he has come to be respected, and for many something of a legend where the lines between fact and fiction blur.

In itself, remoteness is a two-edged sword. It may remove us so much from a person or events that to study them seems irrelevant and to believe them seems foolish. Christ once told his disciple Thomas, "Because you have seen me, you have believed; blessed are those who have not seen and yet have believed."[8] On the other hand, closeness, as Smith pointed out, is also susceptible to blindness, sometimes preventing the true importance of achievements from being realized. The credulity of faith thus excludes the immediate, leaving only the people, events, sayings, or scriptures of the remote to be believed. Jesus experienced this when he visited his home town and preached in the synagogue. "Isn't this the carpenter?" people asked. "Isn't this Mary's son and the brother of James, Joseph, Judas, and Simon? Aren't his sisters here with us? And they took offense at him." Jesus replied, "Only in his hometown, among his relatives and in his own house is a prophet without honor."[9]

These are sobering thoughts since most people base their religious beliefs on ancient texts and the teachings of people who lived long ago, often in a foreign land, or on gods that are preternatural (thus remote from the natural world.). Is something more believable or more outstanding because it happened long ago or far away, outside the direct scrutiny of modern science and reasoning? Or does remoteness make it less believable, unproven, fictitious? Mankind has always exhibited a fertile imagination. Fictional *creations* can with time become the myths and legends that people believe to be *fact*. One book on my shelf contains collections of over 100 myths from around the globe that only deal with one subject: the creation of the world.[10] How can one be assured that one's own views, over all the rest, are THE truth about the universe? How do we know that the life of Christ, surely a historical reality, has not become embellished to become a legend that Christians believe? Or, to use terms from the academic world, has the 'Jesus of history' been transformed through imagination and fictionalizing into an exaggerated 'Christ of faith'? Do not the writings that were not incorporated into the Biblical canon, such as the Gospel of Thomas or the Abgar Legend, seem to suggest that the answer to this is "yes"?

I have received the most help on this issue from the writings of C.S. Lewis. Two papers, "Modern Theology and Biblical Criticism" (from *Christian Reflections*) and "What Are We to Make of Jesus Christ?" (from *God in the Dock*), approach the problem from this angle:

> There are characters whom we know to be historical but of whom we do not feel that we have any personal knowledge—knowledge by acquaintance; such are Alexander, Attila, or William of Orange. There are others who make no claim to historical reality but whom, nonetheless, we know as we know real people: Falstaff, Uncle Toby, Mr. Pickwick. But there are only three characters who, claiming the first sort of reality, also actually have the second. And surely everyone knows who they are: Plato's Socrates, the Jesus of the Gospels, and Boswell's Johnson. Our acquaintance with them shows itself in a dozen ways. When we look into the Apocryphal gospels, we find ourselves constantly saying of this or that logion, "No. It's a fine saying, but not His. That wasn't how He talked."—

just as we do with all pseudoJohnsoniana. We are not in the least perturbed by the contrasts within each character: the union in Socrates of silly and scabrous titters about Greek pederasty with the highest mystical fervor and the homeliest good sense; in Johnson, of profound gravity and melancholy with that love of fun and nonsense which Boswell never understood though Fanny Burney did; in Jesus of peasant shrewdness, intolerable severity, and irresistible tenderness. So strong is the flavour of the personality that, even while He says things which, on any other assumption than that of Divine Incarnation in the fullest sense, would be appallingly arrogant, yet we—and many unbelievers to—accept Him at His own valuation when He says "I am meek and lowly of heart."[11]

As a literary historian, I am perfectly convinced that whatever else the Gospels are they are not legends. I have read a great deal of legend and I am quite clear that they are not the same sort of thing. They are not artistic enough to be legends. From an imaginative point of view they are clumsy, they don't work up to things properly. Most of the life of Jesus is totally unknown to us, as is the life of anyone else who lived at that time, and no people building up a legend would allow that to be so. Apart from bits of the Platonic dialogues, there are no conversations that I know of in ancient literature like the Fourth Gospel. There is nothing, even in modern literature, until about a hundred years ago when the realistic novel came into existence. In the story of the woman taken in adultery we are told Christ bent down and scribbled in the dust with His finger. Nothing comes of this. No one has ever based any doctrine on it. And the art of *inventing* little irrelevant details to make an imaginary scene more convincing is a purely modern art. Surely the only explanation of this passage is that the thing really happened? The author put it in simply because he had *seen* it.[12]

The *American College Dictionary* defines legend as "a nonhistorical or unverifiable story handed down by tradition from earlier times and popularly accepted as historical." It also notes, "LEGEND, originally denoting a story concerning the life of a saint, is applied to any fictitious story, sometimes involving the supernatural, and usually concerned with a real person, place, or other subject."[13] These match Eugene Smith's descriptions well, even though they do not comment on *why* humans love legends. I do know, though, that it is easier to believe a legend than to research the truth. As Samuel Johnson once said, "It is more from carelessness about truth than from intentional lying, that there is so much falsehood in the world."[14]

And so it goes. Discernment and accuracy will belong to those who seek them. Gullibility and dogmatism belong to those who don't.

Keep seeking.

Family Trees and Pedigrees

Some parts of the Bible are easier to read than others. Pedigrees, partitions, and tabernacle measurements, for example, are more important than they are interesting.

> And on the left hand were their kinsmen the sons of Merari: Ethan the son of Kishi, the son of Abdi, the son of Malluch, the son of Hashabiah, the son of Amaziah, the son of Hilkiah, the son of Amzi, the son of Bani, the son of Shemer, the son of Mahli, the son of Mushi, the son of Merari, the son of Levi.
> I Chronicles 6:44-47

> And for the width of the court on the west side shall be hangings of fifty cubits with their ten pillars and their ten sockets. And the width of the court on the east side shall be fifty cubits. The hangings for the one side of the gate shall be fifteen cubits with their three pillars and their three sockets. And for the other side shall be hangings of fifteen cubits with their three pillars and their three sockets.
> Exodus 27:12-15

> Now the fifth lot fell to the tribe of the sons of Asher according to their families. And their territory was Helkath and Hali and Beten and Achshaph, and Allammelech and Amad and Mishal; and it reached to Carmel on the west and to Shihor-libnath. And it turned toward the east to Beth-dagon, and reached to Zebulun, and to the valley of Iphtahel northward to Beth-emek and Neiel; then it proceeded on north to Cabul, and Ebron and Rehob and Hammon and Kanah, as far as Great Sidon.
> Joshua 19:24-28

David Graham

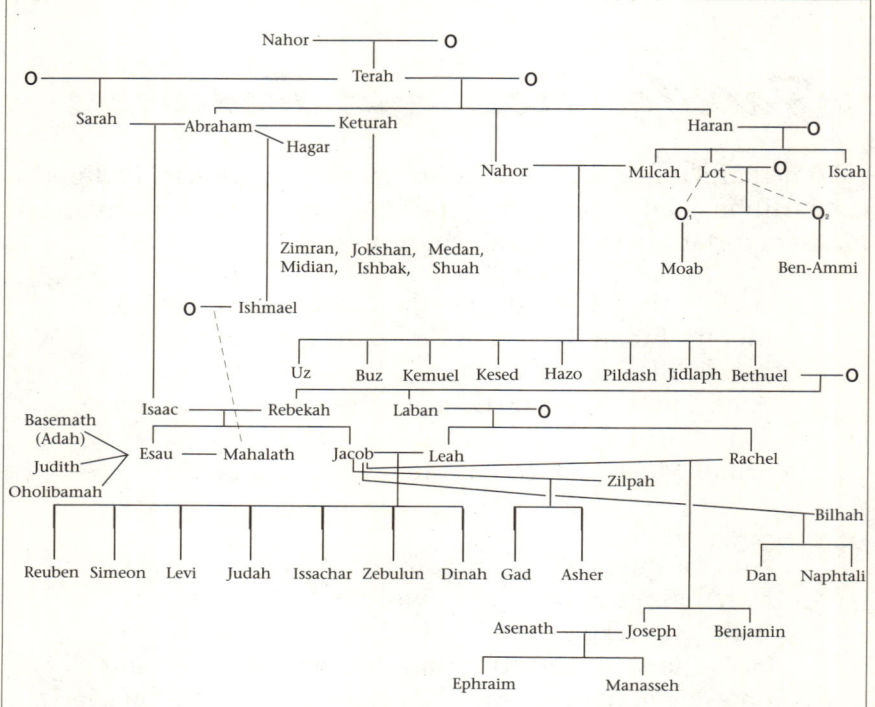

Isaac—Rebekah's a) first cousin once-removed and b) husband.
Jacob—Leah and Rachel's a) second cousin once-removed and b) husband.
Abraham—Uncle to Lot, a) great uncle and b) father-in-law to Rebekah, 1) half-brother and 2) husband to Sarah.
Esau—Married his half-cousin Mahalath.
Lot—Father of his daughters and oddly, father of his grandsons (because of the incest with his daughters).
Nahor—Milcah's a) uncle and b) husband.
Leah—Rachel's a) sister and b) fellow wife.
Jews—Descended from Abraham (and Isaac and Jacob).
Israel—12 tribes named after Jacob (Israel's) 11 sons and two grandsons.
Moabites—Descended from Lot.
Ammonites—Also came from Lot's incest with his daughters.
Midianites—Descended from Midian and probably Ishmael and Medan.
Edomites—Descended from Esau.   (Figure 1)

Thoughts Along the Way

I am thankful for passages like these since they lend historical credibility to my Christian roots, even though my brain tends to balk at reading them. Perhaps if I had guided tours through the nation of Israel or drew my own tabernacle illustrations (or built a model of them), these scriptures would easily come to life and be imbued with meaning. I have done neither. Fortunately, I have done one thing that has helped me to take a greater interest in all of those pedigrees: I went to medical school.

Medical school may not seem to be an obvious place to study theology or philosophy or to attend for more enlightenment of the scriptures, but I found it quite helpful for doing all that. In addition to other benefits, it gave me the chance to study and interpret "family trees" (i.e., pedigrees) while studying genetics. This has led to a better personal understanding of many genealogy lists found in the Old Testament. It has also pointed out some interesting familial relationships (see Figure 1) that might otherwise have gone unnoticed. Though stiff-looking, mapping out the pedigrees brought the scriptures to life while giving me the "big picture" when studying a particular individual. Here is one such example involving the Aaronic priesthood.

> "Then a man of God came to Eli and said to him, 'Thus says the Lord,'...Why do you kick at My sacrifice and at My offering which I have commanded in My dwelling, and honor your sons above Me, by making yourselves fat with the choicest of every offering of My people Israel? Therefore the Lord God of Israel declares, 'I did indeed say that your house and the house of your father should walk before Me forever'; but now the Lord declares, 'Far be it from Me—for those who honor Me I will honor, and those who despise Me will be lightly esteemed. Behold, the days are coming when I will break your strength and the strength of your father's house so that there will not be an old man in your house...this will be the sign to you which shall come concerning your two sons, Hophni and Phinehas: on the same day both of them shall die. But I will raise up for Myself a faithful priest who

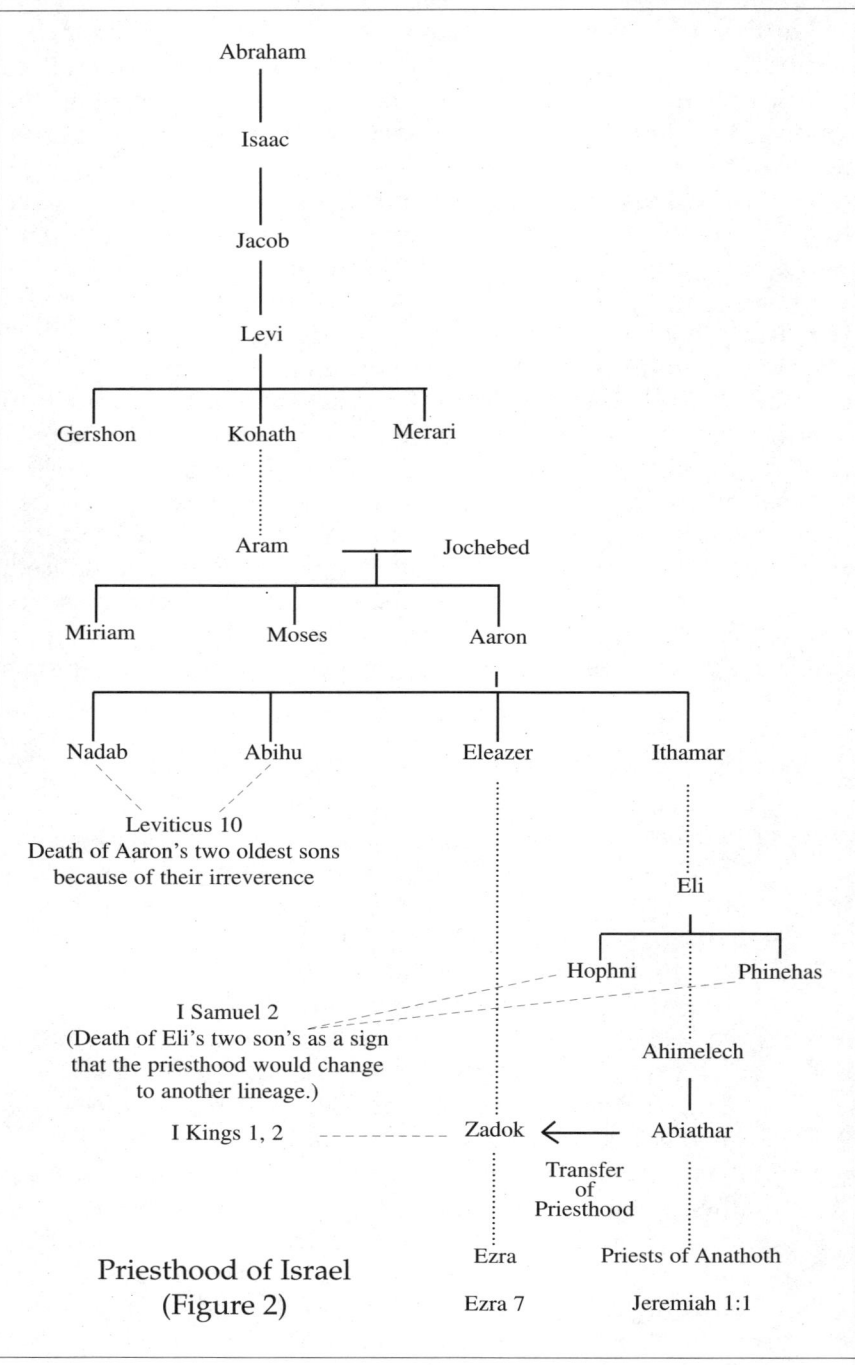

Priesthood of Israel
(Figure 2)

will do according to what is in My heart and in My soul; and I will build him an enduring house.'"
>
> I Samuel 2

"Now Nadab and Abihu, the sons of Aaron, took their respective firepans, and after putting fire in them, placed incense on it and offered strange fire before the Lord, which He had not commanded them. And fire came out from the presence of the Lord and consumed them, and they died before the Lord. 'By those who come near Me I will be treated as holy.'"
>
> Leviticus 10

Adonijah has gone down today and has sacrificed oxen and fatlings and sheep in abundance, and has invited all the king's sons and the commanders of the army and *Abiathar* the priest, and behold, they are eating and drinking before him; and they say, "Long live King Adonijah!"...Then King David said, "Call to me Zadok the priest, Nathan the prophet, and Benaiah the son of Jehoiada...and let [them] anoint him (Soloman) as king over Israel, and blow the trumpet and say, 'Long live King Solomon!'"
>
> I Kings 1

Then to Abiathar the priest the king (Soloman) said, "Go to Anathoth to your own field, for you deserve to die; but I will not put you to death at this time, because you carried the ark of the Lord God before my father David, and because you were afflicted in everything with which my father was afflicted." So Solomon dismissed Abiathar from being priest to the Lord, in order to fulfill the word of the Lord, which He had spoken concerning the house of Eli in Shiloh.
>
> I Kings 2

David Graham

For some reason, making my own study guides seems to be more helpful than using those made by others. Perhaps you find this to be true for you as well. If so, I hope you will try your hand at making pedigrees or maps of the Holy Lands or whatever else will enhance your reading of the Bible. God made man in His own image: a little creativity seems appropriate for studying the scriptures of a creative God.

Birthdays, Inheritance, and Booker T. Washington

Without pausing to think about it or stopping to look it up, I can tell you with certainty where I was born, the date of my birth, how old I am, who my parents and grandparents are, and how old I was when I first rode an airplane, graduated from high school, and when I married. Much of my identity—and therefore my self-understanding and outlook on life—is determined by knowing my age and my ancestry. When we complete an application for a school, mission, job, hospital admission, or passport, we all give this information without difficulty since what we are giving is the information *by which we define ourselves*. This is why Booker T. Washington's autobiography *Up From Slavery* is so startling and sobering:

> I was born a slave on a plantation in Franklin County, Virginia. I am not quite sure of the exact place or exact date of my birth, but at any rate I suspect I must have been born somewhere and at some time. As nearly as I have been able to learn, I was born near a cross-roads post-office called Hale's Ford, and the year was 1858 or 1859. I do not know the month or the day. The earliest impressions I can now recall are of the plantation and the slave quarters—the latter being the part of the plantation where the slaves had their cabins.
>
> My life had its beginning in the midst of the most miserable, desolate, and discouraging surroundings. This was so, however, not because my owners were especially cruel, for they were not, as compared with many others. I was born in a typical log cabin, about fourteen by sixteen feet square. In this cabin I lived with my mother and a brother and sister till after the Civil War, when we were all declared free.
>
> Of my ancestry I know almost nothing. In the slave quarters, and even later, I heard whispered conversa-

tions among the colored people of the tortures which the slaves, including, no doubt, my ancestors on my mother's side, suffered in the middle passage of the slave ship while being conveyed from Africa to America. I have been unsuccessful in securing any information that would throw any accurate light upon the history of my family beyond my mother. She, I remember, had a half-brother and a half-sister. In the days of slavery not very much attention was given to family history and family records—that is, black family records. My mother, I suppose, attracted the attention of a purchaser who was afterward my owner and hers. Her addition to the slave family attracted about as much attention as the purchase of a new horse or cow. Of my father I know even less than of my mother. I do not even know his name. I have heard reports to the effect that he was a white man who lived on one of the near-by plantations. Whoever he was, I never heard of his taking the least interest in me or providing in any way for my rearing.[15]

Washington's words came to mind while recently reading through the book of I Chronicles in the Bible. The Chronicler gave the Jews a strong sense of history and identity with his meticulous recording of their ancestry and division of labor in the government and priesthood. Reading these annals is a profitable, though ofttimes wearying process. The highlights of God's work in the lives of His chosen people are recorded succinctly; the chronologies are not. Pedigrees are painstakingly traced out with thorough scholarly effort and detail. For the Chronicler, ancestry of family histories was important to record accurately: it is no light matter to be called a son of Abraham.

I can trace my own lineage farther back than Booker T. Washington, yet not as far as someone like Ezra or Zadok could theirs. I am thankful, though, that my *spiritual* heritage does not depend on old files in well-preserved archives for authenticity. In Paul's letter to the church in Rome, he wrote that Gentiles, too, were part of God's family, like a wild olive branch grafted on to a tree. By grafting in to the tree whose root was the Abrahamic Covenant, the believing Gentiles became recipients of God's promised blessing to Abraham, "and in you all the families of the earth shall be blessed."[16] Whether born in or out of wedlock, to slaves or free men, to thieves, extortioners, embezzlers, murderers, kings, merchants, fishermen, or engravers, our spiritual heritage depends only on our faith in Christ. In God's family, pedigrees are perfect. No wonder the Apostle John could be so buoyant, "See how great a love the Father has bestowed upon us, that we should be called children of God; and such we are."[17]

The Missionary Spirit

Go into all the world and preach the gospel to all creation.
                              Mark 16:15

Go therefore and make disciples of all the nations, baptizing them in the name of the Father and the Son and the Holy Spirit, teaching them to observe all that I commanded you.
                              Matthew 28:19, 20

And just as you want people to treat you, treat them in the same way.
                              Luke 6:31

For nearly two millennia, Christians have been going into all parts of the world to preach the gospel. Since Christians believe in the basic truth of the gospel and therefore the need for others to know and accept it, why is it so painful to read about many of the ways this is done? Benjamin Franklin, for example, in his "Remarks Concerning the Savages of North America" reports of a "Swedish minister, having assembled the chiefs of the Susquehanna Indians, made a sermon to them, acquainting them with the principal historical facts on which our religion is founded; such as the fall of our first parents by eating an apple, the coming of Christ to repair the mischief, His miracles and suffering, &c. When he had finished, an Indian orator stood up to thank him. 'What you have told us,' says he, 'is all very good. It is indeed bad to eat apples. It is better to make them all into cider. We are much obliged by your kindness in coming so far, to tell us these things which you have heard from your mothers. In return, I will tell you some of those we have heard from ours. In the beginning...' (upon which the Indian orator began his narration of the origin of their crops.) The good missionary, disgusted with this idle tale, said, 'What I delivered to you were sacred truths; but what you tell me is mere fable, fiction, and falsehood.' The Indian, offended, replied, 'My brother, it seems your friends have not done you justice in your education; they have not well instructed you in the rules of common civility. You saw that we, who understand and practice those rules, believed all your stories; why do you refuse to believe ours?'"[18]

Christian missionaries have struggled over the years to find the right balance between Christianity and culture. Unfortunately, this is not an easy task, nor is it uncommon for missionaries—and the organizations who support them—to overestimate their success. Missionary reports to congregations, especially when given in person, usually seem to be glowing with progress and evangelization success, while the full effects of the missionary encounter on the indigenous peoples are often missed. As one Native American recently wrote, "The Makah elders alive in 1991 remember potlatches (song fiests) that went for two weeks without a song being repeated. Today a potlatch lasts but a night. We have no way of knowing how many songs were lost in the epidemics, how many were lost through the persistent efforts of missionaries and federal Indian agents to suppress our language and culture. I am a Christian; I am not sorry the missionaries came. But I wish they had known how to let their news change peoples' lives from the inside, without imposing their culture over our ways."[19]

C.S. Lewis, himself a proponent of the gospel, once wrote, "But can even missionaries be trusted? 'Gun and gospel' have been horribly combined in the past. The missionary's holy desire to save souls has not always been kept quite distinct from the arrogant desire, the busybody's itch, to (as he calls it) 'civilize' the (as he calls them) 'natives.'"[20]

Missionary societies seem to have the capacity for often attracting ill-informed, dogmatic people into their ranks, whose stubbornness prevents them from understanding any viewpoint other than their own and whose actions often soil the work of the majority. I find the stories of narrow-minded criticism that my older sister has been subjected to as a missionary school teacher rather exasperating, for example, and can only shake my head in admiration of her patience. (Having worked with two different mission societies in two vastly different countries, she knows that this criticism is neither geographically nor denominationally limited.) Hearing these stories angers me, adding to the feelings of confinement and subservience to petty rules that I myself have experienced with the missions with which I have worked. In John 8:32, Christ said, "and you shall know the truth, and the truth shall make you free," and yet, ironically, the times I have felt the least amount of freedom have been when I was doing work on "mission trips," overseas. Although I was not greatly restricted, it gave me more appreciation for the North American Indian philosophy that I heard of the Sioux, "No man can tell another man what to do;" a sign of true respect, to my way to thinking.

I am not, as it may seem, opposed to Christian missions nor repulsed by missionaries. The majority that I know are hard-working, God-fearing people who have respect for those they have come to evangelize. They observe Christ's command to preach the gospel to all creation while following the Golden Rule. Their task is a challenging one, for they must be able to balance culture with gospel, preserving what is good and changing what is bad. This can be difficult. Many issues are not clearly black and white, right or wrong, and require much prayer as well as a keen, yet sensitive intellect—one that is willing to search out the heart of a matter BEFORE issuing a pronouncement on it. Because this process is also fraught with subjectivity, humility is of paramount importance. When prayer, curiosity, work, fairness, and more prayer DO combine to produce the "fruit of the spirit," the results can be very satisfying. Here are a few samples:

> These words spoke of an incredible change in the heart of a Condoshi Indian chief in Peru. For as long as his people could remember, killing had been a way of life! Children were taught to kill a wounded enemy. It would build courage. In their lives revenge killings were a cultural mandate. Head hunting was done as a sign of strength and worth...Not long after many of these people had come to Christ, outsiders suggested that they might be happier returning to their old ways. One of the Indian leaders responded, "Years ago when my mother's brother was killed, Mother was forced to carry his head in a basket to the home of her captors. Do you think people enjoy living like that? We are people. We have hearts just like everyone else."[21]
>
> (*JAARS* newsletter April, 1993)

Despite all the protestations of modern anthropologists, the fact remains that the Africans to whom Dad came as the Master's servant were sunk in debauchery and total degradation of the darkest hues. Witchcraft, superstition, and shrinking fear of evil spirits shackled the souls of the natives around our home...To the uninitiated they appeared ferocious. But to Dad and Mother they were friends trapped in the tyranny of their own tribal traditions and grinding poverty.

Most of the men were notoriously indolent. Given to excessive debauchery they lolled in the shade of scrubby trees most of the day, then spent their nights in ribald revelry. They would stagger past our place shouting and chanting in the darkness, hoping to drive away the demons they dreaded.

Women were abused and maltreated as though of less value than even a dog or donkey. They not only bore the babies, most of whom perished in infancy, but also bore the entire work load of digging, planting, harvesting, gathering wood, and carrying water in clay pots on their heads.

It never ceased to astonish me how brutal was the behavior of the men in beating their wives and children. Throughout the nights the throb of the beer drums, the animal-like shouts of intoxicated men, all mingled with the screams of women and children beaten with clubs & whips.

The huts and villages built of mud and sticks, plastered with cow dung, were crude and filthy hovels in which human beings, goats, chickens, and a few scrub cattle lived together at a bestial level. With utter boldness and unflinching courage, Dad and Mother entered these places to bring help and healing. Their love and compassion was shed abroad so freely in their visits that many of the villagers were drawn from their despair to discover a new life in God.[22]

(W. Phillip Keller, *Chosen Vessels*)

Kok-Me accepted what had been said and then nodded. "Now I want to say something," he began. "We Damals had nothing before you came with God's message from the Bible." His voice rose with emotion as he continued. "We thank God that He sent Gordon Larson and John Ellenberger and you, Damal-Neme, to bring us the words of Jesus. Hai, the hope of eternal life, has come to us through Jesus Christ."

"The coming of the gospel has stopped our wars. Women are no longer killed as witches. Before the gospel came many babies born here were handicapped and dumb. The sores from yaws killed so many people that travelers from the Ilaga used to sit on their own rain mats lest they be contaminated with our disease. People were always hungry and our pigs didn't prosper. Spirit appeasement filled every part of our lives, but still it didn't help us. The younger generation doesn't even know what it was like in the Berga before the gospel came, but my generation does. This was the only way of life my ancestors knew."

"Now you have come with the gospel, and we want to thank the Christians in America who sent you to us. Damal-Neme and Damal-In, when you grow old and leave us, we want new missionaries to take your place. We will give these new missionaries the same symbolic names we have given you. We will love them as we have loved you, and they will continue to teach us and lead us on God's trail."[23]

(Alice Gibbons, *The People Time Forgot*)

In the journal I kept on my African trip, I wrote the following after reading Alice Gibbons' report, "Primitive people do not enjoy disease and famine and war and spirit appeasement. If they have a chance to live a better life, they will. Missions are justified; the anthropologists' beef about destroying culture is answered thus: if culture is wrong, it is not wrong to change culture. If people desire a better way of life, then they should be granted that." This represents the core of what I truly believe about Christian missions, though this core is covered with the discomfort and cynicism of what I know to be the truth and

Thoughts Along the Way

"success" of missionary involvement in many cases. I am trying to gradually pull off this rind of disenchantment by reminding myself that there are certain freedoms one gives up when a missionary—"No soldier in active service entangles himself in the affairs of everyday life, so that he may please the one who enlisted him as a soldier,"[24] wrote Paul—and that just as the church is supposed to be a "hospital for sinners" (and not a "haven for saints"), so too, its missionary ambassadors will be comprised of "hospitalized sinners." There will be those who follow the Golden Rule and others who won't, just as there will be many wise and some foolish in being "fishers of men" (and in living all of life as well). This is probably why the author of Hebrews wrote about lifting the visual field higher, "looking unto Jesus the author and finisher of our faith."[25]

Holiness

When one of His disciples asked for instruction on prayer, Jesus replied by telling him to say when praying, "Father, hallowed be thy name."[26] When Christ addressed this issue during the Sermon on the Mount, He again started by saying "Our Father who art in heaven, hallowed be Thy name."[27] Each week, millions of people around the globe follow Christ's example by repeating this very phrase during worship services. And during each week millions ignore its message. They tell God to damn this or to damn that, they utter His son's name in anger, and they even refer to the Omnipotent Himself irreverently and absentmindedly. God's name is not treated with respect. His existence usually isn't either.

In the scriptures, the name and person of God are inseparably related. As Baker's *Encyclopedia of the Bible* puts it, "When the Scripture employs the phrase "name of God," God in his fullness is meant. When men and women call on the name of God, God himself is worshipped (Gn 21:33); when they forget the name of God, they depart from God himself (Jer 23:27); when they take the name of God in vain, God himself is personally profaned and affronted (Ex 20:7)."[28] In other words, to treat God's name unholy is to treat God Himself unholy.

For some time now, I have had a growing respect for those people who have a strong sense of holiness. Here in America, where holiness is foreign to our cultural lifestyle, encounters with those who seek it are rare. In part, this is because holiness is a process, not an event. It takes time and effort to cultivate. It doesn't happen quickly and is therefore not appealing to a society drawn toward instant gratification. In part, holiness is impeded by our curiosity, especially about that which is forbidden. In Israel, for example, the Holy of holies in the temple was forbidden to anyone but the high priest (who was only allowed entrance on one day of the year). Curiosity makes one want to peep in, to see what it looked like. Author Earl Wilson says this is true of human sexuality, too. "Fear and danger may also contribute to sexual arousal with unfamiliar persons or events. A man may become highly aroused by seeing a woman other than his wife partially clothed or nude. Even if his wife is physically more attractive, the fact that he is familiar with his wife's body but not the other woman's may affect his arousal state. He may then try to sneak another peek at the other woman, because viewing her body is forbidden by existing cultural standards. Many men report that they are stimulated by women at topless bars and in X-rated movies, not because of their exceptional beauty, but because they aren't supposed to go see them."[29] Of course, holiness is also impeded by lack of desire. Those who haven't tasted it don't want it. They are too self-satisfied to care or to seek anything better.

I respect the opinions of those who recognize the holy and who can convey its appeal. They reveal that which is vital, yet so often missing in our existence. Sometimes, this revelation is simply making others aware of the presence of holiness. In writing about the presence of a holy day, for example, Abraham Joshua Heschel stated, "The higher goal of spiritual living is not to amass a wealth of information, but to face sacred moments. . . The meaning of the Sabbath is to celebrate time rather than space. Six days a week we live under the tyranny of things of space; on the Sabbath we try to become attuned to holiness in time."[30] Others, such as C.S. Lewis in writing *Perelandra* or John Milton in writing *Paradise Lost* show the appeal of holiness through obedience. Many others such as John the Baptist or Dietrich Bonhoffer or Mahatma Gandhi have shown that holiness was worth more than anything, even one's own life. This desire for the holy, for recognizing and desiring the sacred—be it God's name, God's day, God's word, or God's people—is something vital to our existence in becoming fully human. When I daily hear someone taking God's name in vain, it tends to turn me away from atheism. I don't want a life of irreverence. That is ultimately an empty existence on a road that leads to nowhere. I *want* purity, sacredness, and divinity (even though my own life is often impure, profane, and always mortal). I can see that those who *have* thirsted after, and tasted this, are never quite the same. The fruit of holiness turns out to be delicious. "Blessed are those who hunger and thirst after righteousness," said Christ. "For they will be filled."[31]

Quoting

I often begin my essays with a quote, and almost invariably incorporate at least one (and usually several) within my composition. I will deviate for once, although even now I find the urge to quote someone to explain why I am not going to quote. But I won't.

There is not any single reason for why I, and others, quote. It seems to come easily, even reflexively, because I am seeking to express something and need help in saying it just right. A quote can grasp the essence of what I want to say, and rather than trying to present something in my own words, I let the quote say it for me. Sometimes I quote so much that I feel as though my essays are more like brief commentaries interspersed among some quotes I enjoy rather than being true "compositions." My role becomes more like an editor (picking out and grouping quotes) than an author. It is not too dissimilar from the grade-school practice of cutting pictures out of magazines and pasting them together to make a collage. The only originality comes in the arrangement, not from what is said.

Quotes are also used to broaden my discussions. I have never been a college professor, traveled to Greece, written a novel, run for political office, lived in another century, drunk hock, been stung by a scorpion or bitten by a shark, but I can read about those who have and vicariously share in their experiences. Quotes enlarge, magnify, and illuminate things that I cannot say on my own. They help to tell the tales and share the ideas of others, to be compared and contrasted with my own. Quotes help to tell life's story. We are all too small to tell it on our own.

Quotes also bring with them some feeling of authority. Some, such as those from the Bible, seem to carry more weight because the quotes are either from God or from writers inspired by God. Whether or not a *feeling* of authority is the same as *authority* itself depends on the faith one places in the truthfulness of one's source. In this respect, everyone must judge for themselves. The Jews look to the Talmud and the Old Testament scriptures. Christians look to the Old and New Testament scriptures with Catholics accepting the Apocryphal books and the

Pope's sayings to boot. Muslims look to the Koran for their authority on life. Buddhists look to their own sacred writings just as Taoists do theirs. Hindus look anywhere (the Vedas with their Upanishads, The Mahabharata with its Bhagavad Gita, The Puranas, the Ramayana—it is basically a religion of preferance in which one can be a pantheist, polytheist, monotheist, or even agnostic. It is not unlike sitting in a restaurant, picking out items from a large menu. Each meal, or in this case, religion, can be created to one's preference.) Members of each group feel that their *own* authority reveals the truth about the universe, the nature of reality, and the way we should behave. How does one decide which is correct? As I said, everyone must judge for themselves. It's a matter of faith, even for atheists (who look nowhere).

I suppose I will always be dependent on quoting, be it medical statistics or theological statements. I rely heavily on the authority and experience of others to build my own. The prayer of the humble and the prudent is for discernment to find the right authority, to separate the wheat from the chaff, the true from the false. In a phrase: to know truth. It's the only thing worth seeking; and it is a lifelong journey.

Bon voyage.

The Unknowable Future

Less than 24 hours after running the second fastest 5,000-meter race in American track and field history, Steve Prefontaine lay dead. Prefontaine was one of the world's premier distance runners in the early 1970s and America's best hope for winning a gold medal in track in the distance races of the 1976 Olympics. He was young, popular, and superbly fit. While driving home in the early morning hours after his successful race in May 1975, he fell asleep at the wheel. His car crashed, pinning him inside, and he died of asphyxiation. The sports world mourned his death.

Thoughts of Prefontaine and his tragic death came to mind while recently reading from the book of Ecclesiastes. The author of that book points to an obvious but painful fact of life when he states, "Since no man knows the future, who can tell him what is to come? No man has power over the wind to contain it; so no one has power over the day of his death."[32]

How little we can know about the future occasionally leads to predictions of comical proportions. A sixteenth-century French essayist named Michel de Montaigne wrote the following while commenting on the importance of horses in war.

> It is much more sensible to rely on a sword that we hold in our hand than on the bullet that escapes out of our pistol, in which there are many parts—the powder, the flint, the lock —the least of which, by failing, will make your fortune fail. You strike with little certainty the blow that the air carries for you:
>
> Let the winds waft their blows where'er they will.
> A sword has strength; and every manly race
> Makes war with swords.
>   Lucan
>
> But as for the pistol, I shall speak of it more amply when I make a comparison of ancient arms with ours;

and except for the shock to the ear, with which by now everyone has become familiar, I think it is a weapon of very little effect, and hope that some day we shall abandon the use of it.[33]

Montaigne could not see into the future, could not envision that the gun would someday become the primary means of waging war, nor realize that war horses would eventually be rendered obsolete. It is a surprising world we inhabit, full of unforeseen twists and turns. One never knows exactly how events will unfold.

I think this has much to do with the widespread practice of and interest in religion around the world. Whether or not they give it much thought, most people would like to believe that there is a power(s) that is in control, that gives meaning to life, that can be prayed to for aid in times of need, and that can grant the gift of life after death. We are surrounded by death, disease, confusion, and crime as well as life, health, order, and beauty. It seems far too complex to have come about by chance, far too mystifying and wonderful to have "just happened." So Hindu gurus, Buddhist monks, Tibetan lamas, tribal witch doctors, shamans, Islam imams, Jewish rabbis, Christian pastors and priests attempt to teach the masses what they believe to be the truth about the universe. Their answers vary considerably, as do their views about the future.

Since people view the future in terms of their *own* lives, it was to the individual, not the corporate, that Christ directed his remarks when He told His disciples, "do not worry about tomorrow, for tomorrow will worry about itself. Each day has enough trouble of its own."[34] Christ had good reason for saying this since he could also say, "Come to Me, all who are weary and heavy-laden, and I will give you rest."[35] Rest from the unknowable future, from the worry of uncertainty, is a theology of comfort. It's a good theology for life; and for death.

Cultural Relevance and the Search for Absolute Truth

> The more sacred a text is, the more subject it is to glosses and strained interpretations.
> — C.S. Lewis[36]

There is a sense in which no two people share identical religious beliefs. It is the sense of individuality, in which everyone sees the world from a different viewpoint than their neighbor. Although many groups hold to a common set of values and doctrines, the "flavor" of understanding them varies with each individual. Moreover, differences within a group often prove to be more than variations of "flavor" or "seasoning": some of them are outright disagreements. It is during quarrels over these disagreements that people of otherwise likemindedness occasionally part ways. Down through the ages, corporately and individually, schisms have come over differences of interpretation over the practice of "life's rules."

Knowing mankind's vast intellectual capacities and disputational temperament, I am not puzzled by schisms in religion, but I am sometimes baffled by the issues that cause them. The issue of cultural relevancy and its relation to absolute truth (e.g., "it's unlawful to drive on the left side of the highway *in the United States*" (*cultural* law) versus "it is wrong for *anyone* anywhere to stab a baby to death in its sleep" (*moral* law)) is one of the toughest issues to ponder, and not infrequently lies at the roots of a schism. Yet the relationship of culture to truth must be discussed when considering the legions of Jews and Christians throughout history who have ordered their lives according to their interpretation of a multi-authored, culturally flavored book that purports to teach absolute truth. (Culture vs. law has wide variations of interpretation in Islam, too. An Islamic female in Canada, for example, is apt to differ in interpretations of 'modesty' and 'submission' from a woman in Saudi Arabia.) It is here that Lewis's statement about sacred texts comes to mind. ("The more sacred a text is, the more subject it is to glosses and strained interpretations.") Lewis also said something else that bears repeating when considering the issue of truth: "In every age nearly every conceivable opinion is held by somebody."[37] Conversely, one might also say that in every age, no conceivable opinion is held by everybody. In his writings, Lewis addressed this by concentrating on those beliefs that constitute "mere Christianity," beliefs supposedly common to all Christians. He purposely avoided delving into specific ecclesiastical difficulties. This continues to make his writings popular among many diverse branches of Christianity, because he avoided taking sides on the very doctrinal differences that divide. Yet these doctrinal differences are often the very things that bring up the issues about truth: What is absolute and permanent, and what is relative, temporal, and culturally conditioned? How does one go about deciding these things? A look at some specifics reveals some of the difficulties.

Homosexuality has been present throughout history. Its existence is not a secret, though its presence is often not openly discussed. The "coming out" of homosexuals merely reflects that people now discuss this more openly, not that the numbers of homosexuals are increasing. Because of this openness—and the AIDS epidemic—Christians have had to again encounter this issue. The fact that many homosexuals are also practicing Christians has led to disagreements over the authority and interpretation of scriptural statements about the morality of homosexuality (typically having one side say that biblical statements condemning this are culturally limited, while the other side says that homosexuals are blatantly disobeying the permanent truths of scriptures).

The nature of women's participation in church politics and practices has undergone more change and been discussed even more frequently than homosexuality. Women's liberation in the working and sporting worlds has been followed by increasing participation in the church's "hierarchy" and a questioning of the submissive roles that women have played in marriage and worship. If a woman can capably carry on as a senator or parliamentary member in government, then why not as an elder or priest in the church? If she can teach a college course in biology to young men, why should she not preach a homily in worship? The bulk of church policy has been dictated over the years by interpretation of one portion of the Bible—the Pauline epistles. "A woman should learn in quietness and full submission."[38] "I do not permit a woman to teach or to have authority over a man; she must be silent."[39] "Wives, submit to your husbands as to the Lord."[40] "Women should remain silent in the churches. They are not allowed to speak, but must be in submission, as the Law says. If they want to inquire about something, they should ask their own husbands at home; for it is disgraceful for a woman to speak in the church."[41] Taken out of their cultural context, such statements seem biased and chauvinistic. Is this the opinion of Paul—a man simply reflecting the patriarchal culture he inhabited—or is this really the law of God, permanent and binding for all time? (If this is God's law, is it then disgraceful for women to pray aloud, recite the Apostle's Creed, the Lord's Prayer, or participate in responsive reading?? Were women created for the purpose of being subdued??)

Whether people refer to Saturday or Sunday as "Sabbath," most people still maintain a careless attitude toward a holy day. Sabbath, as observed through the years by the Jews (and more recently by Seventh-Day Adventists and the Worldwide Church of God) has been kept from sundown Friday night to sundown Saturday. The importance of a holy day is demonstrated in the Pentateuch, where the Sabbath is not infrequently discussed. "Remember the Sabbath day by keeping it holy,"[42] God told Moses. Once again, though, Paul seems to confuse the issue. Though a Sabbath keeper himself, he argues forcefully against its observance being necessary to the Christian faith. "Who are you to judge someone else's servant? To his own master he stands or falls. And he will stand, for the Lord is able to make him stand. One man considers one day more sacred than another; another man considers every day alike. Each one should be fully convinced in his own mind. He who regards one day as special, does so to the Lord. He who eats meat, eats to the Lord, for he gives thanks to God. For none of us lives to himself alone and none of us dies to himself alone. If we live, we live to the Lord; and if we die, we die to the Lord. So, whether we live or die, we belong to the Lord."[43] Which leaves one asking yet again, what is true—permanently true—and what is temporary requirement? Which rules in the Bible are still binding and which ones are not? What freedoms can a Christian now take? What can a woman be allowed to do in worship and in marriage? Can a Christian practice homosexuality without offending God? Is the Sabbath really necessary to keep? Was Paul giving personal (and therefore nonbinding) opinions or passing on God's word? ("I have no command from the Lord, but I give a judgment as one who by the Lord's mercy is trustworthy," he writes to the Corinthians.[44] "When you received the word of God, which you heard from us, you accepted it not as the word of men, but as it actually is, the word of God," he wrote to the Thessalonians.)[45]

These issues crop up again and again because they won't go away. Each generation grapples with them anew and the answers often change. Slavery, for example, was something Paul was knowledgeable about, but he never wrote about ending the practice or commanding masters to free their slaves. He simply told slaves to obey and masters to be fair. Abolitionists in the eighteenth and nineteenth centuries were the ones who 'went for the jugular' and aimed to eliminate slavery. They felt that the Bible supported their cause. Likewise, many a feminist, homosexual, heterosexual, abortionist, ecologist, or pastor has used the Bible to support or justify a particular cause or program. Each has sought to rid society of an evil or to right a wrong. For the abolitionist, it was to rid the world (or at least their country) of slavery. For the feminist, to combat prejudice and establish sexual justice. For the homosexual, to align human sexuality with religious beliefs. For the abortionist, the combat poverty, broken lives, overpopulation, etc. For the ecologist, to prevent and correct abuse of material resources. For the reformer, to combat racism and prejudical treatment. Each of these goals are worthy (even if the means of achieving them sometimes are not). But the dangers of such practices can be subtle. Perhaps chief among them is the tendency to turn Christianity from a religion of revelation into a religion of common sense. C.S. Lewis alone, of all the writers I have read, seems to have understood this. In his essay "Priestesses in the Church?" from *God in the Dock*, he writes, "This is what common sense will call 'mystical.' Exactly. The Church claims to be the bearer of a revelation.... We should expect to find in the Church an element which unbelievers will call irrational and which believers will call supra-rational. There ought to be something in it opaque to our reason though not contrary to it—as the facts of sex and sense on the natural level are opaque. And that is the real issue. The church...can remain a church only if she retains this opaque element. If we abandon that, if we retain only what can be justified by standards of prudence and convenience at the bar of enlightened common sense, then we exchange revelation for that old wraith Natural Religion."[46]

I once took a college course entitled "New Testament Criticism," which, among other things, looked at how various people view the scriptures. Some see the scriptures as human creations, while others, we learned, see the scriptures as a mixture of divine revelation and human ideas (with no satisfactory formulas for determining which parts are "divine" and which parts are "mortal"). Protestants see their canonical scriptures as 'divinely' inspired but the apocryphal scriptures as 'humanly' inspired—a views Catholics do not accept. The class made it clear that one's views about anything—tithing, fornication, circumcision, lying, life after death, or whatever else—were dependent on one's beliefs about scriptural composition (man-made vs. God (through man)—made or 'fiction' vs. 'non-fiction') and the personal interpretation of the passages in question (permanent truths vs. cultural requirement, binding vs. nonbinding). These two things (scriptural composition and interpretation) determine how one thinks about Paul's remarks regarding slavery, marriage, or women's submissiveness; Amos's remarks about injustice (since they were only addressed to *one* nation, at a *particular* time, rather than being general pronouncements to the world at large); psalmists' expression of pride in Israel (is it okay for us to "crow" about how great our own country is? Are we considered righteous when we do so? Or are we only supposed to sing the praises of ancient Israel?); or John's writing to Gaius, discussing the problem of a man called Diotrephes (is III John merely of historical interest or is it a pamphlet to be used for church discipline today?). These sorts of questions begin in Genesis and continue through Revelation. Some of the answers are readily apparent (or at least we think they are), while others remain elusive. These difficulties and confusions should make everyone humble, prayerful, and considerate of others whose theological beliefs do not match their own. After all, it seems doubtful that anyone even practices ALL of the things they DO believe.

Mark 9 quotes the father of a demon-possessed boy as saying, "I do believe; help my unbelief."[47] To this plea, we should add our own, "I do believe; help my perplexity."

Motivation

Many an accusation has been leveled against a hated tyrant, but sometimes a passing commentary can be more devastating. The Israeli king Jehoram died in 841 B.C., and when he did, his subjects shed no tears for him. The author of I Chronicles candidly recorded the feelings of those whose lives the king had touched by simply stating, "and he departed with no one's regret."[48] He was unanimously hated. A more condemning epitaph could not be made: "He died to no one's regret."

Most people live their lives between the extremes of universal love and universal hatred. They have neither the notoriety of an exhaustingly evil life nor the fame of a beloved benevolent one. They live somewhere in the "middle ground." The apocryphal book of Ecclesiasticus has a passage that describes the fate of most people's influence after they die. "All these were honored in their generations, and were the glory of their times. There are some of them who have left a name, so that men declare their praise. And there are some who have no memorial, who have perished as though they had not lived; they have become as though they had not been born, and so have their children after them."[49] And so it is. Given the fact that the "out of sight, out of mind" rule eventually applies to nearly all people, what then gives us the motivation to act in any particular fashion? If no one misses us or thinks about us 500 or 5,000 years after we die, what governs us to make choices about anything we do? Why should a surgeon-in-training, for example, bother to record his musings about the world, type them on paper, and send them out to his friends and family? In 100 years, all of the recipients will be dead, the essays will probably be destroyed (or the paper recycled), and the author long forgotten. Alternatively, even should we live a life where we "die to no one's regret," how could this deter our cruelty if, in five millennia, no one knows about it? If, in five millennia it will be as though we had not been born? For good or for ill, what motivates us?

Motivational questions are commonly discussed in the fields of psychology, sociology, and anthropology, but ultimately all of these questions turn to the metaphysical, religious nature of existence; and each religion seeks to answer those questions. Some of those answers ring truer than others. Those promoting goodness and civic duty for their own sake (such as Confucianism or Roman Stoicism) seem stupid (since they fail to provide motivational reasons for behavior. "Why act good?" we ask. "Just because," they answer.). Those promoting goodness for fiction's sake (Hinduism, New Age, Theosophy—all obviously human creations/fictions) seem futile. The religions rooted in history that purport to give divine reasons for human motivation seem to merit the most consideration. Islam, Christianity, Judaism and atheism fall into this category (atheism because it says there is no divine, thus giving a "divine reason" for human behavior.)

Rather than launching into a full-scale (and undoubtedly inept) discussion of the world's major religions, I would rather turn autobiographical for a moment and end by saying what provides motivation for me and for my writing. As a Christian, any aspiration for good or lawful actions is based on the belief in a divine being who rewards good and evil appropriately (in this life and in the life after death.) If then in some measure, great or small, I can live a godly life and affect those whose lives I touch, it will not matter when I become part of those "who have no memorial, who have perished as though they had not lived." I live and act for something other than myself—for God, who will one day judge all of us, for humans who may benefit from my actions in this life, and for humans who may benefit in the life to come because of how I affect them in this one. So I write and live my life in certain ways because it matters—at least to God, if not to others in the generations to come. Whether it be writing essays or working to feed the hungry, clothe the cold, befriend the stranger, encourage the downtrodden, rear the child, teach the ignorant, school the young, or bring joy to others through entertainment, our actions matter—even if we can't see that they do.

The Printed Word

Samuel Johnson

It is more from carelessness about truth than from intentional lying, that there is so much falsehood in the world.
— Samuel Johnson[1]

James Boswell's *Life of Johnson*, written in the late eighteenth century, is still considered by most literary critics I know to be the greatest biography ever penned. Its readable style, extensive research, insight, and subject matter made it a superb work. It was the rage among London's readers when first published and is still in print over 200 years later. Why is it, then, that its readers today are almost exclusively those in the academic world, professors and their students who are required to read selections from it for their obligatory literature classes?

There are probably several reasons for the unpopularity of Boswell's *Life*. Its length is somewhat formidable. The standard edition is six volumes long and the one-volume paperback work is 1,400 pages in length. This is about twice the length of a long Tom Clancy or James Michener novel. It is not given much marketing publicity, either. *If* you can find a copy of this book in a bookstore, it is located way back in the "Classics" section, not up front among surrounding advertisements. Another detractory factor is the antiquity of its subject and gossipy reporting. Two hundred years ago, this was fresh stuff. Today, it is old hat. No longer 'contemporary *biography*,' it almost seems more appropriate now to label it 'literary *history*.' Readers gravitate toward current literature, and a 200-year-old lengthy biography cannot compete with a fresh-off-the-press-sordid-details-and-all story of a modern public figure's life.

Richard Armour dedicates his wonderfully humorous book *The Classics Reclassified* "to that amazing device, the Required Reading List, better even than artificial respiration for keeping dead authors alive."[2] My hope is that the "RRL" would not be the only thing that could motivate you to read some older literature, "classics" such as

David Graham

Tolstoy's *Anna Karenina*, Dostoyevsky's *Crime and Punishment*, or Boswell's *Life of Johnson*. Perhaps a few more quotes will entice you to give Boswell's biography a try. In this book you will find plenty of: Wit (Johnson single-handedly compiled the first comprehensive English dictionary):

> Dr. Adams found him one day busy at his *Dictionary*, when the following dialogue ensued. "ADAMS. This is a great work, Sir... But, Sir, how can you do this in three years? JOHNSON. Sir, I have no doubt that I can do it in three years. ADAMS. But the French Academy, which consists of forty members, took forty years to compile their Dictionary. JOHNSON. Sir, thus it is. This is the proportion. Let me see; forty times forty is sixteen hundred. As three to sixteen hundred, so is the proportion of an Englishman to a Frenchman."[3]

Humor (Johnson actually took seven years to complete this work):

> Mr. Andrew Millar, bookseller in the Strand, took the principal charge of conducting the publication of Johnson's *Dictionary*; and as the patience of the proprietors was repeatedly tried and almost exhausted, by their expecting that the work would be completed within the time which Johnson had sanguinely supposed, the learned author was often goaded to dispatch...When the messenger who carried the last sheet to Millar returned, Johnson asked him, "Well, what did he say?"—"Sir" (answered the messenger) "he said, 'thank God I have done with him.'" "I am glad" (replied Johnson, with a smile) "that he thanks God for any thing."[4]

Honesty: Pity is not natural to man. Children are always cruel. Savages are always cruel. Pity is acquired and improved by the cultivation of reason.[5]

Wisdom:

> Every man is to take existence on the terms on which it is given to him.[6]

Even without artificial respiration, I think you'll enjoy this book.

A Book Sampler

I can't recall the year in which our exchange occurred, but I do remember the essential bits of discussion my older sister and I had one day when I was in high school. We were debating the merits of athletics versus books: I who had grown up playing sports, defending the former, while she, the avid reader, advocated the latter. She said that if I ever wanted to amount to anything, I was going to have to learn to read other things besides what I was merely assigned in school. She said I needed to establish good reading habits. It wasn't enough just to read what I *had* to read. I needed more. I countered by telling her that she needed more exercise. "All you ever do is go sit in a corner and read all day. You need to get outside. You're as pale as a ghost." From this exchange, the seeds of my reading habits were planted, and before too long, my sister was going outside to run every day. Of the two of us, I consider myself to have gotten the better advice, and have always been glad that she pushed me into becoming an avid reader.

Without pretending to place any order on my selections, I present here some of my favorite and least favorite selections from my readings. It is a list that will continue to change as long as my mind and eyesight and access to books will last.

The Bible is required reading, but I recommend the help of several good commentaries.
Funniest Novel—*Don Quixote* by Cervantes. Even though I can't read the Spanish original text (and thus enjoy his puns), I still think this the funniest novel I've ever read. It made me guffaw numerous times.
Funniest Children's Books—*Green Eggs and Ham* by Dr. Seuss, *Where the Sidewalk Ends* by Shel Silverstein, and *Alexander and the Terrible, Horrible, No Good, Very Bad Day* By Judith Viorst.
Funniest Cartoon Books—*Calvin & Hobbes* by Bill Watterson. I find these even funnier than Gary Larson's *The Far Side*. I would hate to be a real-life parent of Calvin's, but as a cartoon character, he's hysterically funny.
Best Adventure Novel—*Kidnapped* by Robert Louis Stevenson. I couldn't put it down. I thought it a gripping yarn.
Most Boring Novel—*Phantastes* by George McDonald. I only finished

this book by sheer determination, and when I did, I said "Never again"; ironically, I picked this phrase up from C.S. Lewis, one of the book's greatest admirers. It pronounces a moratorium on ever returning to a book.

Best Novel Series—*The Chronicles of Narnia* by C.S. Lewis, hands down. They were even a greater pleasure to read as an adult, though I liked them as a kid. Lewis's fine sense of humor and fertile imagination make these good reading at any age (though you may be interested to know that J.R.R. Tolkien despised them).

Best Novel—*War and Peace* by Leo Tolstoy. It's the type of book that ought to be re-read every 10 years or so. When I finished it this last time, I shook my head in admiration and said, "Wow."

Honorable Mention—*Anna Karenina* by Leo Tolstoy, *Crime and Punishment* by Fyodor Dostoyevsky, *Till We Have Faces* by C.S. Lewis, and *Huckleberry Finn* by Mark Twain.

Best Trilogy (fiction)—A tie between *The Deptford Trilogy* by Robertson Davies and *The Lord of the Rings* by J.R.R. Tolkien (well, okay, it's actually four books if you count *The Hobbit*). The first is infused with Davies' keen sense of humor, talent for storytelling, fascinating characters, and love of a good mystery. The second reveals Tolkien's awe-inspiring prodigality of invention in creating the middle earth and populating it with creatures, language and geographical landmarks, while his able storytelling capabilities imbue it with history.

Best Trilogy (Nonfiction)—*The Civil War: A Narrative* by Shelby Foote. A novelist by trade, his style of writing greatly enhances the narration of America's most divisive war, without compromising historical accuracy. You don't get the feeling of reading a secondhand account of the war so much as actually sharing in the experience.

Best Biography—*Life of Johnson* by James Boswell. As I've said before, it's in a class by itself.

Most Overrated Novelist—Ernest Hemingway. Kurt Vonnegut said it best, "I am struck, though, by how little Hemingway's work resembles Twain's. He has no ear for dialects, he severely limits his vocabulary, he is enchanted by violence, he can't tell jokes."

Most Overrated Novel—*This Present Darkness* by Frank Peretti. Sure, it was a racy story, but the language was insufferable (too many people speaking in clichés and glib phrases) and the characters too flat and predictable.

Best Diary—*Brothers and Friends*, by Warren Hamilton Lewis. Here was an observant man with a high capacity for extracting enjoyment out of even the common things in life. After reading this, I

Thoughts Along the Way

had a heightened sense of perception whenever I stepped outside.

Best Mysteries—The Sherlock Holmes stories written by Arthur Conan Doyle. This is still great stuff even a hundred years later.

Most Boring Book—*Knowing God* by J.I. Packer. Many people have enjoyed reading this. While I hope they found it helpful (and that many others will in the future, too), if I want to know more about God, the Bible is not only a *primary* source, it's also better reading.

Best Nonbiblical Books on Pain—a) *Pain: The Gift Nobody Wants* by Dr. Paul Brand and Philip Yancey. I highly recommend this. It won't answer all of the questions about pain (no book can), but it will enrich your understanding of its crucial role in our lives.
b) *Where is God When it Hurts?* by Philip Yancey. Philip Yancey takes a different approach in this book by examining pain more from a theological and personal angle: Why do we suffer? Honest, compassionate and hopeful, without being dogmatic, this book deserves its high reputation.

Best Playwright—William Shakespeare. (I know, I know, everyone already knew that. But do try to see some of the movies that have come out such as *Hamlet, Henry V, Othello,* or *Much Ado About Nothing*. Like the stage productions, they really bring his works to life.)

Best Love Story—*A Severe Mercy* by Sheldon Vanauken. A spiritual pilgrimage combined with a story of love and grief that brought tears to my eyes when I first read it.

Best Books on Reading—*An Experiment in Criticism* by C.S. Lewis and *Literature Through the Eyes of Faith* by Susan Gallagher and Roger Lundin are books that examine the things we read and how reading affects us. The latter book was so good that I almost felt like highlighting and underlining everything.

Most Enjoyable Essayists—C.S. Lewis and Philip Yancey are my two favorite writers, and each has written several books of essays that can be read with pleasure. One of the reasons that essays are appealing is that they can be taken in 'bite size morsels' and lend themselves to reading aloud to a group as well as perusal when time is limited (such as lunch breaks or prior to bedtime.) Two such books of Lewis's I have enjoyed are *God in the Dock* and *The World's Last Night And Other Essays* while Philip Yancey's *I was Just Wondering* and *Finding God in Unexpected Places* were both stimulating and enlightening.

Happy trails. . .

A Heroic Bard

Poets are unlikely heroes. Although admired for their language skill and communicative powers, is there anyone who, in the late twentieth-century, considers someone their *hero* because of the poetry she/he writes? If there is, they are unusual. Poets may be loved and their poetry admired, but they aren't mentioned if the subject of heroes is broached.

My poetic tastes are simple. I eschew the chaotic free verse of many twentieth-century writers, admire the technical difficulty of the sonneteers and englyn experts, laugh and smile at "children's poetry" (especially that of Dr. Seuss and Shel Silverstein), and meditate on the likes of Emily Dickinson or Robert Frost. Each kind of poetry manifests a different aspect of human creativity, making it unfair and foolish, for example, to compare the merits of "Green Eggs and Ham" with "Stopping by Woods on A Snowy Evening." Each has something different to offer. While I enjoyed their work, I never considered any of these people to be heroes or heroines until I looked up the definition in the dictionary. The first definition, "a mythological or legendary figure endowed with great strength, courage, or ability, favored by the gods, and often believed to be of divine or partly divine descent,"[7] certainly excluded poets from this category. But the second invited their admission. A hero(ine) was defined as someone of "distinguished valor or performance, admired for his/her noble qualities."[8] If these are the criteria for judgment, then the first poet to come to my mind for distinguished performance and qualities I admire would be Henry Wadsworth Longfellow.

Longfellow was born in Portland, Maine, in 1807, and when he died 75 years later in 1882, he left a legacy of being the most popular poet in America, a fame that no other poet ever surpassed and probably none—except perhaps Robert Frost—has ever equaled in their lifetime. His fame was not cheap, for he worked hard at his craft. To his gift for writing, he added his talents as a linguist, serving 25 years as professor of modern languages at Bowdin and Harvard colleges, publishing several textbooks along the way. His poetry was also enriched by his travels, including two trips to Europe while undertaking his language study. His two marriages gave him insight not only into the fairer sex and domestic life, but also into the grieving human heart and the tragedy of life, for both of his wives preceded him in death—the first following a miscarriage and the second in a fire. His work was often a reflection of his Christian beliefs—a fact that made his poetry the subject of much abuse long after his death.

Without realizing it, I first became familiar with Longfellow's work as a child when my mother recited portions of "The Landlord's Tale" from *Tales of A Wayside Inn*: "Listen my children and you shall hear/Of the midnight ride of Paul Revere,/On the eighteenth of April, in Seventy-five;/Hardly a man is now alive/Who remembers that famous day and year."[9] It was also during my grade school years that I first heard Longfellow's "Christmas Bells" sung by Johnny Cash. "I heard the bells on Christmas Day/Their old, familiar carols play,/And wild and sweet/The words repeat/ Of peace on earth, good-will to men!"[10] Over the years I encountered Longfellow's work from time to time, usually in the schoolroom through such works as "The Courtship of Miles Standish"[11] (a tale with a great twist) and "Evangeline."[12] It was during my third year of medical school that I expanded my contact with the poet by purchasing the Cambridge edition of the poetical works of Longfellow. When I began to slowly wade into the book, I found repeated satisfaction with each reading. His varied rhyme schemes, the numerous subjects covered, the changing moods, his lucidity, and his strong sense of right and wrong all combined to stir me deeply. Whether in mirth or sadness or admiration, I found a man who spoke to the inner recesses of my spirit. If greatness is measured in the ability of someone to change how we view the world, then Longfellow was a great man. His work has stamped itself indelibly on some of my deepest emotions. In this, I am not alone. His poetry moved many, whether read privately or in large audiences. (It was not unusual for crowds of several hundred or even a few thousand to gather together for a "reading" of poetry in nineteenth-century New England). Of his poem about The Union, "The Building of the Ship," a man named Noah Brooks related that he found President Abraham Lincoln one day attracted by some stanzas from this poem that were quoted in a political speech. "Knowing the whole poem as one of my early exercises in recitation, I began, at his request, with the description of the launch of the ship, and repeated it to the end. As he listened to the last lines, his eyes filled with tears, and his cheeks were wet. He did not speak for some minutes, but finally said, with simplicity: 'It is a wonderful gift to be able to stir men like that.'"[13]

Lest I leave the impression that Longfellow only wrote solemn stuff, I recall one of my many joyous celebrations of life in connection with him. During my internship on one of my rare days off, I walked to a nearby field in the middle of the woods. It was one of those sunny, cloudless days where a mild breeze blows through from time to time to cool things off and keep the temperature in a very comfortable zone. With no physician's beeper on my belt, no responsibilities on my shoulders, and a feeling of perfect healthiness, I sat down in this field, away from all traffic, people, and interruptions, and read "A Day of Sunshine." It gave me the unusual experience of having a book describe exactly the kind of day and weather I myself was experiencing during my reading.

> O gift of God! O perfect day:
> Whereon shall no man work, but play;
> Whereon it is enough for me,
> Not to be doing, but to be!
>
> Through every fibre of my brain,
> Through every nerve, through every vein,
> I feel the electric thrill, the touch
> O life, that seems almost too much.
>
> I hear the wind among the trees
> Playing celestial symphonies;
> I see the branches downward bent,
> Like keys of some great instrument.
>
> And over me unrolls on high
> The splendid scenery of the sky,
> Where through a sapphire sea the sun
> Sails like a golden galleon,
>
> Towards yonder cloud-land in the West,
> Towards yonder Islands of the Blest,
> Whose steep sierra far uplifts
> Its craggy summits white with drifts.[14]

Thoughts Along the Way

Like music, poetry is much better experienced than described. By this I mean that attending a concert or listening to a stereo recording will teach far more about Mozart or Michael Jackson's music than reading a book about it will. Likewise, I can only convey my enthusiasm for Longfellow, not his substance. To get that, you will have to read him yourself. If you do, you may find yourself admiring an unlikely hero.

The Re-reading of Books

While growing up, it was not my practice to read something more than once (unless it was a text from school that required studying). I did not understand why someone would voluntarily subject themselves to reading something they had already finished. There was no appeal to that practice. It was a waste of time (or so I thought). Yet times and opinions change, and over the years I have come to realize that there is much pleasure and profit that comes from re-reading books. To say, "Oh, I've already read that" is akin to saying things like, "I've already seen a sunset" or "I've already told my wife that I loved her. I told her that when we married." Furthermore, "I've said a prayer before." "I know what blueberry pie tastes like. I've already had it." "Sure, but I've seen an ocean already." "Yes, I've already read the Bible. Why read it again?" "Okay, so now I've exercised. Why do it again?" "I read that chapter from my medical text. So what?" The fact is that a book's qualities cannot be exhausted with a single reading. So I have come full circle and now consider it profitable to re-read books. I also enjoy "comparing notes" on books with others and have decided to offer a few more of my favorite and not-so-favorite selections to sample.

Great Fairy Tale—*The Silver Trumpet* by Owen Barfield (especially the edition illustrated by Josephine Spence). Barfield's friend, C.S. Lewis, lent the book to J.R.R. Tolkien (author of the all-time best-selling fairy tale, *The Lord of the Rings*), after which he reported back to Barfield with the following results. "I lent *The Silver Trumpet* to Tolkien and hear that it is the greatest success among his children that they have ever known. His own fairy-tales, which are excellent, have now no market: and its first reading—children are so practical!—led to a universal wail 'You're *not* going to give it back to Mr. Lewis, are you?' All the things which the wiseacres on child psychology in our circle said when you wrote it turn out to be non-sense. 'They liked the sad parts,' said Tolkien, 'because they were sad and the puzzling parts because they were puzzling, as children always do.' The youngest boy liked Gamboy because 'she was clever and the bad people in books usually aren't.' The tags of the Podger have become so popular as to be almost a nuisance in the house. In fine, you have scored a direct hit."[15]

Thoughts Along the Way

Delightful Tale—*The Wind in the Willows* by Kenneth Grahame. This is an adventure along an English riverbank involving, Rat, Mole, Badger, and Toad. Each has memorable personalities—Mole, the domestic cleaner; Water Rat, the unlikely sailor; Toad, the careless adventurer whose exploits with gypsy caravans and fast motor cars get himself and his friends in trouble; and Badger, of whom Lewis once wrote: "Consider Mr. Badger...—that extraordinary amalgam of high rank, coarse manners, gruffness, shyness, and goodness. The child who has once met Mr. Badger has ever afterwards, in its bones, a knowledge of humanity and of English social history which it could not get in any other way."[16] (A fine sequel to this story (by William Horwood) came out 85 years later, entitled *The Willows in Winter*.)

Books that Exceeded my Expectations—a) *The Education of Little Tree* by Forrest Carter. This is an excellent example of why a book should not be judged by its cover. I had seen this work in book stores but had never considered buying it since it appeared to have a simplistic, "juvenile" cover masking its contents. But a friend gave the book to me as a birthday present and I began to read it. . . and was soon caught up in a story of growing up that was unlike any I had ever encountered. Little Tree is the Indian name of the narrator (Forrest Carter), who shares his autobiographical memories of life with his Eastern Cherokee Hill country grandparents in the 1930s. The reader is treated to an alternative way of viewing the world, of seeing things from one native American's perspective, at once similar yet foreign to the 20th century western-world way that most caucasions view life. There is both naivety and wisdom to share, as well as a love for—and communion with—nature, that is appealing and enviable. The incidents are often comical, and humor is richly suffused throughout the book. Rennard Strickland, who wrote the introduction to the 1985 paperback edition, was right: "After reading *Little Tree*, one never again sees the world in quite the same way."[17] b) *The Search for God at Harvard* by Ari L. Goldman. In 1985, Ari Goldman took a year's sabbatical from his job as a religion reporter for *The New York Times* and enrolled in the Harvard Divinity School. What began as a project to deepen his knowledge of world religion turned out to be an extraordinary odyssey of spiritual illumination. This is one of the few books that truly IS hard to put down. It is well-written, lucid, searching, instructive (especially of

Goldman's Jewish faith), and (perhaps best of all) quite personal. I give this book my "Highly Recommended" stamp of approval.

c) *Seeing Voices: A Journey into the World of the Deaf* by Oliver Sacks. If I could only recommend one book about the phenomenon of language and its influence on epistemolgy (the study of the nature of knowledge) it would be *Seeing Voices*. I have been thinking about the relationship of language to thought (and the bearing that language has on our very humanity) ever since I returned from my trip to Africa during medical school. Reading this book shook my preconceptions about the deaf and opened my eyes to seeing some of the fascinating relationships between two things we all take for granted—language and thought. I enthusiastically endorse this book, but with the caveat that it should be read with a pen or pencil in hand to highlight it and make notes in the margins, lest the numerous footnotes and asides prove too distracting or muddling.

Best Second-Chance Book—*The Reivers* by William Faulkner. The first time I tried to read this book, I made it as far as the end of the first chapter before closing the book, never intending to open it again. Faulkner's style, especially his wordy, run-on sentences, was distasteful for me. For some reason, I gave it another try later that year and wound up somewhat intrigued by the style and wholly interested in the story. It is an amusing misadventure involving three unusual thieves, or reivers: 11-year-old Lucius Priest and two of his Mississippi family retainers, Boon Hogganbeck and Ned the coachman. In 1905, they steal the family car and drive from their home in Mississippi to Memphis, Tennessee. The book is a reminiscence of this episode and the events that followed.

No Chance Book—Unlike *The Reivers*, I could never catch the cadence of Walker Percy's *The Message in the Bottle*. I struggled manfully through the first nine chapters before 'going under for the last time.' Percy has some valid points to make, and the first chapter wasn't bad, but things degenerated after that. The writing is esoteric and needlessly obscure. "What is he saying?" I kept asking myself.

Long Overdue—*To Kill a Mockingbird* by Harper Lee. After many years of negligence, I finally opened the book (thanks to a birthday present from my older sister). Inside, I found a marvelously crafted story of growing up in twentieth-century southern America. The characters, from Jean Louise (Scout) Finch, the narrator, to Boo

Radley, the mysterious tenant down the street, are appealingly vivid and odd. The story is superb because Harper Lee is that rare novelist who succeeds in *showing* a story rather than *talking* about it. Like my sister, I now consider this one of my favorite American novels.

Angriest Reaction—*Let Justice Roll Down* by John Perkins. I was seething while reading this. As Perkins told the story of his torture in the hands of white law-enforcement officers down in Mississippi, I became furious at the injustice being perpetrated. Perkins's response of forgiveness and magnanimity was more than brave and noble. It was ample testimony of an ability to forgive because of a life changed by God's love.

Below Expectations—a) *Peter Pan* by Sir James Barrie. The story itself isn't too bad, but Peter was a conceited, selfish brat, not a hero to be admired or envied. The Darling household was repulsive, especially Mr. Darling, who was such a hypocritical pansy. Selfishness or self-centeredness seemed to permeate most of the characters. By contrast, if you read tales like Tolkien's *Lord of the Rings* or Lewis's *Chronicles of Narnia*, you will find nobility, loyalty, courage, generosity, kindness, severity, sacrifice, justice, and mercy in many varied characters, vividly contrasted with real wickedness, folly, or evil demonstrated in others. The landscapes are robustly described and the whole quality of these works puts them on a different plane from *Peter Pan*. Despite its popularity and story appeal, I found Barrie's book a little lame.
b) *A History of the English Speaking Peoples* by Winston Churchill. Churchill was a superb writer and a fine speaker. His style is the best part of this four-volume work. Yet his chronicling is too narrow in scope. He focuses on military and political matters to the exclusion of nearly everything else. He mentions very little about disease, and when he does—as when briefly discussing the Black Plague—he doesn't linger long over it (even though disease and medicine have had as big an impact on history as war). Music, dress, art, and architecture are ominously absent from his work. Sport, too, is missing, and religion is mostly discussed within the political sphere. Science and invention are only mentioned if they contribute something to the art of war. He omits mention of many prominent writers and infrequently explores the links between national legends and historical events or places (such as

Canterbury and Chaucer's tales, Glastonbury and the Holy Grail, Winchester and the Round Table of Camelot, or Robin Hood and medieval England). J. Henri Fabre, the nineteenth-century French entomologist, was right on target when he said, "History pays but little attention to these details: it celebrates the battle-fields whereon we meet our death, it scorns to speak of the ploughed fields whereby we thrive; it knows the names of the Kings' bastards, it cannot tell us the origin of wheat. That is the way of human folly."[18] To sum, Churchill's style is excellent, but his work is myopic and therefore unsatisfactory.

Poor Biography—*C.S. Lewis: a Biography* by A.N. Wilson. Wilson's book is extensively researched, lucid, easy to read, and shows true insight in many places. But it is also misleading, error-prone, and unbalanced. He believes the truth of many Freudian psychological assumptions and too often uses subjective guesswork to reach conclusions, inaccurately assessing his subject with these methods. Wilson also struck me as someone who has difficulty recognizing holiness. *Jack: C.S. Lewis and his Times* by George Sayer is more accurate and free of the psychological rot, misinterpretation of motive, and twisting of facts that are Wilson's downfall.

Seminal Book—*Shantung Compound* by Langdon Gilkey. Gilkey's experiences as an American prisoner in China during World War II made quite an impression on me when I read his book during college. It was from him that I first learned the function of law. "Matthew Read and I used to talk by the hour about the strange relation of law to society which this whole problem highlighted. Somewhat to our surprise, we found we agreed that the law was made necessary because of self-interest, and that therefore its primary function was not, as I had always thought, that of stating what is abstractly just and right, but rather that of controlling self-interest, and molding it into socially creative rather than socially destructive patterns."[19]

Company Aytch

"A better book there never was."
Margaret Mitchell (author of *Gone with the Wind*), commenting on Sam Watkins *Co. Aytch*[20]

I am a creature who seeks comfort. I like to have a roof over my head when it rains, clothes that fit well on my body, a shelter to keep me warm in winter, a breeze or a fan to cool me in summer, clean water to drink, appetizing food to eat, a bed to rest on, a reasonable amount of sleep every night, protection from dangerous animals, freedom from war and crime, and health without sickness. Because I am also a creature who likes satisfaction, I appreciate having an enjoyable job, good books to read, and an appropriate amount of human contact. I have had such an abundance of these things in my life that it makes my vocational lack of one comfort—sleep—more tolerable. Conversely, during the times when I have had little to eat (such as my two-week trek in the Michigan wilderness when I was 18), I have never lacked sleep. When my home lost electricity (a modern luxury) and therefore heat during a snowstorm one March, I still had blankets and coats and walls to block the wind. Even in places like Haiti and Honduras and Benin, I always had clean water to drink and satisfying food to eat; and no one has ever pointed a gun at my head. What hardships I have endured have been mild.

Unlike myself, mankind has had a plethora of discomforts. Written accounts of these abound, and the one I have most enjoyed reading was written by a one-book author over 100 years ago. The book is entitled *Co. Aytch: A Side Show of the Big Show*. Sam Watkins was a private in the H ("aytch") Company of the First Tennessee Regiment in the Confederate Army from 1861 to 1865, and his memoirs, written 20 years after the start of the American Civil War, read like a fictional spy novel (such as a James Bond adventure), with the difference being that his account is true. He fought in all of his regiment's major battles from Shiloh to Nashville, was captured twice, shot in the hand, finger, thigh, heel, arm, through the hat, through his cartridge-box, and through his coat (eight times); survived a tornado, a cannonball that knocked his hat off (and killed the comrade next to him), hypothermia in a snowstorm, marches in freezing winters and fights in hot, parched summers, scant food rations, and the ravages of disease, which killed twice as many soldiers as battles did. When his unit finally surrendered on April 26, 1865, only 65 of the 3,200 men from the first Tennessee Regiment were still left to present arms, and Sam was one of only seven who were still living from the original 120 who had enlisted in the Maury Grays H Company in 1861. . . War is harsh.

Although his cause and his "country" were defeated, Sam was able to accept the outcome. Unlike many southerners, who carried their resentfulness with them when all else had been taken from them (and in turn passed down their hatred to succeeding generations), Sam was not bitter. His memoirs are infused with good will toward his fellow men and sprinkled with humor. Of his promotion to corporal, for example, he relates his conversation with a friend following this act. "Why, hello, corporal, where did you get those two yellow stripes from on your arm?" "Why, sir, I have been promoted for gallantry on the battlefield, by picking up an orphan flag, that had been run over by a thousand fellows, and when I picked it up I did so because I thought it was pretty, and I wanted to have me a shirt made out of it."[21] In stating his philosophy of fighting, he also offers a wag's view of his superiors: "I always shot at privates. It was they that did the shooting and killing, and if I could kill or wound a private, why, my chances were so much the better. I always looked upon officers as harmless personages."[22]

Sam's writing reflects a rare mixture of country shrewdness and formal academic learning. (He had attended Jackson College in his home town of Columbia, Tennessee before the war.) His style is learned but informal, with good insight into understanding the war. Although he occasionally errs in relating minor facts and in misspelling a few names (as well as indulging in humorous hyperbole) his skill as a historian and storyteller is superb, and he describes with clarity what it was really like to be a soldier. "A soldier's life is not a pleasant one. It is always, at best, one of privations and hardships. The emotions of patriotism and pleasure hardly counterbalance the toil and suffering that he has to undergo in order to enjoy his patriotism and pleasure. Dying on the field of battle and glory is about the easiest duty a soldier has to undergo."[23]

Thoughts Along the Way

As a soldier, of course, he saw as much horror as could be expected from war. One such instance demonstrates not only Sam's powers of empathy but also shares his response for why bad things happen to good people. His regiment had come to a place in Virginia called Hampshire Crossing and there, to their amazement and horror, had found a band of 11 soldiers who had frozen to death at their post of duty. "Two of them, a little in advance of the others, were standing with their guns in their frozen hands! The tale is told. Were they true men? Does He who noteth the sparrow's fall, and numbers the hairs of our heads, have any interest in one like ourselves? Yes, He doeth all things well. Not a sparrow falls to the ground without His consent."[24] Sam does not try to explain "why" these things happen—he can't. Instead, he places his trust in the One in charge of everything. As he wrote elsewhere, "The ball struck him on his knapsack, knocking him twenty feet, and breaking one or two ribs and dislocating his shoulder. He was one of God's noblemen, indeed—none braver, none more generous. God alone controls our destinies, and surely He who watched over us and took care of us in those dark and bloody days, will not forsake us now. God alone fits and prepares for us the things that are in store for us. There is none so wise as to foresee the future or foretell the end. God sometimes seems afar off, but He will never leave or forsake anyone who puts his trust in Him. The day will come when the good as well as evil will all meet on one broad platform, to be rewarded for the deeds done in the body, when time shall end, with the gates of eternity closed, and the key fastened to the girdle of God forever. Pardon me, reader, I have wandered. But when my mind reverts to those scenes and times, I seem to live in another age and time and I sometimes think that "after us comes the end of the universe." I am not trying to moralize, I am only trying to write a few scenes and incidents that came under the observation of a poor old Rebel webfoot private soldier in those stormy days and times."[25]

Sam Watkins' discomforts and adventures, his reflections and memories, made me realize again how horrid and how noble the human race an be; how terrible and even, yes, how wonderful war can be. As Jefferson Davis put it, "Revolutions develop the high qualities of the good and the great, but they cannot change the nature of the vicious and the selfish."[26] And finally, for we humans who seek comfort, who enjoy, as the prophet Amos phrased it, being "at ease in Zion,"[27] Sam Watkins' memoirs are also a reminder that being cozy is not the chief purpose of living.

Mystery

Crystallization

Once upon a time, one of my college chemistry professors told our class that he never ceased to be fascinated by the process of crystallization. Crystallization is a process used to separate impurities from an organic compound. When an impure organic compound is placed in a liquid solvent and heated to a high enough temperature, it dissolves. As the solution then cools, the organic compound will crystallize, while the impurity remains dissolved. The pure crystals may then be filtered from the solution. No matter how many times he had watched this process of crystallization, my professor was always intrigued by it. That moment when the crystals first began to form was amazing and delightful: an experience of wonder.

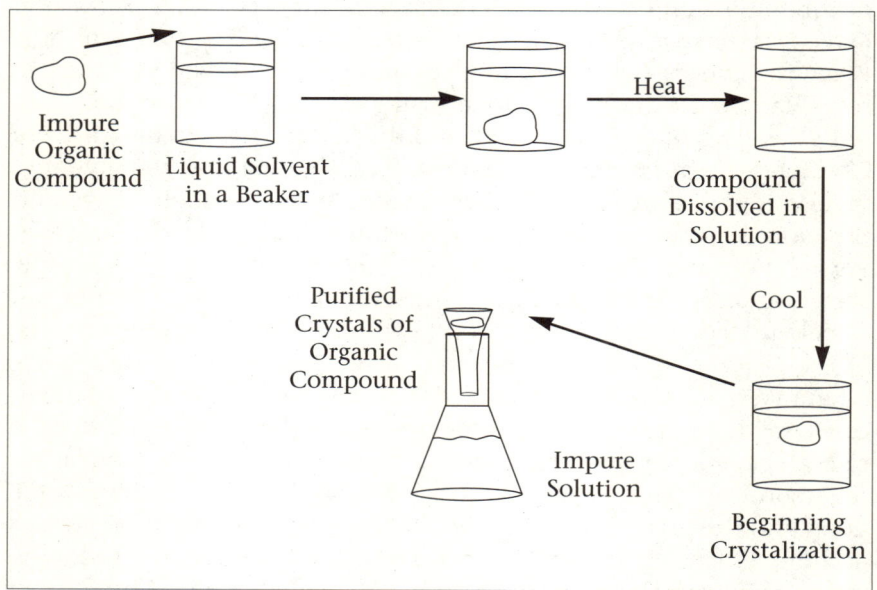

Moments of crystallization, of discovery, enlightenment, or the "Ah-ha!" experience—when the amorphous solidifies into a definite form—are indeed exciting, whether one is thinking about chemistry, religion, mathematics, family matters, cooking recipes, or a passage in a book. We don't know exactly how these moments of insight come about, but they quicken the soul's pulse. Many result in grand discoveries: Archimedes, the famous Greek mathematician, determining the proportion of silver and gold in a wreath by weighing it in water (later named the "Archimedes principle," after which legend reported him leaping from his bath, where he received his revelation, to run through the streets—still naked—and shout repeatedly "Heureka!" meaning "I have found it") or James Watson and Francis Crick suddenly enlightened with the ideas for formulating the molecular model of DNA as consisting of a double helix and thus revolutionizing the field of genetics. Some moments lead to new religious insight, such as Siddhartha Gautama's "enlightenment" (while sitting under a fig tree), which led to his becoming the Buddha ("the Enlightened One"). Other moments of crystallization result in decisions after much deliberation, as, for example, when pediatric surgeon C. Everett Koop finally settled on his firm stance against all abortions, a decision that was to surround him with controversy during his later tenure as America's Surgeon General. "It all crystallized for me one Saturday in 1976. My residents and I had spent the entire day operating on three newborn babies with defects that were incompatible with life, but were nevertheless amenable to surgical correction. Surgery on newborns is time-consuming, and although we started at 8:00 A.M., we did not have the third youngster safely in his incubator with his immediate future assured until early evening. As the three of us sat in the dimly lit corner of the cafeteria having a meal that had been held for us while it grew cold, I said to my two colleagues: 'You know, we have given over two hundred years of life to three individuals who together barely weighed ten pounds.'

"One of my residents answered, 'And while we were doing that, right next door in the university hospital they were cutting up perfectly formed babies of the same size just because their mothers didn't want them.' I knew then that as a surgeon of the newborn, I had to do something about the slaughter of the unborn."[1] Sometimes it may simply be "seeing" something for the first time when reading a familiar passage from a book such as the Bible; "I read the passion narratives in the Gospels all the way through. In Matthew 24-25 I noticed a pattern I had never before seen"[2]; "When I read straight through the Bible, I saw the life of Elijah in a very different light."[3] "I was familiar with James's stern admonitions, but I had not noticed his formula for obtaining holiness."[4]

David Graham

I had one of those experiences of crystallization while sitting in a church service one day. The New Testament lesson was one that I was quite familiar with, containing a verse I had memorized back in grade school, "The next day John saw Jesus coming to him and said, 'Behold, the Lamb of God, who takes away the sin of the world!'" (John 1:29) The phrase "Lamb of God" directed my thoughts to the Old Testament sacrificial system. Leviticus records how individuals were to bring their own lambs to be killed for fellowship offerings or sin offerings. In my case, "David's lamb" would be sacrificed to pay for my own sins. It could not pay for others. Jesus, however, was God's lamb or "Lamb of God." Jesus was God's offering. Unlike "David's lamb," though, the payment of God's lamb was permanent, an atonement that didn't need repeating. Also unlike David's lamb, God's lamb paid for everyone, not just a family or an individual. John stressed this point when he wrote, "He is the atoning sacrifice for our sins, and not only for ours but also for the sins of the whole world." (I John 2:2)

I used to associate the phrase "Lamb of God" with innocence or gentility, a title to reflect Jesus's sinlessness and love. This changed during the moment of "crystallization" when I quietly realized the true significance of this title. When I read this phrase now, I think not of gentility but of sacrifice; God's sacrifice: Jesus.

"And Isaac spoke to Abraham his father and said, 'My father!' And he said, 'Here I am, my son' And he said, 'Behold, the fire and the wood, but where is the lamb for the burnt offering?' And Abraham said, 'God will provide for Himself the lamb for the burnt offering, my son.' (Genesis 22:7-8)
"The next day he saw Jesus coming to him, and said, 'Behold, the Lamb of God who takes away the sin of the world!'" (John 1:29)

My chemistry professor was right. Crystallization is fascinating.

The Puzzle of Sex

Yet she became more and more promiscuous as she recalled the days of her youth, when she was a prostitute in Egypt. There she lusted after her lovers, whose genitals were like those of donkeys and whose emission was like that of horses. So you longed for the lewdness of your youth, when in Egypt your bosom was caressed and your young breasts fondled.[5]

This graphic quote did not come from *Playboy* magazine or a softcover novel from the "Romance" section of a bookstore. It comes from the Bible and is, in fact, a quote from God Himself, as recorded in the twenty-third chapter of Ezekiel. God is not embarrassed by masturbation or sexual intercourse. As creator of the animal kingdom in general, and humanity in particular, He established the sexual drive in our constitution. This side of humanity is rarely discussed in depth from the pulpit except to point out its woes when abused. On those occasions when the topic does come up, it is discussed in a rather coy fashion. That human sexuality is not readily canvassed can be ascertained by asking yourself how often you hear a body part like arm, leg, eye, ear, or hand, or a function like eating, sleeping, or seeing mentioned in a sermon. Then ask yourself when the last time was that you heard other God-created body parts like penis or vagina and God-created functions like orgasm or ejaculation mentioned in church. Rarely, if ever, right? Granted, these are not words that need to be used when discussing coveting, greed, lust, or even sex, but their lack of employment is reflective of the indirect, circumferential manner in which this aspect of humanity is approached by the church.

God does not inhibit His language when addressing human sexuality. Without even quoting from the Bible's most amorous book—The Song of Songs (Song of Soloman)—it is easily seen that God is not mortified by sensuality. He used plain, open language when addressing the Jews on sexual behavior. "You are a swift she-camel running here and there, a wild donkey accustomed to the desert, sniffing the wind in her craving—in her heat who can restrain her? Any males that pursue her need not tire themselves; at mating time they will find her." (Jeremiah 2:23-24) "In all your detestable practices and your prostitution you did not remember the days of your youth, when you were naked and bare, kicking about in your blood." (Ezekiel 16:22) "These are the regulations for a man with a discharge, for anyone made unclean by an emission of semen, for a woman in her monthly period, for a man or a woman with a discharge, and for a man who lives with a woman who is ceremonially unclean." (Leviticus 15:32-33) "If a man has sexual relations with an animal, he must be put to death, and you must kill the animal. If a woman approaches an animal to have sexual relations with it, kill both the woman and the animal." (Leviticus 20:15-16) This is not polite language, but this is often not a polite side of human behavior either. (The impolite word "fuck" is really an acronym: "For Unlawful Carnal Knowledge," a phrase used several centuries ago by the Puritans in labeling the offense of a person placed in the public stocks for fornication. Ironically, what was once a polite word for a heinous offense is now a scurrilous term for any coitus.)

There are few things in life as perplexing as human sexuality. It is such an emotionally and morally charged subject, and the lack of consensus about any one aspect of it—even among people of similar religious views—baffles me. As part of nature, it is seen throughout the animal kingdom; yet human sexuality, because of its occurrence in a reasoning, moralistic species, is treated differently in both scientific discussions and in informal table talk among friends. My confusion increases, as it does with other subjects, after spending time in a library or bookstore. A foray in the medical library at the hospital brought me into contact with some of the books on human sexuality, including Havelock Ellis's extensive works published early in this century and the Kinsey reports on human sexuality in the male and female (which involved interviewing over 20,000 test subjects). They examined such issues as religious background (Catholic, Protestant, Jewish, and Agnostic, as well as subcategories of orthodox, devout, active, or inactive), age, and educational background in relation to incidence and frequency of nocturnal emissions, masturbation, premarital petting to climax, postmarital petting to climax, premarital intercourse, extramarital intercourse, and homosexual outlet. Their findings include, for example, that "there is much more homosexual activity among males of lower educational levels than there is among males of the college level. Within any particular educational level the differences between religious groups are not so great." "The differences between religiously devout persons and religiously inactive persons of the same faith are much greater than the differences between two equally devout groups of different faiths. In regard to total sexual outlet the religiously inactive groups may have frequencies that are 25 to 75 percent higher than the frequencies of the religiously devout groups." [6]

In discussing premarital petting, comments about this practice are compared to other members of the animal kingdom. "Among most species of mammals there is, in actuality, a great deal of sex play which never leads to coitus. Most mammals, when sexually aroused, crowd together and nuzzle and explore with their noses, mouths, and feet over each other's bodies. They make lip-to-lip contacts and tongue-to-tongue contacts, and use their mouths to manipulate every part of the companion's body, including the genitalia. They may nip, bite, scratch, groom, pull at the fur of the other animal, pull out fur, urinate, and repeatedly mount without, however, making any serious attempt to effect a genital union. Such activity may continue for a matter of minutes, or hours, or even in some cases for days before there is any attempt at coitus. The student of mammalian mating behavior, interested in observing coitus in his animal stocks, sometimes may have to wait through hours and days of sex play before he has an opportunity to observe actual coitus, if, indeed, the animals do not finally separate without ever attempting a genital union. Extensive sex play has been observed in such widely diverse mammals as cattle, horses, hogs, sheep, cats, lions, dogs, raccoon, rats, mice, guinea pigs, chinchillas, hamsters, porcupines, rabbits, mink, sable, ferrets, skunks, otter, monkeys, chimpanzees, and still other species. A wide variety of petting techniques is employed by many of these. There are few situations or techniques in human petting behavior which are not widespread among the other mammals."[7]

In terms of the physical acts of sex, humans are not really different from the rest of the animal kingdom. The comments by the biblical authors acknowledge this. Where humans differ is in their moral perception of sexual acts. It is common to hear or read of people who "struggle" with their sexuality—I doubt there are many who have not at some point in their life. Yet this seems strange. If God created the sex drive in animals (including humans), then why are humans the only ones who struggle with it? A monkey will masturbate repeatedly because the act feels good. Many religious people practice this as well, and yet are left with feelings of guilt and shame afterward. Why should a monkey wear a smile while the human prays for forgiveness? If a bull elephant may chase, catch, and mount a virgin only half his size, then why do humans punish rapists and abhor their actions? If pigs can practice homosexuality so casually, why is this lifestyle so controversial among humans? Why are so many Jews, Christians, and Muslims against homosexuality? Why do so many permit it? If rabbits may breed freely and horses are actually encouraged to do so by professional breeders, why is extramarital sex considered wrong by so many from the religious fold? If a bull moose defeats his male rival, he wins the right to copulate with all of the females in his territory. Is there anything wrong, then, with a king or a rich businessman keeping a harem? If dogs freely engage in petting and stroking without ever obtaining a marriage license, is this practice morally acceptable among teenagers whose hormones are so "juiced up?" If many animals have multiple sexual partners, why does the book of Proverbs speak of drinking "water from your own cistern, running water from your own well"? ("Should your springs overflow in the streets, your streams of water in the public squares? Let them be yours alone, never to be shared with strangers. May your fountain be blessed, and may you rejoice in the wife of your youth. A loving doe, a graceful deer—may her breasts satisfy you always, may you ever be captivated by her love." Proverbs 5) With no moral code present in the rest of the animal kingdom, is there any reason to believe that the ones present in human societies and religions are anything more than convention? Are any of these codes representative of an absolute truth? If so, then who do we believe? If a Muslim says the Koran or a Jew the Torah or a Christian the Bible, then why are there so many diverse beliefs and practices within each one of these groups? Which authority hits closest to the mark? Or are atheists right? Is there really no God or moral law? Are we simply the most evolved species in the animal kingdom with nothing but arbitrary rules to govern our sexual conduct (or *any* moral behavior, for that matter)?

If anyone glibly thinks that these questions are easily answered, then a look into Havelock Ellis or the Kinsey books is in order. I, for one, think it would be healthy for the church to talk frankly about these things. It may be correctly said, for example, that human sexual standards are different from any behavioral standard in the animal kingdom because humans alone are made in the image of God, with souls and spirits that were made to do more than act on a level of pure instinct and learned behavior. It would be helpful if the specifics such as masturbation, nocturnal emissions, petting to orgasm before marriage, homosexuality, or oral sex were talked about in an open yet unembarrassing way. Though I am sure He is saddened by the misuse of it (as He is with all sin), God is not embarrassed by the sexual conduct of humanity nor by the sex drive within us. We should not be, either.

Hauntings

> Haunting—"a lingering in the consciousness: not readily forgotten."
> — *Webster's Third New International Dictionary*

Words are inadequate to describe those things in life that make profound impressions on us. "Patriotism," for example, only approximates the feelings engendered by those who returned to France 50 years after landing as soldiers on its shores during D-Day in World War II. "Sorrow" cannot measure the breadth or depth of a spouse mourning the death of their loved one. "Anger" doesn't always capture the exact feeling of someone betrayed, just as "happiness" falls short of describing a satisfying marriage or graduation from school. Whether for better or for worse, we feel things more truly than we can ever say them.

Like patriotism or joy, haunting experiences are also hard to describe. They have an eerie, lingering quality to them. Sometimes they can be troubling and disturbing, such as the hauntings that come after an act of violence. But for other hauntings, there is something mysterious, perhaps even numinous, about the way they affect us. At times, this effect is almost paralyzing in its intensity and power. At others, it is less dramatic, simply returning to haunt our consciousness. We can't explain why they affect us so. We only know that they do.

Haunting can come in many idioms. I have found that music is the muse most frequently employed on me. Even 2,500 years ago, Socrates realized that music had a slippery quality to it, affecting us in ways that reason could not. I enjoy a fairly wide variety of music, yet only a few pieces have that haunting quality to them, and the one that most frequently comes to mind is Johann Sebastian Bach's Passacaglia. (A passacaglia is a musical form consisting of variations on a theme. The theme is usually eight bars long, in 3/4 time, and is continuously repeated while each new variation is performed.) Bach's Passacaglia and Fugue in C minor has always had a haunting quality for me, regardless of the medium in which it is performed. I have heard it played on the organ, by a brass quintet, and by an orchestra with equal effect. I can't explain why I find it so gripping, except to note that music played in a minor key has a greater tendency to unsettle the spirit. Music critics, such as John McClure, may impassively describe the Passacaglia's technical aspects, "Yet after exploring to the full the possibilities of the recurring bass, Bach commences a fugue on the Passacaglia subject, adding a couple of counter melodies—the first a slurred off-beat fragment, and the second a running series of 16th notes—and, after the fugal pattern has run its course, rounds it all off with a resounding summation."[8] But these remarks mean little to me. The real effect on the listener is closer to what another musician named Robert Schumann once said, when he described the 21 variations of the piece as "intertwined so ingeniously that one can never cease to be amazed."[9]

There are, of course, other haunting experiences besides those in music. My visit to Alcatraz Prison was one such occasion, cloaked as it was in cold, rain, fog, and memories of those who lived and tried to escape from there. Certain movies, such as *Fiddler on the Roof*, or beautiful locales, such as a particular woods on a mountain, or even a poem by J.R.R. Tolkien from *The Lord of the Rings* have all had that eerie, mysterious, emotionally moving quality about them.

> Three Rings for the Elven-kings under the sky,
>   Seven for the Dwarf-lords in their halls of stone,
>   Nine for Mortal Men doomed to die,
>   One for the Dark Lord on his dark throne
>   In the Land of Mordor where the Shadows lie.
>   One Ring to rule them all, One Ring to find them,
>   One Ring to bring them all and in the darkness bind them
>   In the Land of Mordor where the Shadows lie.[10]

Even a given conversation or sermon may come to exercise a lingering power on our thoughts. Though these experiences are rare, they are intriguing and enriching, even nourishing. They are mysterious and elusive, beyond the ability for full comprehension. Yet I am glad that the world is full of such wonder, of experiences that awe and mystify us. I am glad, too, that we can't explain everything our senses encounter. I am thankful for the capacity to be amazed and perplexed. And I am pleased that we can be haunted, because a world without mystery is a world of boredom.

The Handicap of Divine Gnosis

In his book *The Man Who Mistook His Wife for a Hat*, neurologist Oliver Sacks writes of two autistic twins named John and Michael whom he met in the 1960s. Their remarkable mathematical abilities had made them the subject of detailed scientific and popular reports, including appearances on radio and television. They were the paradoxical idiots savants or moronic geniuses, with IQs in the 60s that prevented them from doing simple mathematics such as addition or subtraction, or even from comprehending the meaning of multiplication or division. Yet in other ways they had astonishing numerical powers. "Give us a date—any time in the last or next 40,000 years," they would say. When a date was offered, they almost instantly responded by stating what day of the week it would be. They could also state the date of a given Easter with equal accuracy during this 80,000-year stretch. Alternatively, one could ask them to repeat a given number and they would—three, 30, or 300 digits long—it didn't seem to matter. They could repeat all with equal ease. Many who studied them believed that the twins did this by a secret method, using an unconscious algorithm for calendar calculations. Indeed, they had been called "calendar calculators." Yet Sacks doubted this, asking—with a healthy dose of skepticism—how two people without the wherewithal to calculate even simple arithmetic problems could do this. How could those who could not calculate, who lacked even the rudimentary powers of computing arithmetic, be considered 'calculators'?

In discussing the twins, Sacks recalled Sir Herbert Oakley, a nineteenth-century Edinburgh professor of music who was once taken to a farm, where he heard a pig squeak. He instantly cried, "G Sharp." Someone ran to the piano and G sharp it was. This "feeling," this "knowing," this instant "understanding" of music has been called "perfect pitch." In the same way, these twins instantly "knew" a number. For example, a box of matches once fell on their table, discharging its contents onto the floor. "111," they both cried simultaneously. Then John said "37." Michael repeated this and John said it yet again. Sacks then laboriously counted all of the fallen matches. There were 111. When he asked the twins how they could count the matches so quickly, they replied that they hadn't counted. "We *saw* the 111," they said. When he then asked why they had murmured 37 three times, they said in unison "37, 37, 37, 111." (37 x 3 = 111) Sacks was puzzled, astonished. That they should *see* 111—"111-ness"—in a flash was extraordinary, a sort of "absolute pitch" for numbers; but they had gone on to "factor" the number 111—without having any method, without even "knowing" (in any ordinary way) what "factors" meant. They seemed to have simply *seen* it, to have an extraordinary sense of immediate, *felt* reality. Was it possible that they could somehow 'see' numbers' properties? They did not understand abstract concepts like arithmetic, but could they see numbers' properties as *qualities*, being somehow felt in a sensuous, , immediate, concrete way? And not simply, Sacks mused, as isolated qualities (like '111ness') but as qualities of *relationship*? Perhaps akin to Sir Herbert Oakley's gift in judging musical relationships between notes on the musical scale?

By comparison, Sacks discusses Russian chemist Dmitri Mendeleev, father of the periodic table of elements. Mendeleev carried cards around with him on which were written the numerical properties of elements, until they became utterly familiar to him. They became so familiar that he no longer thought of them as aggregates of properties, but as familiar faces. He saw the elements iconically, as faces that related, like members of the family, and that made up the whole formal face of the universe. Such a scientific mind, Sacks notes, is essentially 'iconic', and 'sees' all nature as faces and scenes, and perhaps even as music.

Seventeenth-century physician Sir Thomas Browne wrote that, "whoever is harmonically composed delights in harmony . . . and a profound contemplation of the First Composer. There is something in it of Divinity more than the ear discovers; . . . a sensible fit of that harmony which intellectually sounds in the ears of God. . ."

Thoughts of the remarkable "knowing" abilities of John, Michael, and other idiot savants have come to mind when reading about the size of the universe and pondering the existence of a God who could *know* it all. Our own galaxy, the Milky Way, for all its vastness (over 70,000 light years or 410 quadrillion miles in diameter) is only one of 200 billion galaxies in the universe. How could any entity possibly know the intimate details about each living being on one planet from one huge galaxy from one huge universe? The idea of this kind of God is far beyond, almost infinitely beyond, the grasp of the human imagination. It strains credulity. And yet, John and Michael give a hint of the possibility of such knowledge. They seem to show that the very essence of something (numbers, in their case) can be known intuitively, even if that something be vast and complex. If they, being "idiots" can know, then should not the "First Composer," who is far, even infinitely, greater than they, be able to *see* (feel, know, understand, etc.) *all* of reality? It suddenly seems possible.

I like the way C.S. Lewis put it in *God in the Dock* (pp. 41*ff*): "We are inveterate poets. Our imaginations awake. Instead of mere quantity, we now have a quality—the sublime. Unless this were so, the merely arithmetical greatness of the galaxy would be no more impressive than the figures in a telephone directory. It is thus, in a sense, from ourselves that the material universe derives its power to over-awe us. To a mind which did not share our emotions, and lacked our imaginative energies, the argument from size would be sheerly meaningless. Men look on the starry heavens with reverence: monkeys do not...

"And this drives me to say yet again that we are hard to please. If the world in which we found ourselves were not vast and strange enough to give us Pascal's terror, what poor creatures we should be! Being what we are, rational but also animate...I do not see how we could have come to know the greatness of God without that hint furnished by the greatness of the material universe. Once again, what sort of universe do we demand? If it were small enough to be cozy, it would not be big enough to be sublime. If it is large enough for us to stretch our spiritual limbs in, it must be large enough to baffle us. Cramped or terrified, we must, in any conceivable world, be one or the other. I prefer terror. I should be suffocated in a universe that I could see to the end of. Have you never, when walking in a wood, turned back deliberately for fear you should come out at the other side and thus make it ever after in your imagination a mere beggarly strip of trees?

"... We are in no position to draw up maps of God's psychology, and prescribe limits to His interests. We would not do so even for a man whom we knew to be greater than ourselves. The doctrines that God is love and that He delights in men, are positive doctrines, not limiting doctrines. He is not less than this. What more He may be, we do not know; we know only that He must be more than we can conceive. It is to be expected that His creation should be, in the main, unintelligible to us."[11]

Thoughts Along the Way

In Paul's letter to the Corinthian church, he wrote that God had "chosen the foolish things of the world to shame the wise, and God has chosen the weak things of the world to shame the things which are strong, and the base things of the world and the despised, God has chosen. . . that no man should boast before God."[12] John and Michael provide what I like to think of as glimpses into the Divine, whose thoughts are not our thoughts nor His way our way (as Isaiah wrote).[13] They are the idiot savants, the "foolish" things that shame the wise. Many arguments have been proposed to prove the existence of God. The ontological argument which states that the idea of God infers His existence, was championed by St. Anselm of Canterbury. The cosmological argument, stating that the created world implies a creator God, has been pushed by many, such as St. Thomas Aquinas. The teleological argument proposes that the order in the world proves God's existence, as advocated by William Paley and others. The moral argument seeks to show that certain features of the existence of a moral law point to a lawmaker. Men such as Immanuel Kant and C.S. Lewis certainly felt so. The argument from religious experience has been voiced by numerous people. Along these lines, one is almost tempted to argue for God's existence from autism—surely an unusual philosophical approach! ("Note how Graham argues from autism—the ability to see as God sees.") Of course, idiot savants do not prove God's existence nor His competency, but there does seem to be a bit of Divine humor—made at our own expense—in allowing these "learned idiots" to experience a part of omniscience that we "intelligent" humans cannot grasp. We "normal" ones who care for and lord it over them are on the outside, looking in. They are the ones who know this reality, this bit of the omniscient. We can only marvel at it; and the joke, of course, is on us.

How We View the World

Many medical-school lectures are endured rather than enjoyed. Because the subject matter is factually detailed, lectures stress substance over style, making it difficult to arouse enthusiasm in the audience. Good lecturers are therefore both helpful and welcome. Ironically, when memory of the substance they taught fades, the appreciation of their style remains.

One of the more memorable lectures I heard during my own sojourn in medical school was given by a neurology professor at the end of my first school year. It was a lecture on vision, which even to this day still excites my admiration. Although this was a complex topic, it was presented in a lucid fashion, analyzing the process of "seeing" by separating this act into its component parts. Complex concepts such as "Center-Surround Concentric Receptive Fields" were explained in great detail and the fundamental process of vision was amply illustrated when the professor paused for a simple demonstration. He held a long, cylindrical, white piece of chalk in his right hand and a fat, square, yellow-orange one in his left. Turning to one of the students he asked, "What are these?" Rather than replying, "I see an oblong, tubular shaped, white-colored, solid-textured object being motionlessly presented to my left inferior visual field and a large, square, yellow-orange object of similar appearing material in my right superior visual field," she merely said, "They look like chalk." The light reflecting off of the chalk had hit her eye (sensation), been converted into electrical signals (carried in the optic nerve), decomposed (into elementary sensations of size, shape, color, texture,

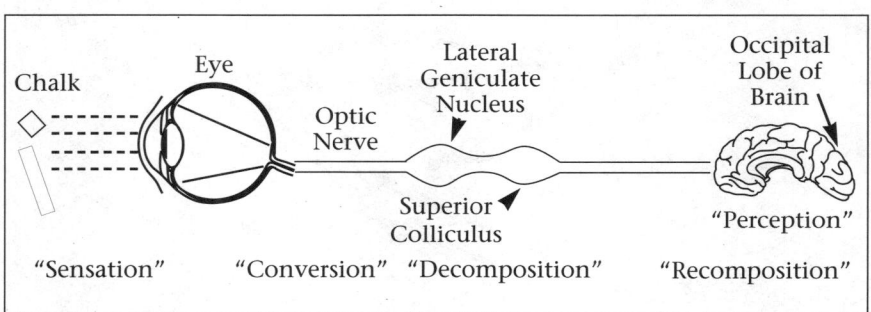

and location in space) and then recomposed into perception ("they look like chalk,") in the visual cortex of the brain. It was an amazing process to ponder. The professor eventually ended the lecture by saying, "This is the first rudimentary examination at the cellular level of how pure sensation is converted to electrical impulses, then transformed to perception. This concept of decomposition, recomposition, and receptive fields is fundamental to neuroscience—it is not just a visual phenomenon, but also occurs in auditory and somatosensory pathways." He then took a sip of water, paused, and looked back up at the class, saying with conviction, "and this provides the basis... (pause)... for how we view our world."

"For how we view our world," he had said. Such a simple statement for such a complex process. How do we do it? The phenomenon of transformation, of turning sensation into perception, continues to intrigue the human mind.[14] How do we *know*? How do we *recognize* things? Why can we see *one* face in a *crowd* of faces—all of which have two eyes, two cheek bones, a set of lips, a couple of ears, a chin, and eyebrows—and recognize it as familiar ("That's Jan," "There's my mother," "I see the President.")? Why do we perceive those other faces as "strangers"? To get to the root of these questions would be to ultimately ask, "How does the brain—on a cellular, microscopic level—learn?" Investigators continue to study the matter, trying to understand it. This is a fascinating, challenging task.

C.S. Lewis gave a layman's thoughts on the matter in his excellent book *Miracles*. The book discusses how God intervenes in nature and human affairs. The text is addressed to the doubter, the skeptic, the agnostic who is interested in taking the subject—and possibility—of miracles sincerely. In the chapter "The Cardinal Difficulty of Naturalism" (and one may substitute "materialism" or "atheism" for Lewis's "naturalism"), he points to the shortcomings of a world view that excludes the existence of the supernatural. Naturalism, Lewis argues, fails to bridge the gap between sensation and perception. For example, seeing (a sensation) does not, by itself, evolve into insight (perception). A dog may see a billboard, but only the human can read it and understand (perceive) it. Even the human could not understand it unless the human mind had been given the ability to perceive. So how could naturalistic evolution—a process based on random chance—ever do this? Surely something *outside* of Nature, something *super*natural, had to step in to insert this ability into the human mind, this capacity to transform sensation into perception. "Now natural selection could operate only by eliminating responses that were biologically hurtful and multiplying those which tended to survival. But it is not conceivable that any improvement of responses could ever turn them into acts of insight, or even remotely tend to do so. The relation between response and stimulus is utterly different from that between knowledge and the truth known. Our physical vision is a far more useful response to light than that of the cruder organisms which have only a photo-sensitive spot. But neither this improvement nor any possible improvement we can suppose could bring it an inch nearer to being a knowledge of light...Knowledge is achieved by experiments and inferences from them, not by refinement of the response. It is not men with specially good eyes who know about light, but men who have studied the relevant sciences."[15] It is here that the theist digresses from the naturalist (atheist, materialist). The theist "is not committed to the view that reason is a comparatively recent development molded by a process of selection which can select only the biologically useful."[16] For the theist, reason really means the reason of God. Reason is not an evolutionary development, derived somehow from repetitive stimulus-response events. Reason is a gift, a gift whereby insight and knowledge are possible. "The human mind in the act of knowing is illuminated by the Divine reason."[17] One thinks of the Psalmist's words, "In Thy light we see light." (Psalms 36:9) Seen this way, the act of knowing is supernatural, because it comes from reason, a gift inserted into the natural mind of mankind by God. ("Who has put wisdom in the innermost being, or has given understanding to the mind?" Job 38:36)

It is the sense of beauty, though, rather than reason, that comes to mind when I hear a lecture that describes "the basis, for how we view our world." From whence does this sense of beauty come? Why do we not only recognize a song, but find it beautiful or ugly as well? Why do we not only see a "vertically oriented, cylindrically formed branching structure manifesting green, pointed, flexible-stemmed outcroppings," but perceive it as a "tree", perhaps identify the kind ("it's a maple"), and further still retain the capacity for sensing "beauty" in it?[18] Why are authors like Lewis or G.K. Chesterton able to discuss beauty—to speak of longing for it or wanting to plunge into it? The remainder of the animal kingdom does not exhibit this passion. Some animals may be attracted to a particular plant or species mate, may have certain colors or odors they are drawn toward, but do they really have a sense of beauty or a sense of understanding beauty? It seems only humans do. True, aesthetic judgement is subjective, and people disagree about what is or what is not beautiful; but recognizing the *existence* of beauty, in any form, suggests the presence of the numinous in our world. That vision is a means of apprehending such beauty is itself a mysterious wonder.

Perhaps the real thrill of obtaining even a rudimentary understanding of the basis "for how we view our world," lies in the exciting sense of detecting the divine spark in our existence; of sensing the ultimate source of our understanding by which we can even know something about anything; of seeing the natural because of the supernatural. And so we echo the words of the psalmist. "In Thy light, we see light."

Observations

Requisite for a Surgeon

On July 1, 1990, I began a six-year residency training program in general surgery at Erlanger Hospital in Chattanooga, Tennessee.

Because the system in the United States for training physicians continues to change, I'll say a few things about its current status. The first-year internship following graduation from medical school has been incorporated into most residency programs and thus does not exist autonomously as a prerequisite to the residency. For instance, the training of a surgeon formerly consisted of a one-year internship followed by a four-year general surgery residency. Training now consists of five years of residency. The overall training time has not changed, but the structure has. (Though first-year residents are still referred to as "interns," they are receiving training that is related to their specialty rather than general training in several different medical fields.) Many surgery programs, including the one at Chattanooga, are adding a year of research to their programs for a total of six years training. My own time scheme looks like this:

Kindergarten Graduation			B.S. Degree	M.D. Degree		Boards
1 Year	12 Years	4 Years	4 Years	6 Years		2-3 Years
		High School	Wheaton College	Medical School University of Tennessee Memphis	General Surgery Residency University of Tennessee Chattanooga Branch	Fellowship?

After training as a general surgeon, one may opt to study a further surgical subspecialty in a postresidency program called a "fellowship." Fellowships vary from 2-3 years and include plastic, hand, vascular, oncology, colorectal, cardiothoracic, critical care, pediatric,

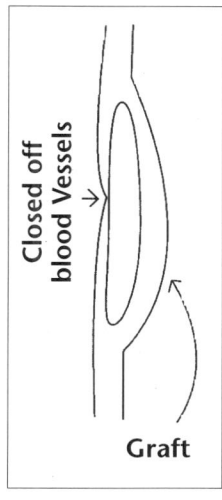

transplant, or trauma specialty training. Note: fellowships are optional. Most people who do them are planning on practicing in that particular subspecialty rather than general surgery.

Residency is really an apprenticeship and a general surgeon trains in the areas of trauma (bad falls, automobile accidents, gunshot wounds, etc.) vascular surgery (such as bypassing closed-off blood vessels with grafts), thyroid, breast, pancreas, or colon operations for cancer, appendectomies and cholecystectomies for appendicitis or gallbladder disease, stomach and small intestinal surgery for things such as ulcers or tumors, hernia repairs, amputations, biopsies, and many, many other things. Surgeons do more than just operate, though, and training includes treating nonoperative problems seen in the clinic or emergency room and caring for pre- and postoperative patients. Upon completion of the residency program, a surgeon becomes eligible to take the board certification exams in general surgery. This is not a mandatory requirement, but hospitals prefer most of their physicians to be board-certified. Currently, surgery boards (which were valid for *life* before 1975) are good for only 10 years, at which time retesting for certification is required (a foolish requirement, in this author's opinion).

Surgeons are made, not born. My strong belief is that becoming a good physician requires diligent, steadfast work and study. Though one desires to be a good surgeon, there are no guarantees that this will become true, so this wish must be fulfilled through hard work and perseverance. There are no shortcuts, because competence must be earned, not assumed. Once earned, competence should then be cultivated, or it will be lost. Passion for excellence, compassion for patients, and the gift of proficiency are the requisites for surgical expertise. Happy are they who attain it. . .

Work

Work may produce rather ambivalent feelings. There is something attractive yet tiring about it. It can be a necessary burden yet give satisfaction when completed. Its presence as well as its absence both provide grounds for complaint. Adam was cursed to work by the sweat of his brow, though good work is praised throughout the Bible. For millennia, work has caused endless pain and endless progress, while happy friendships and bitter enemies have been formed there.

I first noticed my own ambivalence toward work while trekking on a two-week wilderness program before my freshman year of college. Being deprived of the daily luxuries found in latter twentieth-century America, while at the same time hiking, canoeing, camping, and eating just enough to stay alive (I lost 12 lbs.—and I was thin when I started the course) gave me a better appreciation of the leisure I had once enjoyed. In my journal, I wrote that it was the difficult times in life that made the easier moments more pleasing. Perhaps there really was some truth in the cliché, "Nothing ventured, nothing gained." The effort and toil in work enhanced the enjoyment of one's private hours, when the "real living" took place: sport, romance, familial gatherings, worship, entertainment, and the like occurred away from the shop. Work was the contrast that heightened these pleasures, so work was good, and besides being a means to earning a living it contributed something positive to society.

> There is nothing better for a man than to eat and drink
> and tell himself that his labor is good.
> Ecclesiastes 2:24

Does "real living," however, only occur off-duty? With the passage of time, my views on work have shifted so that my answer to that question is "No." Part of this change has come after reflecting on the jobs that I have not just tolerated but actually enjoyed. Working on a farm *was* fun. Masonry *was* pleasurable. Chemistry *was* satisfying to learn. My vocational experiences, including the disagreeable jobs, proved to be pieces that were woven into my life, not set apart from it. I began to think that the enthusiasm and attentiveness that I had lavished on the things I enjoyed would be well spent if applied to the things I didn't. To my surprise, I found that when I did this, the wearying aspects of my job became less tiresome and some of the boring tasks were made a bit interesting. Tolstoy's description of the peasants gathering hay in *Anna Karenina* captures the right spirit.

> All that had been swallowed up in the sea of their joyful common toil. God gave the day and God gave the strength for it. Both the day and the strength for it were devoted to labor, and *that was its own reward.* [1] (italicized emphasis is mine)

Work is not always a great enjoyment. Moments of dissatisfaction or fatigue are inevitable. Perhaps it will always produce ambivalent feelings. But work is not just a means to a living. It *is* living. Since this is so, it seems reasonable that a spirited interest and determined effort will yield their own rewards, even during the uninviting moments. The preacher of Ecclesiastes said it well,

> Here is what I have seen to be good and fitting: to eat, to drink, and enjoy oneself in all one's labor in which he toils under the sun during the few years of his life which God has given him; for this is his reward. [2]

The Unchanging Human Heart

A twenty-first-century historian might look back an eon and write,

> Trade and commerce flourished, and there was a pronounced drift of labor from the land to the city. A generation from whom the ever-present threat of military attack had been removed began to concentrate upon more material things, and this quickly resulted in a demand for luxury items that had previously been the prerogative of only the highest levels of society. Such preoccupation with materialistic goals went hand in hand with moral and religious depravity, and struck hard at the traditional concepts of social justice. Bribery of officialdom was frequently employed by unscrupulous individuals who wished to amass lands and wealth in a comparatively short time. This trend was carried to its extreme in the corruption of the judiciary, with the result that one who was illegally deprived of his property or other holdings could seldom if ever expect to receive justice in the courts of the land.
>
> Self-interest of this kind soon created a powerful aristocracy of wealth, and this was accompanied by the virtual disappearance of the middle class in society. Since there was then no social level that could maintain the tensions necessary for a healthy communal climate, the gap between rich and poor became ominously wide.
>
> In the area of religion the depravity of worship had reached its fullest point of development. Self-interest in social affairs made for self-indulgence in matters of religion. The sanctuaries were crowded with worshippers who, in the main, were rejoicing in the prosperity of the times...Priests associated with the sanctuaries

profited from the lavish gifts of the worshippers, and naturally condoned these exercises in the name of religion, appearing completely oblivious to the conditions of rapid decay which lay immediately underneath the surface of social life. [3]

The writer, however, is not a commentator on North American or European history but a biblical scholar (R.K. Harrison), and the text is taken, slightly modified, from his description of the social conditions in ancient Israel under the reign of Jereboam II, when the prophet Amos delivered his messages. How "modern" this sounds! Yet it demonstrates well Harrison's contention that the human spirit "in basic character has remained unchanged to all intents and purposes throughout recorded history."[4] As C.S. Lewis put it, "Humanity does not pass through phases as a train passes through stations: being alive, it has the privilege of always moving yet never leaving anything behind. Whatever we have been, in some sort we are still."[5]

I sometimes hear or read—usually from Christian sources—about the moral decline of the world or a particular country or society. While it is true that political climates change and work ethics differ, I think that there is some truth to Lucius Priest's comments in William Faulkner's novel *The Reivers*. "You have heard—or anyway you will—people talk about evil times or an evil generation. There are no such things. No epoch of history nor generation of human beings either ever was or is or will be big enough to hold the un-virtue of any given moment, any more than they could contain all the air of any given moment; all they can do is hope to be as little soiled as possible during their passage through it."[6]

Reading the Bible, and the Old Testament in particular, has been my greatest help in trying to understand the world I inhabit. A history lesson from Chronicles or a pronouncement from one of the prophets like Amos or puzzlement about the triumph of injustice pondered in the Psalms continue to be understood generation after generation because of the unchanging character of human nature and the presence of evil or "un-virtue" in all peoples of all cultures. Likewise, the experience of announcing a birth or celebrating marriage was as joyful 3,000 years ago as it is today, while the pain of divorce or bereavement of death has not diminished with time. The Bible remains "modern," as Frederick Buechner writes, "because it is a book about both the sublime and the unspeakable, it is a book also about life the way it really is. It is a book about people who at one and the same time can be both believing and unbelieving, innocent and guilty, crusaders and crooks, full of hope and full of despair. In other words it is a book about us.

And it is also a book about God. If it is not about the God we believe in, then it is about the God we do not believe in. One way or another the story we find in the Bible is our own story."[7]

Trying to evaluate the present, especially in making moral judgments about people, culture, society, or countries, requires good information. If I were forced to choose only one news source to aid my conclusions, you can bet it wouldn't require a switch to turn on or a carrier to deliver it.

Studying the Little Things in Life

There is nothing, Sir, too little for so little a creature as man. It is by studying little things that we attain the great art of having as little misery and as much happiness as possible.
Samuel Johnson [8]

Ultrasound of the Prostate,[9] has yet to make it to *The New York Times* bestseller list. It hasn't even been reissued in paperback. The demand for it just isn't there. Its approach is highly specialized with limited appeal even for many a specialist. The focus centers on *one* test of *one* gland that is present in only *half* of the population in the body of *one* species, diseased in a small *proportion* with only a *subset* of these needing this *particular* exam to be interpreted by a *fraction* of professionals in *medicine* who have specialized in one area of practice and who will use this test as *part* of their diagnostic work-up. . . It is not a popular book.

Some things, such as love, are easier to sense than they are to explain. Thomas à Kempis wrote "I would far rather feel contrition than be able to define it."[10] Such is the case for the things that interest us: it is easier to discuss our enthusiasm for something than it is to explain why it is that we have chosen it. A biologist writing about tropical rain forests in the December 1991 issue of *National Geographic* spoke of his lifelong interest in ants. One particular archaeologist featured in the April 1991 issue of *National Geographic* had spent a lifetime studying Ramses II and ancient Egypt. I once saw an advertisement for a posthumous book containing a historian's thoughts on a lifetime of researching and writing about the American Civil War. Sports fanatics are easily found across the nation, while varied sports trivia books are by no means unpopular. Just the other day, I found out that a friend of mine was an aficionado of Batman lore, quite informed about the minutia of this fictitious character's life. Why does one man enjoy working on car engines, while another loves science fiction novels? Why is one woman a connoisseur of French recipes, while another likes golf? Nobody knows. I myself have had to provide "reasons" for entering into my profession (interviewers usually ask, "So why did you choose to go into surgery?"), but in the end, all that can be said is, "I like it."

Of course, there is always a danger in any indulgence. C.S. Lewis wrote of "the deeply ingrained conviction of narrow minds that whatever things they themselves are chiefly exercised on are the only important things, the only things worth adult, informed, and thoroughgoing interest."[11] On the other hand, a genuine interest in something outside ourselves, no matter how small, can be healthy. As Lewis's senior devil Screwtape writes to his nephew in training, Wormwood, "I would make it a rule to eradicate from my patient any strong personal taste which is not actually a sin, even if it is something quite trivial such as a fondness for country cricket or collecting stamps or drinking cocoa. Such things, I grant you, have nothing of virtue in them; but there is a sort of innocence and humility and self-forgetfulness about them which I distrust. The man who truly and disinterestedly enjoys any one thing in the world, for its own sake, and without caring two pence what other people say about it, is by that very fact forearmed against some of our subtlest modes of attack. You should always try to make the patient abandon the people or food or books he really likes in favor of the 'best' people, the 'right' food, the 'important' books. I have known a human defended from strong temptations to social ambition by a still stronger taste for tripe and onions."[12] I like the way Annie Dillard puts it: "I have often noticed that even a few minutes of this self-forgetfulness is tremendously invigorating. I wonder if we do not waste most of our energy just by spending every waking minute saying hello to ourselves."[13]

No, *Ultrasound of the Prostate* isn't popular. But to those who read from it, its contents instruct them in their area of professional interest. No matter how obscure its contents when judged by the public's standards, or how many "little things" it teaches, it can still be read with interest by the students of that field. Even a book such as this can aid its readers in attaining "the great art of having as little misery and as much happiness as possible."

I hope you continue to enjoy even the little things in your own areas of interest.

Sketch of a General Surgery Residency

> If practitioners attempted to keep up with the literature by reading two articles per day, by the end of one year, they would be 5 centuries behind.
>
> C.L. Bernier and A.N. Yerkey[14]

(There are now more than 20,000 different biomedical journals published yearly with an annual growth rate of 6 to 7 percent. Over 300,000 articles are indexed each year, with over 25,000 devoted primarily to surgical problems.)[15]

I began my residency on July 1, 1990, one month after graduating from medical school. In some ways, learning to become a good surgeon is like learning to walk as an infant or learning to fly as a bird: it takes lots of effort, involves plenty of mistakes, and requires repetition. With time, the effort and repetition remain unchanged, but the errors (thankfully) lessen with experience. It is at once a challenging and profoundly humbling journey.

A surgery resident's work is divided up into rotations on the various "services." These "services" will vary from one training program to another, but over the course of five or six years, the goal is to give everyone an equivalent (not equal) training experience. These rotations usually last for one or two months and give the resident experience working in the different areas of general surgery such as trauma, vascular, or oncology surgery.

In the early stages of one's residency, one's duties are more geared toward assisting and observing, progressing to operating and more important decision-making with time. By the last year—referred to as the "chief" year, in which one is a "chief resident"—the resident is expected to be operating, reading, and running his own surgery service just as a fully trained surgeon would do. He discusses all of his operations beforehand with a fully trained "attending" surgeon, and when necessary asks an attending surgeon to actually help him in the operating room (OR).

Being "on call" for a resident means being readily available. This means not leaving the hospital when on call. On call, or simply "call" averages about 10 times a month, or every third night where one never goes home. This accounts for the number of hours a surgery resident spends at the hospital, ranging from 80 to 90 on an easy week to 110 or 120 on a hard week, with the average around 90-100. During a call night, there are "call rooms" where a resident can (try to) sleep, but the beeper usually prevents much rest. Calls can come from anywhere—intensive care units, nursing calls about patients in regular hospital beds, the operating room, or the emergency room, with the last two usually requiring a personal visit rather than a telephone conversation alone.

The "index of annoyance" is rather high with my job because of the constant interruptions. One of the orthopedics residents once told me that the hardest thing about his work was to try concentrating on the patient he was seeing while his beeper kept going off. It would be a luxurious day to have things proceed in an orderly, uninterrupted fashion. This rarely happens. It takes a good deal of effort not only to respond to several things in short order, but to keep from being angered by it. Doctors typically succeed in the former and fail in the latter. The sudden interruptions—whether working or trying to sleep—coupled with the long hours are the most wearying aspects of my job. (In reading through Shelby Foote's Civil War narrative, I found much empathy with the soldiers who not infrequently fought or marched on very little [if any] sleep. In fact, considering the conditions *they* were under, I am amazed that they performed as well as they did.)

I have often heard the comment, "I wouldn't want someone who had been up all night to operate on me." The common thinking is that someone who has been up for more than 24 hours would be more likely to make a serious mistake in the OR. While this is potentially true, I have never seen it happen. When seeing someone in the emergency room (ER) or operating in the OR, one's adrenaline is up and this keeps doctors not only awake but alert as well. Sleep deprivation does not affect me in the critical-care setting. It does affect me, however, when I *assist* in the OR on a long, slow case, since the assistant is sometimes required to do the noncognitive job of holding retractors (and therefore not *doing* the operation). In that situation, the mental stimulation is gone and it is not difficult to get sleepy. This, however, does not affect patient care.

"General surgery" is an oxymoron because it seems to imply that one gets a little training in everything but specializes in nothing.
"What are you training in?"
"General surgery."
"What's that?"
"It's surgery on many different parts of the body, but most of it is on the breast and abdomen. For example...(multiple examples given)."
(Pause) "...Well, do you think you will specialize after that?"
(Silently miffed) "General surgery IS a specialty."
(Surprised and baffled) "...Oh..."
A general surgeon is a specialist in many diseases and their treatment—breast disease, thyroid disease, colon disease, hernias, trauma, and stomach ulcers, just to name a few.

Though it is not widely known, within any given specialty, physicians have their own subset of problems that they treat. In orthopedic surgery, for example, some doctors do hand surgery; others don't. Some do spine surgery; others don't. Some do only pediatric orthopedic work; others concentrate on adults or specialize in artificial joint replacements. In gynecology, most do obstetrics and deliver babies; others do not. Some gynecologists specialize in oncology, others in fertility. Some plastic surgeons concentrate on correction of congenital malformations (such as cleft lips, cleft palates, craniosynostosis [skull deformity]), others on hand surgery, while still others may only do cosmetic surgery (providing the stereotype of what a plastic surgeon does) or perhaps a little of many things while directing care toward burned patients. Ophthalmologists have their own subspecialists within the realm of eye care, and the same is true of general surgeons. Some general surgeons do vascular surgery; others don't. Some incorporate endoscopy into their practice; others don't. Some limit their practice to thyroid and parathyroid surgery, while others stick to colon and gallbladder or stomach or liver work. In short, a physician's practice is a tailored one, depending on her/his interests and the politics of the hospitals they work in. No one ever does *everything* that they received training in.

David Graham

PEANUTS by Charles M. Schultz

PEANUTS reprinted by permission of United Feature Syndicate, Inc.

Do surgeons have big egos? You bet they do. In some ways, the job requires it. Self-confidence is important to a surgeon, especially when the going gets tough. The four biggest temptations a surgeon faces are pride, anger, lust, and greed. Pride is something that any successful person struggles with, anger is usually expressed inside the operating room (due, quite frankly, to lack of self-control), numerous opportunities for lust are present when a prestigious, male-dominated profession interacts with the female-predominant nursing and ancillary care professions, and greed is especially appealing to someone who has spent so many years in school, often piling up a huge debt. (Almost 80 percent of those gradating from medical school are in debt, and the average liability exceeds $50,000.) Prayer for humility, self-control, and contentment should be offered alongside requests for good judgment and surgical skills. Like the Christians Paul addresses in Romans 8, I do not know how to pray as I should, and I too infrequently pray for these qualities to develop in me. Fortunately, "the Spirit Himself intercedes for us with groanings too deep for words."[16]

How does an intern (i.e., first-year resident) fresh out of medical school know how to take care of a patient with a complicated problem? Isn't that endangering the patient's life? The answers are "he doesn't" and "no." What the intern does know how to do is a history and physical. After that, he/she can call a senior or chief resident to talk about or to come see the patient. The intern learns by watching how the chief handles things ("Increase the pressure support on her ventilator to 20 centimeters and give her aerosol breathing treatments every four hours") and by asking questions ("Why did you do a peritoneal lavage instead of a CT scan?"), as well as assisting in operations ("This peritoneal reflection is the line of Toldt. Stay in this avascular plane when mobilizing the colon."). The chief, in turn, learns from reading, the patient (patients are the best teachers, whether teaching—through example—disease presentation or anatomy lessons) and from attending physicians who have finished their *training* (but not their *learning*. No one ever finishes that.).

One of my former chief residents, who is now in private practice, once commented on the biggest limitation to his skills as a surgeon. In classic Southern style, he said, "I can cure a lot of things, but I can't cure a dumb-ass." While the majority of patients I encounter are fairly reasonable, there are many who are not. They are exasperating to deal with. I have seen a lot of self-destructive, abusive, irresponsible behavior since I began my residency: the numerous people who drink alcohol to intoxication and then get behind the wheel of an automobile, ending up in the ER with major injuries (and many who do survive will do it again and again); or those who have repeated bouts of life-threatening pancreatitis because of alcohol abuse; lung cancer and the development of abdominal aortic aneurysms from smoking; knifings and gunshot wounds from fighting; drug-seeking individuals who lose their emotional balance or ruin their livers from drug abuse or who die from smoking cocaine; promiscuous sexual activity that leads to disease transmission and sometimes death; and refusal to accept the truth. All of these people are humans, made in the *image* of *God*. Sometimes this baffles me; can it really be true??!!

While it never ceases to amaze me, it also reminds me that I am called as a physician to help these people, too. When Christ was on earth, he didn't just minister to the reasonable or the intelligent or the interesting. As a Christian, I feel that as Christ emphasized God's command to "Love the Lord your God with all your heart, and with all your soul, and with all your mind"[17] and "love your neighbor as yourself"[18] I am to share God's love with everyone—lovely or unlovely. This, of course, is easier said than done. At the same time, I am humbled by God's immense goodness to me and grateful for the life I have lived. My job is not easy, but it is fascinating and stimulating. I really do like it. It gives me a high level of happiness and satisfaction.

Name-calling

I wish I had a book that chronicled the social history of the way humans address one another. It is not as simple a matter as one might think. Familial relationships are usually straightforward, with siblings enjoying a casual, first-name basis with each other. Parents have the respectful yet familiar titles of Papa, Mama, Dad, Mom, Father, Mother, Mammy, or Pappy. Grandparents, aunts, and uncles also have a respectable yet intimate first-name address: "Uncle Rick," "Aunt Janice", "Grandpa Ron," "Grandma Eunice." Things are a little more complicated in stepfamilies and in the working world. Circumstances of introduction, age barriers, timing, and familiarity all play a role in determining how we address others. If an infant's mother remarries, for example, that child will probably grow up calling the paternal figure "Dad." On the other hand, if the mother remarries when her child has become an adult, the stepfather will probably be called by his first name. The older age of the offspring changes the mode of address.

Missionaries working in Third World countries tend to address each other on a first-name basis, regardless of vocational status. Thus a mere medical student may address a fully trained doctor in this setting on an informal, first-name basis. "Good morning, Craig, how are you?" But if these same two individuals were to meet in the hospital wards of America, things would be different. "Good morning, Dr. Klatskin, how are you?" The age and vocational status would be the same, but the different cultural circumstances dictate the change in address. Sometimes it is timing that determines how we address each other. For example, during a medical residency the "resident" physicians address each other on a collegial, first-name basis. When a resident completes training and becomes an "attending" physician, he/she still maintains a familiar, first-name basis with the residents they already know who still happen to be in training. Thus when Dr. R. finished his residency and became an attending surgeon (and therefore one of my bosses) I still addressed him as "Michael." But when a New York resident transferred into the Chattanooga program a couple of years later (having started his residency the same year I had), he addressed the attending surgeon as "Dr. R." The only difference between us was timing—I called the attending physician "Michael" because I met him when he was a resident, and my colleague called him "Dr. R." because he met him after Dr. R. had become one of the attending physician staff.

Social matters are complicated by relationship changes as well. Several nurses, including the one who later became my wife, addressed me as "Dr. Graham" when I first began working in the hospital, yet with time, familiarity and friendship changed that. The same thing usually occurs if a doctor joins the group of physicians that trained him/her. Former bosses become colleagues and first names are substituted for surnames when addressing them. The opposite process occurs sometimes, too, as when someone is elected President of the United States. No longer do reporters address that man as "Mr. Clinton" or "Governor," but "Mr. President."

Reflection about these matters arouses a certain historical curiosity. It would be interesting to know how things worked in times past and in other cultures. How were the elderly, the authorities, or the employers addressed? Surely we would not say "Mister Socrates" when addressing the sage, would we? Or "Doctor Galen," "Mister Archimedes," or "Miss of Arc" (as Joan of Arc was once addressed in a movie)? The book I seek would be able to answer such questions.

Social titles hold more than an academic interest for me. Having been a student in school for more than two decades, I must admit that I felt enamored by the change of address after I received my medical degree. Being simply "David" all of my life had accustomed me to that role, and when people first addressed me as "Dr. Graham," it felt a bit odd. At first, it seemed inappropriate (embarrassing, really) because I felt so inadequate to the title. With time and experience, though, I gained confidence, and the "doctor" title seemed fitting. More than that, I subconsciously came to expect it. I enjoyed the respect it carried. It catered to my pride. At the same time, I enjoyed being on a first-name basis with some of the attending surgeons who my younger resident colleagues addressed as "Doctor." (Pride enjoys personal elevation and inclusion while seeking to lower and exclude others.)

Detecting such pride can be an elusive undertaking. Like becoming a surgeon, inflating pride is an insidious process, accruing slowly with time. Subtlety is an effective mask of change. So sometimes it takes an outside stimulus to illuminate what has happened, and Longfellow's poetry did this for me when I read his work *Christus: A Mystery*. In "Part I, The Divine Tragedy," he expanded several gospel scenes from the life of Christ into a poem, including a section from Matthew 23 that convicted me of my love for social entitlement when I read it. The passage was a familiar one, yet I paused for reflection when it began describing the learned scholars in another field of endeavor—in this case, the religious elite. "They love the uppermost rooms at feasts, and the chief seats in synagogues, and greetings in the markets, and to be called of all men Rabbi, Rabbi!" [19] Those scribes and Pharisees enjoyed the title of "Rabbi," which meant "teacher," although the connotation was "My great one," or "My superior one." They obviously delighted in the fringe benefits of being a "Rabbi" just as physicians do "Doctor" today. The self-love is the same. Only the vocations and setting are different. (As I've asserted before, the human spirit has remained basically the same throughout the ages.)

Yet herein lies the rub: while being elite is rewarding, it is not wrong. Good work *should* produce rewards. If hard work happens to make someone elite, then so be it. And there is a certain amount of pride that *is* justified in seeing good works rewarded. It is when pride begins to gloat that it subtlety changes character to a reprehensible trait. Knowing this, I try to view my own position of authority and elite entitlement with modesty, since humility is expected of God's children. In that same passage from Matthew 23, Christ went on to say, "The greatest among you will be your servant. For whoever exalts himself will be humbled, and whoever humbles himself will be exalted."[20] Nobly stated. Yet this continual humbling is easier said than done. The ability to take pride in one's work and remain humble in nature requires a whole lifetime of balancing; and humans do not balance opposites easily. I hope this book I am looking for discusses that, too.

Wisdom

Remember

In one corner of my study I have a bookcase shelving nine albums of photographs. Reviewing them brings back times from the past: clowning around with high school friends, teaching Sunday School in a Chicago housing project while in college, missionary construction trips overseas, a memorable vacation in Washington after taking board exams in medical school—thousands of memories triggered by the viewing of these pictures. These photographic memories recall my emotions at the time, conversations, the company I was with, the setting, and what station of life I was in when the photograph was taken. Viewing them brings great pleasure because memory is such a powerful stimulant.

In another corner I have a bookshelf that houses my three personal journals. These go a step in the opposite direction from my photographic albums. Whereas the albums draw me outward to other people and scenes around me, the journals draw me inward to view myself. When I review my journals I not only re-read my former musings, but I am often stimulated to ponder various issues or read passages from books again and again. Most entries were written when I was angry, or confused, frustrated, lonely, ecstatic, pensive, or in some way rather excited, but all of them attempt to be honest—to see the world as it is, keeping a steady gaze on the bad and the good, the lovely and the unlovely. Some issues continue to recur, while others are resolved or I make peace with them. Whatever the issue, reading an entry again is profitable, and I know this principle to be true: remembering my past makes a difference in the way I live the future.

On the corner of my desk lies my Bible. In that collection of books, the exhortation to remember recurs frequently. At the end of the Pentateuch (or Torah, the first five books of the Bible) when Moses was preparing to send the children of Israel into the Promised Land after 40 years of wilderness wandering, he said, "Remember!"

Remember what? "Everything." His reminiscences cover 33 of the 34 chapters of Deuteronomy, and though this is old information to the Israelites, Moses nevertheless outlines all that God has done for Israel from Egypt to the Promised Land. One might sum up Deuteronomy with the short phrase, "Remember, or face the consequences." In fact, from Genesis to Revelation, we find a call to remember ever present. "God remembered Noah."[1] "You shall well remember what the Lord your God did to Pharaoh and to all Egypt,"[2] "and it shall be a tassel for you to look at and remember all the commandments of the Lord,"[3] "Remember the former things long past, for I am God and there is no other."[4] "Jesus, remember me when you come in your kingdom."[5] "Remember therefore what you have received and heard."[6]

It is the Apostle Paul who gives the reason as to *why* remembering is important, *why* the scriptures were written, and *why* we should repeatedly read them. In a letter to the church at Corinth he wrote, "These things happened to them as an example, and they were written for our instruction,"[7] and to the Romans he wrote, "For whatever was written in earlier times was written for our instruction, that through perseverance and the encouragement of the Scriptures we might have hope."[8]

Collecting photographs, admittedly, is a less then two-century-old phenomenon that people have functioned without for thousands of years. However, like story telling, seeing home movies, reviewing journal entries, re-reading a book, or pneumonics, it is a device for helping us to remember. As we review the good and the bad, the correct and incorrect, the lovely and the unlovely, we grow up as humans and grow stronger as children of God.

Communication

Doctors have horrid handwriting. This is not myth but fact. And it is lamentable because this is the means by which doctors communicate with nurses and with each other regarding patient care. As more than one nurse can tell you, things are often easier to write than to read. Why would a doctor write out orders or jot down progress notes that require such laborious efforts to decipher? Why make the effort to write if the result is illegible or nearly so? What's the use? Why bother to write at all? And why scribble a "signature" that no one can read? Such practices are a waste of time and paper. I think they are inane.

Like others, I enjoy music. What I do not like are unintelligible renditions of the lyrics in a song. "What is she singing?" "What was that line?" Why sing it so that people can't understand it? Or why compose a piece of instrumental music that is so bizarre and contains so much dissonance that a soul finds it repulsive? As with music, art has many different expressions, ranging from the concrete to the abstract, mixing dissonance with consonance. I readily acknowledge this. What puzzles me, though, is how some creations of chaos and randomness can be labeled as art or touted as being works of "genius." Why paint a canvas that only a modicum of people who see it will *claim* to understand or appreciate?—I'll take a meaningful Norman Rockwell painting over an abstruse Jackson Pollock product any day. C.S. Lewis once wrote that a puddle is not a work, no matter which rich wines or oils or medicines went into its making. "Many modern novels, poems, and pictures, which we are brow-beaten into 'appreciating,' are not good work because they are not *work* at all. They are mere puddles of spilled sensibility or reflection. When an artist is in the strict sense working, he of course takes into account the existing taste, interests, and capacity of his audience. These, no less than the language, the marble, or the paint, are part of his raw material; to be used, tamed, sublimated, not ignored nor defied. Haughty indifference to them is not genius nor integrity; it is laziness and incompetence."[9]

Communication: it is the important ingredient in singing a song, writing a note, painting a picture, or learning in school. It also is the means by which we enlarge our view of the world. My older sister was once a schoolteacher for Wycliffe Bible Translators in the Philippines. Her life there allowed her to observe many fascinating aspects of Filipino culture. While back in the United States for a month of furlough once, she related to me the fascinating story of the people of Barlig who lived up in the mountains. The translators from Wycliffe who lived there were working on translating the Bible into the Konkenay language and having difficulty with the passages containing aquatic terminology. Unlike our mobile society, the people of Barlig, like many others around the globe, had not traveled far from their birthplace. Even though they lived on an island, they had remained up in the mountains, not venturing out to see the things around them—the ocean, the sailboats, or the nets used to catch fish (spears worked well enough for catching river fish). How then, does one find the words to explain these things, or to relate the sense of *awe* that comes from seeing a sea storm desist? "Then He arose," wrote Matthew in his gospel, "and rebuked the winds and the sea; and it became perfectly calm. And the men marveled saying, 'What kind of man is this, that even the winds and the sea obey him?'"[10] How does one communicate the miraculous nature of a dividing Red Sea for the Israelites to a people who don't know what a sea is? My sister remarked, "I didn't see an ocean until I was six, but I knew what one was. I didn't see a camel until I was 20, but I knew what one looked like from TV, books, talking with others, movies. . . ." The difference between my sister's knowledge and the Barlig people's ignorance was not intelligence, nor basic living needs, nor levels of curiosity, nor inquisitiveness. It was communication, the opportunity to see the world through the experiences of others.

In *Telling the Truth: The Gospel as Tragedy, Comedy, and Fairytale*, Frederic Buechner writes of the need for good communication from preachers. To communicate, they must speak to the needs of the people by being honest. The preacher does not live inside a bubble. He is a sinful man preaching to a congregation of sinners. He is not called to be an actor or a magician in the pulpit, but to be himself, telling the truth as he has experienced it. If he tries to avoid discussing the difficulties of life by only speaking about the truths that people love to hear, he will not meet the needs of the congregation. His communication is suspect because it only conveys part of the truth, and doesn't address the dark truths of life that need to be confronted.[11]

Thoughts Along the Way

The importance of effective communication is proven in its need for winning a war, excelling in sport, bringing salvation (physical or spiritual), cultivating a relationship or sharing God's love. The clarity of transmission and the effort to communicate will determine how effectively our lives impact upon others. Pictures, whether painted or photographed, abstract or concrete, should have meaning. Music should be performed well. Writing should be legible. Speech or song should be intelligible. And if communication needs clarity, it requires contact as well. This may involve writing a letter to a friend even if one doesn't feel like making the effort, taking an extra moment from a busy schedule to stop and talk to a fellow employee or customer, making the effort to spend time with your spouse, preparing thoroughly for a lecture or speech so they will be lucidly presented, or even trying to communicate love through a smile or a handshake. All these things take initiative; and work. If, however, this message to communicate well doesn't move you, and if it fails to express the importance of clarity, and if therefore you get nothing else out of this reading, at least ponder your penmanship. That way, if your legibility is good, you won't ever be accused of being a doctor.

Learning by Imitation

We learn how to do things by doing the things we are learning to do.
Aristotle

Beloved, do not imitate what is evil, but what is good.
St. John

I vividly remember the fear I experienced when an instructor nonchalantly told my group of green, inexperienced, third-year medical students—about to embark on our first hospital rotation—"You all are going to be sewing on people in the ER (emergency room)." I was scared. *"Me*?! Sewing on another human being!!?? I don't know how! What will I do??!"

What I did was watch my instructor sew, practice on models myself, then (with supervision, thankfully, by the surgery resident doctors) begin sewing on patients. Repeated trips to the ER and OR (operating room) taught me how to sew and how to do it well. Upon reading Aristotle's quote, most people would be reminded of how they learned to ride a bike or drive a car, lay bricks, play instruments of music, cook, throw balls, dance, swim, shake hands, or speak a new language. When I read that statement, I remember my learning to sew by sewing.

The Apostle John made a pertinent observation about education. He knew, as did Aristotle, that we learn through imitation and repetition. A child learns how to talk, stir, skip, or whistle by imitating others. Children also learn how to love and hate or share or steal by watching those around them. This process of learning continues into and throughout adulthood, and whether or not we admit it, we all do a good bit of imitating.

"Diotrephes, who loves to be first among them, does not accept what we say. For this reason, if I come, I will call attention to his deeds which he does, unjustly accusing us with wicked words; and not satisfied with this, neither does he himself receive the brethren, and he forbids those who desire to do so, and puts them out of the church. Beloved, do not imitate what is evil, but what is good. The one who does good is of God; the one who does evil has not seen God. Demetrius has received a good testimony from everyone, and from the truth itself; and we also bear witness, and you know that our witness is true." III John 1:9-12

Concretely, John said, "Do not imitate Diotrephes. He is a poor model to follow. Demetrius, however, is well thought of by everyone, and the truth shows him in good favor." Abstractly, he wrote, "Do not imitate what is evil, but what is good."

Aristotle laid down the basic principle of learning. John gave the moral advice of "choosing" what we should imitate to learn. We are the ones who must follow or stray from these dictums. I hope you choose wisely: the model someone else might choose may be you.

"Read Marcus Aurelius,"

Said the cold, impassive voice in very evenly measured tones.[12] Advice from Hannibal Lecter should be dubious, but there was something in his voice, a certain mysterious assurance that aroused my interest. My curiosity was probably heightened by my having purchased a copy of Marcus Aurelius's *Meditations* a couple of years earlier; and so I decided to look into it. Full of sound advice though espousing a philosophy of life I eschewed, it was a pleasure to read. It was, as we say in America, "a good buy."

Thoughts of Marcus Aurelius came flooding back to me when I read a terse editorial by Kevin McHale, the recently retired basketball star who played for the Boston Celtics. In his piece, McHale had mentioned his surprise at the media's heavy-handed worrying about the fate of the league when Michael Jordan suddenly retired. He thought that this concern was nonsense because the league always goes on. Players come and go, but not the league. Other basketball greats such as Wilt Chamberlain, Bill Russell, and Bob Cousy had left without impairing the NBA in the least. "Everybody leaves, and it's out of sight, out of mind." This lesson was demonstrated a few years earlier when McHale was talking at a school and happened to mention basketball legend Julius Erving (who retired in 1987). "Man, you should've seen Dr. J. in his prime," and the kids all went, "Who?" Only two years into his retirement and they had never even heard of him. McHale predicted the same fate for Jordan. In a few years, they'll say, "Michael who?"[13]

Across the ocean, Marcus was observing the same thing 18 centuries ago. "Think how we must follow whither so many great orators are gone before, so many reverend sages—Heraclitus, Phythagoras, Socrates—the heroes of early days, the captains and the kings of after-ages, and with them Eudoxus, Hipparchus, Archimedes, and many another; keen wits, sublime spirits, men unwearied, resourceful, and resolute; those too who made a merry jest of the transience and brevity of this mortal life in the fashion of Menippus and his school. Muse often on these men, all long since laid low in death. How, pray, are they the worse for it now—more especially those whose very names have been forgotten?"[14]

Thoughts Along the Way

Again, "reflect often how all the life of today is a repetition of the past; and observe that it also presages what is to come. Review the many complete dramas and their settings, all so similar, which you have known in your own experience, or from bygone history: the whole court-circle of Hadrian, for example, or the court of Antoninus, or the courts of Philip, Alexander, and Croesus. The performance is always the same; it is only the actors who change."[15]

Many of the important and self-important from ages past are important no more. The fact that more than one name mentioned above is unfamiliar to us is ample evidence of how transient fame is, how fleeting in nature. Today's stars will be tomorrow's memory before vanishing into the future. The people I admire or might try to impress or for whom I work will one day be gone and then forgotten. McHale was right: life goes on; which brings me back to Marcus Aurelius, and yet further back to Ecclesiastes, where the preacher gives a bit of advice for all of us transients living on this planet. "And I have seen that nothing is better than that man should be happy in his activities, for that is his lot."[16] As for the theist, he adds, "the conclusion, when all has been heard, is: fear God and keep His commandments, because this applies to every person."[17] It is simple but sagacious advice. Better to live for enjoyment and a God who remembers than for fame and a race of beings who forget and die. I wonder if Kevin and Marcus would drink to that. . .

Endings

A Panegyric for MJ and BB

The cover said it all: "Why?" Michael Jordan was pictured walking off of the basketball court and symbolically out of life in the NBA. The magazine—*Sports Illustrated* [1]—was asking the same stunned, disappointing question that everyone else was asking: Why? Why would THE premier basketball player in the United States—nay, in the entire world—at the peak of a career as perhaps the most popular athlete in history, suddenly retire and walk away from it all? Why now?

It was not, of course, the first time that an outstanding athlete had retired in his prime. Many others had done likewise, including Rocky Marciano (boxing), Sandy Koufax (baseball), Jim Brown (football), Herb Elliott (track), Mark Spitz (swimming), and Eric Heiden (speedskating), to name a few. Jordan, though, was colossal. He was widely adored, not just in America but throughout Europe and Asia, perhaps more than any athlete since Muhammad Ali or the soccer great Pélé. More than just a superb player, he was flashing and spectacular—a dominating presence on the court. He was a joy to watch, whether it was at the free throw line where, with beautiful form, he would shoot free throws that only touched the net on the way through the hoop, or driving down the lane, spinning, faking, splitting the double team defense for a basket, or playing aggressive, "street-smart" defense. His unexpected retirement was a source of keen disappointment to all of his fans. They felt the loss deeply. In counting myself among their number, I can say that I had not had that kind of shock and disappointment since. . .since. . .well, since 1983 when another immensely popular athlete called it quits in *his* athletic prime. . .and left the sport of tennis lessened by his loss.

Bjorn Borg began attracting attention while still a teenager in the early 1970s as a promising Swedish tennis player with long golden locks and an odd racket grip. Like Jordan, Borg was a superbly conditioned (his resting pulse rate was 35) and gifted athlete with a streamlined physique, quick feet, an accurate eye, strength, endurance, and an inordinately strong will to win. He won his first Gland Slam event in 1974 when, at the ripe old age of 18, he conquered the field at the French Open. By the end of 1981, he had won six French Opens and five Wimbledon championships in addition to 33 straight Davis Cup match wins, several Italian Opens, Masters championships, and a multitude of other tournaments. His only major championship failure came at the U.S. Open, where he was unsuccessful in 10 attempts. When he effectively retired at the age of 26, he left the game without winning either the U.S. or Australian Opens (he never played in the latter) and despite being perhaps the greatest talent in the history of tennis, he never won the Grand Slam (French Open, Wimbledon, U.S. Open, and Australian Open victories in one year—a rare achievement). Arthur Ashe, himself a champion tennis player, felt that Borg's retirement left the game of tennis wanting. He felt Borg could have won the U.S. Open and the Grand Slam as well. But he didn't. As a big fan of Borg's, I find that over a decade later, this still leaves an empty feeling inside. When Borg tried to come back in 1991 at age 35, it didn't make me feel any better, since he was soon defeated by players who, a decade earlier, he would have *pounded* in competition.

By contrast, Jordan won everything a basketball player could possibly win. His retirement at age 30 was disappointing, not because he left without accomplishing all of his goals, but because he, like Borg, left early, snatching away the thrill and excitement of watching them compete. Had either of them continued playing until their skills began to decline, I would not have had such remorse when they retired. Early departures give too much encouragement to the romantic side of humanity—"Oh what might have been! If only. . ." Oh well, enough of this. We sigh, place our epitaph—"Rats!!"—and move on: "I press toward the mark...."[2]

Endings

All things end, and by ending not only find continuance in the whole, but also assure continuance by contributing their droplets, clear or murky, to the stream of history. Anaximander said it best, some 2500 years ago: "It is necessary that things should pass away into that from which they were born. For things must pay one another the penalty and compensation for their injustice according to the ordinance of time."
— Shelby Foote [3]

All essayists reach a point where they end their work. Samuel Johnson, for example, wrote a series of weekly essays for two years entitled "The Rambler" before abruptly retiring. Six years later, he embarked on another series of essays—"The Idler"—and again quit after two years of writing. Everyone has their own reasons for quitting, just as they had reasons for starting. In my case, surgical residency drew to a close, and with that termination, I decided to bring my writing to an end. I had mixed emotions about that. On the one hand, I enjoyed writing and seeing each project completed. On the other hand, it was time to move on, and it seemed to be a good season for endings.

My reasons for embarking on these essays are harder to articulate. In medicine, the terms "diagnostic" and "therapeutic" are used to describe the detection of a disease or condition and the cure for it. Writing has been both diagnostic and therapeutic for me—I have written to expose what I saw of life; doing so made me feel better. I enjoyed sharing book enthusiasms and witty quotes I ran across in my readings as well as some of the unusual statistics I found in my researching. Writing forced me to think through many issues more thoroughly and research a number of topics to improve my perception of reality. It challenged my honesty and preconceived notions about life. My hope was to challenge you, too, and to present you with many subjects worth pondering. I hope my musings made you think (even about things that have no obvious solutions).

Thoughts Along the Way

In reviewing my musings, I was surprised to find out how frequently my Christianity was implicitly or explicitly mentioned. I strive to be ecumenical, to write essays that would interest those of any religious belief or philosophical persuasion. I would like to build bridges of understanding, too, especially with those who share a common heritage (but also a long history of animosity) with Christians, such as Jews and Muslims. A peaceful, ongoing dialogue would be healthy for us all. Inevitably, though, my Christianity, with its attendant lingo, beliefs, and tenants continues to shine through in my writings because it is the cornerstone of understanding for how I see the world. I hope this made things more interesting rather than less enjoyable.

My original intention when I started my residency was to write for only one year. As time went by, however, I kept finding more and more ideas bubbling up to the conscious surface. So I decided to keep writing, churning out my musings each month as long as the topics kept presenting themselves for comment. When residency ended six years later, I still had ideas and topics that begged exploring, but I had been able to convey much of what I wanted to say and could quit feeling satisfied.

The author of Ecclesiastes noted that the writing of many books is endless. For turning your attention to this "droplet" from the endless stream of books, I thank you.

Footnotes

Contents
1. Boswell, James. *Life of Johnson*. Oxford: Oxford University Press, 1980. p. 434.
2. Davies, Robertson. *A Mixture of Frailties*. Ontario: Penguin Books, 1980.
3. "What's bred in the bone will not out of the flesh" is an English proverb from the Latin, dated 1290, and is quoted at the beginning of Robertson Davies' novel *What's Bred in the Bone*.
4. St. Anselm's ontological argument for the existence of God is found in his work Proslogium, a section of which is quoted in Gould, James A. (ed.), *Classic Philosphical Questions*, 4th ed. Columbus, Ohio: Charles E. Merrill Pub. Co., 1982, pp. 413-415.
5. Lewis, C.S. *Surprised by Joy*. New York: Harcourt Brace Jovanovich, 1955, p. 299.
6. Yancey, Philip. *Open Windows*. Nashville: Thomas Nelson Publishers, 1985, p. 9.
7. Psalms 14:3, Psalms 53:3 and Romans 3:12.
8. Foote, Shelby, *The Civil War: A Narrative. Fort Sumter to Perryville*. New York: Vintage Books, 1986, p. 527.
9. Matthew 7:1-2.
10. Matthew 10:30 & Luke 12:7.
11. Psalms 36:9.
12. This quote was reprinted in Brand, Paul and Yancey, Philip. *Pain: The Gift Nobody Wants*. New York: Harper Collins, 1993, p. 289.
13. Boswell, James. *Life of Johnson*. Oxford: Oxford University Press, 1980, p. 307.
14. Lewis, C.S. *Selected Literary Essays*, 'De Descriptione Temporum.' Cambridge: Cambridge University Press, 1969, p. 12.
15. Shirer, William L. *The Rise and Fall of the Third Reich*. New York: Simon & Shuster, 1959, p. vii.

A Global View
1. Only *after* eating a meal and visiting with his divine guests did Abraham find out the important news that Sodom was to be destroyed. In fact, it was not discussed until the visitors got up to leave.
2. Genesis 3:8.
3. Psalms 42:1.
4. John 4:14.

5. Luke 13:20-21.
6. John 13:5.
7. Jonah 3:3.
8. II Kings 3:9.
9. Joshua 5:6.
10. Tolstoy, Leo. *War and Peace*. New York: Nal Penguin, Inc. 1968, pp. 1162-63.
11. *The New Encyclopaedia Britannica*, Vol. 6, Chicago: Micropaedia, 1990, pp. 816-817.
12. Lewis, C.S. *An Experiment in Criticism*. Cambrige: Cambridge University Press, 1961, p. 140.
13. Letter from George Sayer to the author.
14. Lewis, C.S. *Letters*. London: Harper Collins, 1988, pp. 212-213.
15. Lewis, C.S. *God in the Dock*. Grand Rapids, MI: William B. Eerdmans Pub. Co., 1970, p. 202.
16. Richardson, Don. *Peace Child*. Ventura, CA: GL Publications, 1974, p. 43.
17. Richardson, Don. *Lords of the Earth*. Glendale, CA: GL Publications, 1977, p. 20.
18. Tiner, John. *Isaac Newton*. Milford, State: Mott Media, 1975, p. 133.
19. Churchill, Winston S. *A History of the English Speaking Peoples*, Vol. 1. New York: Dorset Press, 1956, p. 3.
20. Amos 6:1, 4-7.

Love
1. I John 4:19.
2. I John 4:10.
3. Romans 5:8.
4. Paul was quoting the Cretan poet Epimenides (ca. 600 B.C.) from his work *Cretica* when he said, "For in him we live and move and have our being," as he spoke to the Athenians in Greece (Acts 17:28).
5. Longfellow, Henry Wadsworth. "Evangeline: A Tale of Acadie," *The Poetical Works of Longfellow*. Boston: Houghton Mifflin, 1975, pp. 70-98.
6. Buechner, Frederick. *Wishful Thinking*. New York: Harper & Row, 1973, p. 2.
7. Buechner, Frederick. *Whistling in the Dark*. San Francisco: Harper & Row, 1988, p. 57.
8. Romans 12:21.
9. Found in *The Norton Anthology of American Literature*, 2nd ed. Vol. 1. New York: W.W. Norton and Company, 1985, p. 2448
10. Lewis, C.S. *The Problem of Pain*. New York: Macmillan, 1940, 1962, p. 10.
11. Lewis, C.S. *The Four Loves*. New York: Harcourt Brace Jovanovich, 1960, p. 154.
12. From Alfred Lord Tennyson's poem "In Memoriam."

13. Carter, Forrest. *The Education of Little Tree*. Albuquerque: University of New Mexico Press, 1976, p. 78.
14. Como, James T. *C.S. Lewis at the Breakfast Table*. New York: Macmillan, 1979, p. 30.
15. *Collected Poems of Emily Dickinson*. New York: Avenel Books, 1982, p. 102.

Frailty
1. Quoted at the beginning of Robertson Davies' novel, *A Mixture of Frailties*.
2. Lewis, C.S. *The Abolition of Man*. New York: Macmillan, 1947, p. 34.
3. Milton, John. *Paradise Lost*. New York: Holt, Rinehart and Winston, 1951, pp. 225, 228.
4. Romans 7:19.
5. "And we know that God causes all things to work together for good..."
6. Lewis, C.S. *A Preface to Paradise Lost*. Oxford: Oxford University Press, 1942, pp. 67-68.
7. Job 42:5.
8. II Corinthians 12:7-10.
9. Davies, Robertson. *The Salterton Trilogy, Leaven of Malice*. New York: Penguin Books, 1986, p. 428.
10. *The Complete Essays of Montaigne*. Stanford, CA: Stanford University Press, 1976, p. 815, 827.
11. Philippians 2:5-7.
12. *The New Merriam-Webster Dictionary*. Springfield, Massachusetts: Merriam-Webster, 1989, p. 248.
13. Psalm 68:19, Psalm 54:4, and Psalm 51:1.
14. *The American College Dictionary*. Syracuse, New York: Random House, 1969, p. 112.
15. Yancey, Philip. *Praying with the KGB*. Portland, OR: Multnomah, 1992, p. 43.
16. James 2:26.
17. Galatians 3:24.

The Dark Side of Life
1. Taken from Strand, Fleur L. *Physiology*, 2nd ed., New York: Macmillan Pub. Co., 1983, p. 615.
2. Proverbs 1:7.
3. From the pamphlet "Military History." Cranbury, NJ: The Scholar's Bookself.
4. "For the creation was subjected to frustration, not by its own choice, but by the will of the one who subjected it, in hope that the creation itself will be liberated from its bondage to decay and brought into the glorious freedom of the children of God." Romans 8:20ff.

The Dark Side of Humanity
1. Lewis, C.S. *God in the Dock*. Grand Rapids, MI: Eerdman's Pub. Co., 1970, p. 124.
2. Matthew 6:14-15.
3. *J'aime l'automne* is French for "I love autumn."
4. Lewis, C.S. *The Letters of C.S. Lewis to Arthur Greeves*. New York: Macmillan Publishing Company, 1979, p. 324.
5. This quotation comes from Hamlet's famous "To be, or not to be, that is the question" soliloquy in Shakespeare's tragedy 'Hamlet, Prince of Denmark'; Act III, Scene I.
6. This quote can be found in *The Mongol Conquests, Time Frame* series. Alexandria: Time-Life Books, 1989, p. 13.
7. Lewis, C.S. *The World's Last Night and other Essays*. New York: Harcourt Brace Jovanovich, 1960, p. 89.
8. From an interview between David Neff and scholar Kay Brigham published in *Christianity Today*: Oct. 7, 1991, p. 27, 28.
9. Chesterton, G.K. *Collected Works: The Everlasting Man*. San Francisco: Ignatius Press, 1986, p. 252-253.
10. Psalms 14:3; Psalms 53:3.
11. Romans 3:23.
12. Luke 12:15.
13. Harris, Thomas. *The Silence of the Lambs*. New York: St. Martin's Press, 1988, p. 227.

Justice
1. Foote, Shelby. *The Civil War: A Narrative. Fort Sumter to Perryville*. New York: Vintage Books, 1986, p. 527.
2. This quote can be found, among other places, in Ward, Geoffrey C., with Burns, Ken and Ric, *The Civil War: an illustrated history*. New York: Alfred Knopf, 1990, p. 284.
3. Matthew 7:1-2.
4. James 1:20.
5. From The Collect on the first Sunday after Easter in *The Book of Common Prayer*.
6. Matthew 27:29.
7. Keefe, Carolyn. *C.S. Lewis, Speaker & Teacher*. Grand Rapids, MI: Zondervan, 1971, p. 76.
8. Foote, Shelby. *The Civl War: A Narrative. Fredericksburg to Merridian*. New York: Vintage Books, 1986, p. 108.
9. *Ibid*, p. 948.
10. Micah 6:8.
11. Foote, Shelby. *The Civil War: A Narrative. Red River to Appomattox*. New York: Vintage Books, 1986, p. 813.

12. McLaughlin, J.G., et al. "Hospitalization and Injury Influence on the Prosecution of Drunk Drivers." *The American Surgeon*. 1993; 59: 484-489.
13. 1992 Statistics from the *1993 Encyclopaedia Britannica Book of the Year*.

Faith
1. Leviticus 17:10-11.
2. Revelation 12, 13, and following.
3. Davies, Robertson, *Fifth Business*. London: Penguin, 1983, p. 58, 59.
4. "A guy named Jason" is an allusion to the notorious character named Jason who terrorized and slaughtered many victims in the popular *Friday the 13th* horror movies. These movies started coming out when I was in high school, and more than one of my friends who went to the movies to see Jason in action later admitted to looking in their closets or under their beds before they went to bed that night.
5. W. Eugene Smith's quote comes from the *1957 American Society of Magazine Photographers Picture Annual*. New York: Simon & Schuster, 1957, p. 7.
6. Both sayings come from Plato's *Protagoras*.
7. Romans 7:19
8. John 20:29.
9. Mark 6:3, 4.
10. Sproul, Barbara C. *Primal Myths*. San Francisco: HarperCollins, 1979.
11. Lewis, C.S. *Christian Reflections*, "Modern Theology and Biblical Criticism." William B. Eerdmans Pub. Co., Grand Rapids, MI: 1967, p. 156-157.
12. Lewis, C.S. *God in the Dock*, "What Are We to Make of Jesus Christ?" Grand Rapids, MI: William B. Eerdmans Pub. Co., 1970, p. 158-159.
13. *The American College Dictionary*. New York: Random House, 1969, p. 696.
14. Boswell, James. *Life of Johnson*. Oxford: Oxford University Press, 1980, p. 899.
15. Washington, Booker T. *Up From Slavery*. New York: Carol Publishing Group, 1989, p. 1-2.
16. Genesis 12:3.
17. I John 3:1.
18. Franklin, Benjamin. "Remarks Concerning the Savages of North America," reprinted in *The Norton Anthology of American Literature*, 2nd ed. vol. 1. New York: W.W. Norton and Company, 1985, p. 384-385.
19. Pascua, Maria Parker. "Ozette." *National Geographic*. October 1991, 180: 4, p. 53.
20. Lewis, C.S. *The World's Last Night and Other Essays*. New York: Harcourt Brace Jovanovich, 1960, p. 90.
21. *JAARS (Jungle Aviation And Radio Service)* newsletter, April 1993.

22. Keller, W. Phillip. *Chosen Vessels*, "Otto C. Keller." Ann Arbor: Servant Publications, 1985, p. 98-99.
23. Taken from the Epilogue of Alice Gibbons' *The People Time Forgot*.
24. II Timothy 2:4.
25. Hebrews 12:2.
26. Luke 11:2.
27. Matthew 6:9.
28. Elwell, Walter (ed.). *Baker Encyclopedia of the Bible*. Grand Rapids, MI: Baker Book House Co., 1988, p. 880.
29. Wilson, Earl D. *Sexual Sanity*. Downers Grove, IL: InterVarsity Press, 1984, p. 37.
30. Heschel, Abraham Joshua. *The Sabbath: Its Meaning for Modern Man*. New York: The Noonday Press, 1951, p. 6, 10.
31. Matthew 5:6.
32. Ecclesiastes 8:7-8.
33. *The Complete Essays of Montaigne*. Stanford, CA: Stanford University Press, 1976, p. 211.
34. Matthew 6:34.
35. Matthew 11:28.
36. Lewis, C.S. *English Literature in the Sixteenth Century (excluding Drama)*. Oxford: Oxford University Press, 1954, p. 517.
37. *Ibid*, p. 41.
38. I Timothy 2:11.
39. I Timothy 2:12.
40. Ephesians 5:22.
41. I Corinthians 14:34 & 35.
42. Exodus 20:8.
43. Romans 14:4-8.
44. I Corinthians 7:25.
45. I Thessalonians 2:13.
46. Lewis, C.S. "Priestesses in the Church?" from *God in the Dock*. Grand Rapids, MI: William B. Eerdmans Pub. Co., 1970, p. 238.
47. Mark 9:24.
48. II Chronicles 21:20.
49. Ecclesiasticus 44:7-9.

The Printed Word
1. Boswell, James. *Life of Johnson*. Oxford: Oxford University Press, 1980, p. 899.
2. Armour, Richard. *The Classics Reclassified*. New York: McGraw-Hill, 1980.
3. Boswell, James. *Life of Johnson*. Oxford: Oxford University Press, 1980, p. 135.
4. *Ibid*, p. 205.
5. *Ibid*, p. 309.

6. *Ibid*, p. 757.
7. *Webster's Third New International Dictionary*. Chicago: Encyclopaedia Britannica, 1986, p. 1060.
8. *The American College Dictionary*. New York: Random House, 1969, p. 567.
9. Longfellow, Henry Wadsworth. *The Poetical Works of Longfellow*, "Tales of a Wayside Inn: The Landlord's Tale: Paul Revere's Ride." Boston: Houghton Mifflin, 1975, p. 207.
10. *Ibid*, "Christmas Bells" p. 289.
11. *Ibid*, p. 164.
12. *Ibid*, p. 70.
13. *Ibid*, p. 98.
14. *Ibid*, p. 202-203.
15. Excerpted from Marjorie Lamp Mead's "Afterword" in Barfield, Owen, *The Silver Trumpet*. U.S.A.: 1986, Bookmakers Guild, p. 121.
16. Lewis, C.S. *On Stories*. New York: Harcourt Brace Jovanovich, 1982, p. 36.
17. From the foreword entitled "Sharing Little Tree" by Rennard Strickland in Carter, Forrest. *The Education of Little Tree*. Alburquerque: University of New Mexico Press, 1985.
18. Fabre, J. Henri. *The Insect World of J. Henri Fabre*. Boston: Beacon Press, 1991, pp. 182-183.
19. Gilkey, Langdon. *Shantung Compond*. New York: Harper & Row, 1966, p. 140.
20. Watkins, Sam. *Co. Aytch: A Side Show of the Big Show*. New York: Macmillan, 1962 (from the back cover).
21. *Ibid*, p. 185.
22. *Ibid*, p. 7.
23. *Ibid*, p. 109.
24. *Ibid*, p. 38.
25. *Ibid*, p. 211.
26. Foote, Shelby. *The Civil War: A Narrative. Fort Sumter to Perryville*. New York: Random House, 1986, p. 798.
27. Amos 6:1.

Mystery
1. Koop, C. Everett. *Koop*. Grand Rapids, MI: Zondervan, 1992, pp. 333-334.
2. Quotation from Philip Yancey's article "Weeping over Jerusalem—Shouting over L.A." in *Christianity Today*, July 20, 1992, p. 64.
3. Yancey, Philip. *Disappointment with God*. Grand Rapids, MI: Zondervan, 1988, p. 84.
4. Quotation from Philip Yancey's article "Imperfect, Codependent, and Unapologetic" in *Christianity Today*, October 26, 1992, p. 92.
5. Ezekiel 23:19-21.

6. Kinsey, Alfred C., et al. *Sexual Behavior in the Human Male.* Philadelphia: W.B. Saunders 1948, p. 486.
7. Kinsey, Alfred C., et al. *Sexual Behavior in the Human Female.* Philadelphia: W.B. Saunders, 1953, p. 229.
8. From the record jacket of E. Power Biggs' recording "Bach Organ Favorites."
9. *Ibid.*
10. Tolkien, J.R.R. *The Lord of the Rings.* New York: Ballantine Books, 1965.
11. Lewis, C.S. *God in the Dock.* Grand Rapids, MI: William B. Eerdmans Pub. Co. 1970, pp. 41-43.
12. I Corinthians 1:27-29.
13. Isaiah 55:8-9.
14. See chapter 27 "Why God Doesn't Intervene" from Philip Yancey's Book, *Disappointment with God,* especially the section entitled "A Way of Life," to see how we daily function and grow through the transformation of sensation to perception using decomposition and recomposition. The lower faculties of sensation carry the meaning for the higher faculty of perception.
15. Lewis, C.S. *Miracles.* New York: Macmillan, 1960, p. 19.
16. *Ibid.* p. 22.
17. *Ibid*, p. 22.
18. See *The Letters of C.S. Lewis to Arthur Greeves*, p. 217-219 to read how baffling a thing like "beauty" can be if attempts to explain it are based on sense impressions alone.

Observations
1. Tolstoy, Leo. *Anna Karenina.* Toronto: Bantam Books, 1960, p. 294.
2. Ecclesiastes 5:18.
3. Harrison, Roland Kenneth. *Introduction to the Old Testament.* Grand Rapids, MI: William B. Eerdmans Pub. Co. 1969, pp. 885-886.
4. *Ibid*, p. 992.
5. Lewis, C.S. *The Allegory of Love.* Oxford: Oxford University Press, 1936, p. 1.
6. Faulkner, William. *The Reivers.* New York: Vintage Books, 1962, p. 52.
7. Buechner, Frederick. *Wishful Thinking.* New York: Harper & Row, 1973, p. 9.
8. Boswell, James. *Life of Johnson.* Oxford: Oxford University Press, 1980, p. 307.
9. Rifkin, Matthew, D. *Ultrasound of the Prostate.* New York: Raven Press, 1988.
10. Thomas à Kempis. *The Imitation of Christ.* London: Penguin Books, 1952, p. 27.
11. Lewis, C.S. *Studies in Words.* Cambridge: Cambridge University Press, 1967, p. 292.
12. Lewis, C.S. *The Screwtape Letters.* New York: Macmillan, 1982, p. 60.

13. Dillard, Annie. *Pilgrim at Tinker Creek*. New York: Harper & Row, 1974, p. 198.
14. Bernier, C.L., and Yerkey, A.N. (eds.). *Cogent Communications: Overcoming Information Overload*. Westport, CT: Greenwood Press, 1979, p. 39.
15. Sabiston, D.C., Jr. (Ed.). *Textbook of Surgery: The Biological Basis of Modern Surgical Practice*. Philadelphia: W.B. Saunders, 1991, p. 2135.
16. Romans 8:26.
17. Matthew 22:37.
18. Matthew 22:39.
19. Longfellow, Henry Wadsworth. *The Poetical Works of Longfellow*. Boston: Houghton Mifflin, 1975, p. 394.
20. Matthew 23:11-12.

Wisdom
1. Genesis 8:1.
2. Deuteronomy 7:18.
3. Numbers 15:39.
4. Isaiah 46:9.
5. Luke 23:42.
6. Revelation 3:3.
7. I Corinthians 10:11.
8. Romans 15:4.
9. Lewis, C.S. *The World's Last Night and Other Essays*. New York: Harcourt Brace Jovanovich, 1960, p. 80.
10. Mathew 8:26, 27.
11. Buechner, Frederick. *Telling the Truth: The Gospel as Tragedy, Comedy & Fairy Tale*. San Francisco: Harper and Row, 1977, p. 40-41.
12. Hannibal Lecter's advice to FBI trainee Clarice Starling in the movie *The Silence of the Lambs*.
13. McHale, Kevin. *Sports Illustrated*, November 18, 1993, p. 146.
14. Marcus Aurelius. *Meditations*. Middlesex, England: Penguin Books, 1964, p. 102.
15. *Ibid*, p. 159.
16. Ecclesiastes 3:22.
17. Ecclesiastes 12:13.

Endings
1. *Sports Illustrated*, October 18, 1993.
2. Philippians 3:14.
3. Foote, Shelby. *The Civil War: A Narrative. Red River to Appomattox*. New York: Vintage Books, 1986, p. 1040.